# Ready fo

## IELTS

2nd Edition

**Teacher's Book
Premium Pack**

Sam McCarter

macmillan
education

+ access to the Teacher's Resource Centre
and Presentation Kit

Macmillan Education
4 Crinan Street
London N1 9XW
A division of Springer Nature Limited

Companies and representatives throughout the world

ISBN 978-1-786-32867-0

Design by Burgess Typography
Page make-up by J&D Glover Limited
Illustrated by Integra Software Services Pvt. Ltd
Cover design by Springer Nature Ltd
Cover photograph by Getty Images/Ascent/PKS Media Inc

Author's acknowledgements
Sam McCarter would like to thank his students at Reache North West. He would also like to say thank you to the team at Macmillan for their expertise and patience, and to everyone who has contributed to this publication directly or indirectly.

The publishers would like to thank Louis Rogers.

The author and publishers are grateful for permission to reprint the following copyright material: p155 Data from 'Employment in sport and average annual growth rate, 2011-2014', published on ec.europa.eu/eurostat, copyright © European Union 1995–2013. Reprinted by permission of the publisher; p163 Extract from 'Learn what you want' by Andrew Downie, copyright © Telegraph Media Group Ltd 2004. First published in *The Telegraph* 09.02.2004. Reprinted by permission of the publisher; p169 Extract from 'And the one in the middle is the joker' by Olga Craig, copyright © Telegraph Media Group Ltd 2007. First published in *The Telegraph* 11.11.2007. Reprinted by permission of the publisher; p176 Data from the statistical bulletin 'Internet Access – Households and Individuals: 2014, p.8' produced by the Office for National Statistics. Contains public sector information licensed under the Open Government Licence v3.0; p182 Material from 'Digital economy and society statistics – households and individuals', published on ec.europa.eu/eurostat, copyright © European Union 1995-2013. Reprinted by permission of the publisher; p184 Extract from 'The Legacy of Krakatoa' by Roger Maynard, copyright © The Independent 2008. First published in *The Independent* 23.08.08. Reprinted by permission of the publisher. www.independent.co.uk; p186 Extract from 'The teenage brain: a scientific analysis' by Steve Connor, copyright © The Independent 2006. First published in *The Independent* 05.11.06. Reprinted by permission of the publisher. www.independent.co.uk; p188 Data from Ofcom's 'Communications Market Report 2010', copyright © Ofcom 2010. Available at https://www.ofcom.org.uk/__data/assets/pdf_file/0013/25222/cmr_2010_final.pdf. Reprinted by permission of the publisher. Sample IELTS Listening and Reading Answer Sheet. Reproduced with permission of Cambridge English Language Assessment © UCLES 2016.

Printed and bound in Great Britain by Ashford Colour Press Ltd.
2021  2020  2019  2018
10  9  8  7  6  5  4

# Contents

# Contents Map

4

| Speaking | Language focus | Vocabulary |
|---|---|---|
| Part 2: Describing a person | 1 Likes and dislikes<br>2 Present simple, present continuous and past simple | Describing people |
| Part 2: Describing an electronic device | 1 Past simple and present perfect<br>2 Habit in the past<br>Adverbs of frequency | Verbs of cause and effect<br>Word building: Evaluating adjectives |
| 1 Part 1: Discussing sport<br>2 Part 3: Discussing physical activity and the benefits of sport | 1 Adjectives with prepositions<br>2 Comparison | Sports<br>Word building: Adjectives ending in *-ing/-ed* |
| 1 Part 1: Discussing food and manufactured goods<br>2 Part 3: Discussing world problems | Countable and uncountable nouns | 1 General nouns<br>2 Developing ideas |
| Part 3: Discussing the future | Ways of looking at the future | 1 Adjective/Noun collocations<br>Word building: Forming adjectives from nouns<br>2 Verbs of prediction |
| Part 2: Describing a place of natural beauty | Transitive and intransitive verbs | 1 Lifecycles and processes<br>2 Conservation |
| 1 Part 3: Discussing goals and career<br>2 Part 2: Describing a job/an achievement | Conditionals 1 | 1 Work<br>2 Collocations |
| 1 Part 1: Describing a neighbourhood<br>2 Part 2: Social interaction with neighbours | Referring in a text | Nouns relating to places |
| 1 Part 2: Describing a building or monument<br>2 Part 3: Discussing buildings and traditions | Modal verbs for evaluating | Beauty<br>Word building: Prefixes *under-* and *over-* |
| 1 Part 3: Discussing the arts<br>2 Part 2: Describing an art form | Defining and non-defining relative clauses | Art |
| Part 2: Describing friendship, relationship, period of your life, membership | Conditionals 2 | The family<br>Word building: Suffixes *-hood* and *-ship* |
| 1 Part 1: Discussing travel<br>2 Part 2: Describing a journey | Articles | Adjectives with multiple meanings<br>Word building: Words related to memory |
| 1 Part 2: Describing a street or square<br>2 Part 3: Discussing transport systems | Concession and developing ideas | Nouns related to systems<br>Word building: Modal verbs to adjectives |
| Part 3: Discussing well-being and money | Substitution and ellipsis | Money matters<br>Word building: Values and beliefs |

# Introduction

The *Ready for IELTS* course consists of the following components:

- Student's Book (with and without answers)
- Digital Student's Book (with answers)
- eBook (with and without answers)
- Teacher's Book
- Presentation Kit
- Teacher's Resource Centre with class audio
- Student's Resource Centre with class audio
- Workbook (with and without answers)

## Student's Book

The Student's Book contains 14 units, each 10 pages in length with an additional two-page *Review*. The focus is on increasing the language competence of your students in the four main skills tested in the academic version of the IELTS examination (listening, reading, writing and speaking). The focus of the course is, therefore, on increasing students' ability to use the necessary language and skills, rather than just knowing about them. In addition, there is a range of activities aimed at building your students' competence in vocabulary and grammar relevant to the skills required for the IELTS exam.

The two-page *Review* section at the end of each unit revises the language covered in that unit. You can use the *Review* section unit by unit as students progress through the Student's Book; and also, periodically, as a quick revision tool in conjunction with the *Wordlist* and *Grammar reference* (see below); or in conjunction with the *Progress Tests* in the Teacher's Book.

There are four *Ready for …* units after every three units up to Unit 12, each dealing with one of the four main skills tested in the IELTS exam: *Ready for Listening, Ready for Reading, Ready for Writing* and *Ready for Speaking*. Each of these sections provides extra practice for the respective skills in the exam and may be used as they occur in the Student's Book. They may also be used as a whole unit, or in part as an addition to a particular unit or units. Alternatively, you may want to keep them for revision purposes. They are meant to be used flexibly, so you can dip in and out of them and revisit as appropriate.

The *Wordlist* and *Grammar reference* are both closely linked to the 14 units in the book.

Students refer to the *Additional material* section and listening scripts for some exercises. The Student's Book is available with or without the answer key, which apart from answers to the exercises contains model answers to all the writing tasks throughout the course.

The following boxes providing tips and advice on performing various tasks are found throughout the Student's Book:

- *What to expect in the exam*: these boxes contain information on what students should be prepared to see, hear or do in a particular type of task in the exam.
- *How to go about it*: these boxes provide advice and guidelines on how to deal with different types of tasks and specific questions.
- *Don't forget!:* these remind students of certain procedures to follow as they perform a task.
- *Useful expressions:* these provide useful language to help students when they complete exercises.

## Teacher's Book

The Teacher's Book contains teaching notes for all the activities in the Student's Book. A typical unit of the Teacher's Book provides you with:

- a summary of the contents of the unit, including the exam question types for each of the skills
- answers to the exercises along with model answers for the writing tasks and comments
- guidelines for using the Student's Book along with suggestions for lead-ins and further activities
- transcripts of the listening tests with the part of the text relating to the answers underlined
- ideas for manipulating exercises.

At the end of the Teacher's Book there are also photocopiable exercises, five photocopiable Progress Tests and a Final Test, a useful list of IELTS strategies and IELTS essentials for students, and sample exam answer sheets for listening and reading.

### Photocopiable activities

For each main unit, there is one photocopiable activity relating to one of the language points taught in the main Student's Book and the Workbook unit. These may be used as further practice at the points indicated in the Teacher's Book, to supplement the corresponding exercise in the *Review* section at the end of each unit, or as revision exercises as your students progress through the units. You may also want to do the exercises as a revision aid before the students do the Progress Tests at the end of the Teacher's Book. At the end of the photocopiable activities there is an answer key with some notes for using the activities.

### Photocopiable *Progress Tests*

These tests are intended to be used after your students have completed Units 1–3, 4–6, 7–9, 10–12 and 13–14. You can use them to assess the progress of your students as they move through the course. Each test contains practice in aspects of listening, reading and writing, along with revision of the language that is presented in the corresponding units in the Student's Book. Apart from the grammar and vocabulary tasks in each test, exam question types corresponding to the various components are as follows:

Test 1: Listening Section 1 (form completion, note completion, selecting items from a list), Reading (matching paragraph headings, *True/False/Not Given* statements, global multiple-choice), Writing Task 1 (describing a graph)

Test 2: Listening Section 2 (labelling a map, multiple-choice questions, sentence completion), Reading (completing a flow-chart, *True/ False/Not Given* statements, answering questions), Writing Task 2 (causes and solutions)

Test 3: Listening Section 3 (table completion, answering questions, selecting items from a list), Reading (matching information to paragraphs, classification, selecting items from a list), Writing Task 1 (plan description)

Test 4: Listening Section 4 (table completion, selecting items from a list), Reading (table completion, summary with a Wordlist, classification), Writing Task 2 (discussing views and giving an opinion)

Test 5: Listening Section 4 (matching, summary completion), Reading (selecting items from a list, diagram completion, *Yes/No/Not Given* statements – claims), Writing Task 1 (describing a chart)

## Final Test

This is a full, photocopiable test, which contains four components relating to the four main skills with model answers for Writing Tasks 1 and 2. You can use the test near the end of the course (at about unit 12 onwards) as a Final Test before students take the IELTS exam.

At the end of the tests, there is an answer key with the listening scripts and model answers.

## Presentation Kit

The Presentation Kit is an interactive version of the Student's Book which can be displayed on an interactive whiteboard. It includes: interactive Listening and Reading exam tasks; embedded class audio; pop-up answers for exercises from the Student's Book and tools to personalise your presentations.

## Teacher's Resource Centre

The Teacher's Resource Centre includes: all the resources on the Student's Resource Centre; communicative activities; downloadable versions of the Progress Tests and Final Test; and Workbook audio and answer key. It can be accessed by a code on the cover of this book.

## Student's Resource Centre

This Student Resource Centre includes: class audio and listening scripts; a complete practice test; speaking videos with student worksheets and video audio scripts; wordlists; and IELTS essentials and strategies.

## Workbook

The Workbook contains 14 units and follows the general topics of the Student's Book. Each unit provides students with further practice, revision and extension of the language presented in the Student's Book, as well as examination practice. Each unit contains the following elements:

### Listening

Each unit in the Workbook provides students with valuable additional practice in listening skills. An example of one of the sections in the IELTS Listening module is found in each unit. The section type and question type mainly follow those in the corresponding units in the Student's Book.

### Reading

The reading practice in each unit mainly follows the question type in the corresponding Student's Book unit so that students can refine their competence and techniques as they go through the course. The vocabulary of the reading passage is sometimes exploited in reading exercises.

### Writing

In each unit, there is writing practice either relating to Task 1 or Task 2 of the exam. There is ample practice of the range of data and diagram interpretation for Task 1, and of the range of question types covered in Task 2.

### Vocabulary

The vocabulary practice in each unit follows closely the vocabulary practice in the Student's Book, with the exercise types being a combination of crosswords, puzzles and exercises similar to those found in the Student's Book (sentence completion, matching, transformation, proofreading, etc.)

### Language focus

This contains further practice of the grammar that the students have learnt in the Student's Book. You can refer them to the relevant section of the Student's Book and the *Grammar reference*.

### Wordlist

The Wordlist at the back of the book contains a list of useful words that are at CEF C1 and above. You can encourage students to complete the definitions for the words as they come across them in the course.

# Using the course to prepare students for the academic version of the IELTS examination

The purpose of *Ready for IELTS* is to prepare students for the academic version of the International English Language Testing System (IELTS) examination. Students preparing for the General Training version of IELTS will also find all the vocabulary and grammar practice, the listening practice and the speaking practice relevant. The Reading and the Writing modules in the General Training version are, however, different.

## Listening

The range of listening practice in this course is a valuable resource for all students preparing for the IELTS examination. In all, there are 52 audio tracks on the Student and Teacher Resource Centres (plus audio CDs to accompany the Workbook) to help develop your students' competence in listening. In the *Ready for Speaking* section there is also an example of the Speaking test, Parts 2 and 3.

Each unit contains one example of a section from the exam, with guidance in the *How to go about it/What to expect* boxes. The *Ready for Listening* section on page 42 contains an example of a full test with explanations. Throughout the Student's Book, there are valuable pre-listening and post-listening activities, with the listening providing a context for the vocabulary and the language in the unit.

As each section of the Listening test in the exam is played only once, it is essential that students are well prepared in techniques that enable them to complete the Listening test efficiently. To this end, the pre-listening activities and *How to go about it/What to expect* boxes provide ample advice and guidance. Students are encouraged to learn prediction techniques for general and specific answers, using the questions as a summary of the listening script. Most listening practices are followed by a discussion, to encourage the students to develop their critical-thinking skills.

The listening practice gives examples of a range of accents. Further listening practice is provided in the Workbook audio CDs and in the online Resource Centres.

## Reading

Each unit contains a reading passage. The *Ready for Reading* section provides general information and further tips on reading, including a focus on *True/False/Not Given* and *Yes/No/Not Given* statements. The reading practices give students examples of the full range of question types that are tested in the exam.

The texts are authentic and provide examples of the range of text types that occur in the exam, e.g., historical, argumentative, descriptive, process, classification, cause/effect, problem/solution.

As with the listening practice, pre-reading activities help students focus on various reading techniques like scanning, paraphrasing, content prediction, etc. After reading, students are encouraged to give their reaction to the text so that they can develop their critical-thinking skills. The reading texts throughout provide examples for the vocabulary and language focus exercises so that the students can see the items they are practising in an authentic context.

At the end of the *Ready for Reading* section of the Student's Book, there is a Reading checklist. Students are encouraged throughout the course to use the checklist.

Further reading practice is provided in the Workbook and in the online Resource Centres.

## Writing

Practice in either Task 1 or Task 2 is provided in each unit of the Student's Book with the *Ready for Writing* section on page 128 providing further practice. Each writing task is preceded by extensive practice with model answers so that students are familiar with the specific writing task covered in that unit before they attempt to write their own answer to a writing task at the end of the writing section. Practice is given in organisation, planning, creating ideas, style/register with proofreading in the *Review* pages, as well as the specific vocabulary and grammar required to perform the various writing tasks.

At the end of the *Ready for Writing* section of the Student's Book, there is a checklist for both Writing tasks to help students check their answers. Students are encouraged throughout the course to use the checklist. For all the Writing tasks in the main units, there is a model answer in the answer key with comments

In the *Ready for Writing* section a wide range of data interpretation is practised, with model answers.

Further writing practice is provided in the Workbook and in the Progress Tests and Final Test in the Teacher's Book.

## Speaking

At least one part of the three-part IELTS Speaking test is found in each unit. The speaking practice generally relates to the theme of the unit and helps practise the vocabulary and grammar presented in each unit. As the grammar and vocabulary in each unit have a context in the reading passage or the listening practice, students are constantly recycling language in different parts of the exam to develop their competence.

Within each speaking section, ample practice is given in the skills students will need to perform efficiently in the IELTS exam, e.g., organsation, vocabulary use, creating ideas, developing ideas and speaking fluently. As with the writing tasks, speaking checklists are provided at the end of the

Student's Book so students can monitor themselves and each other as they progress through the course.

The *Ready for Speaking* section is situated after Unit 12. You may, however, want to refer students to this section earlier in the course and use sections of it to supplement the speaking practice in the main unit. This section contains practice for Parts 2 and 3 of the Speaking test, with practice exercises. It also includes Speaking checklists for each part of the Speaking test.

## Vocabulary

Every unit has at least one vocabulary or word building section. A context for the vocabulary is provided by either the reading passage or the listening practice in each unit. The purpose of the vocabulary section is to provide students with a wide range of words and collocations that they will find useful in all four skills in the exam. The exercises are designed to increase students' competence in using the vocabulary, rather than just learning the words and phrases for their own sake.

The vocabulary items have been selected with a view to being used in a wide range of situations, not just in the contexts in the Student's Book. This should serve students well in all modules of the IELTS exam.

The two-page *Review* at the end of each unit provides further vocabulary practice. The Wordlist at the end summarises the vocabulary items used in each unit. The Workbook provides further practice and the Progress Tests and Final Test provide an opportunity for testing the vocabulary.

## Grammar

Like the vocabulary, the grammar in each unit is selected for its relevance in building students' competence in using language in the IELTS exam, in all four skills. Each unit contains at least one element of grammar in a Language focus section. The context for the grammar selected is found, as for the vocabulary, in either the reading passage or the listening practice. As well as specific speaking activities related to the grammar practice, the writing and speaking tasks provide a wide range of contexts for practising the grammar selected.

*Sam McCarter*

# 1 We are all friends now

Photocopiable activity: Pairwork crossword –
Describing people page 128

Workbook pages 4–11

## Content overview

This unit focuses on people, their
characteristics and relationships.

### Listening SECTION 1

Booking drama classes

Question types: Note completion

### Reading

How teens stay in touch

Question types: Choosing suitable section
headings from a list; Sentence completion;
Identification of information in the text –
*True/False/Not Given*

### Writing TASK 1

Describing a line graph; Verbs of movement;
Analysing main trends and purpose

### Speaking PART 2

Describing a person

**Vocabulary:** Describing people

**Language focus 1:** Likes and dislikes

**Language focus 2:** Present simple, present
continuous and past simple

## Digital overview

### Presentation Kit

Interactive versions of Student's Book exam
tasks

Embedded audio and answer key for all activities

### Teacher's Resource Centre

Communicative activity: Pairwork crossword –
Describing people

Workbook audio, answer key and wordlists

### Student's Resource Centre

Class audio

Wordlist

Speaking Part 2 video and video worksheet

## Vocabulary: Describing people   page 6

### Lead-in

Ask students to look at the title of the unit and
the title of the vocabulary section and predict
the contents of the unit. Give hints by drawing
their attention to the noun *friends* in the title and
elicit what words they know related to *friend*, e.g.,
*friends, friendly, friendship, befriend,* and ways
of describing people, e.g., *physical* and *personal*.
Also elicit from students adjectives to distinguish
between different types of adjectives of personality.
Classify the words on the board under the headings
'positive features/characteristics' and 'negative
features/characteristics'.

**1–6** Students follow the exercises in the Student's
Book. Give them specific times to complete the
exercises so that they increase their awareness of
time management, which is essential in performing
competently in the IELTS exam. This can be
introduced gradually.

**1** 👥 Ask the students to look at the photos in pairs
and discuss them, along with the questions, giving
reasons and examples. Then discuss the photos and
questions together as a whole class.

**2** Make sure students understand all the vocabulary.
Point out that any item can be used more than
once. Elicit examples from the class to check
comprehension. You might want to give your own
example(s) at the end.

> **POSSIBLE ANSWERS**
>
> 1 adventurous, sporty    2 supportive, helpful
> 3 reliable, conscientious  4 artistic, creative

**3** When students have done the exercise in pairs and
checked their answers as a whole class, elicit or
point out the importance of such an exercise. It
helps them to build their vocabulary and, hence,
their confidence.

You might want to elicit more adjectives with
suffixes. This always gives students an opportunity
to bring their own knowledge into the lesson. Keep
your own notes of students' contributions for future
reference.

> **ANSWERS**
>
> 1 talented              2 humorous
> 3 caring/careful         4 generous
> 5 confident              6 social, sociable
> 7 knowing, knowledgeable 8 punctual

**4** After you have checked the students' answers, point out how the sentences can be used to explain the adjective and add more detail, e.g., 1 *My grandfather is (very) humorous, because he …* . For further practice, ask students to give you a few more sentences of their own by way of introducing the next two exercises. Write the sentences on the board.

ANSWERS

| | |
|---|---|
| 1 humorous | 2 knowledgeable |
| 3 talented | 4 punctual |
| 5 confident | 6 generous |
| 7 caring | 8 sociable |

**5–6**  Monitor students during pairwork, trying not to interfere. Give feedback at the end on use of vocabulary and a selection of errors.

## Round up

To round up this section, you could ask students to discuss the following in pairs/groups or as a whole class: *'People generally judge other people just by their appearance without knowing them.' Do you think this is true? Why/Why not? Do you do this yourself?* Monitor the discussion and give feedback on examples of good practice and areas for improvement.

## Listening SECTION 1 page 7

Ask students to read the *What to expect in the exam* and *How to go about it* boxes. Check comprehension by asking specific questions about the content of the boxes and/or by asking students to summarise the information in their words.

**1–2** Point out that the dictation of numbers and letters, as well as spelling, is a feature of the Listening test Section 1. Therefore, students, even advanced students, need to be competent in this area. Encourage students to do further practice outside the classroom by dictating to each other, or recording number and letter sequences, or names, on their phones and playing them to themselves and their colleagues to write down.

**3** It is important for students to remember that they hear the recording only once, so they need to use a wide range of skills to ensure they perform well. Also, it is important that they use what they know about the world, however limited, to predict what is coming. This is an invaluable skill in all aspects of the exam.

ANSWERS

Acting, singing and dancing
Both children and adults

**4** Questions 1–10 can be done as a pairwork exercise followed by global checking. This should then be done for every similar type of question in both the Listening and Reading components so that it is automatic by the time students come to the exam.

Remind students that each section of the Listening test is played only once. However, to build up student confidence, play Section 1 more than once after students have checked their answers. In the exam, students write their answers in a listening booklet and then transfer their answers to the answer sheet at the end of the exam. They have 10 minutes to do so. At an early stage, it is also worthwhile practising this transfer onto a sheet of paper, as many mistakes are made in the transfer process rather than during the completion of the Listening test.

Copy a grid or create a grid for students to use for transferring their answers.

ANSWERS

| | | |
|---|---|---|
| 1 Number | 2 Number | 3 Noun |
| 4 Number | 5 (plural) Noun | 6 Number/Noun |
| 7 Number | 8 Name | 9 Number |
| 10 Number | | |

Point out that in order to get a high score band, e.g., 7 in the IELTS exam, they will need to get all ten answers correct in Section 1.

---

🎧 **Listening script 01**

**(M = Maggie; D = Director)**

**M:** Hi. My name's Maggie. I think I spoke to you yesterday about coming in to see you about the drama classes.

**D:** Oh yes. Hi. How can I help you?

**M:** We're new to the area and I'd like my children, Terry, Andrea and Jasmine, to join the drama classes. They love acting, singing and dancing and they're very energetic and I also thought it would be a good way for them to make friends.

**D:** Oh yes, we offer dancing and singing as well as acting classes and the club's a good place for everyone to meet new people. We have different social and family groups and everyone here's very friendly.

**M:** Great. Can I just ask you some questions about the drama classes?

**D:** Yes sure. What would you like to know?

**M:** Mmm, what classes are there and when are they held?

**D:** Well … during the week, we have classes for different age groups. … By the way, what ages are your children?

**M:** Terry's 8, Andrea's 12 and Jasmine's 16.

**D:** Well, for the youngest age group, those aged 7–11, the times are 5.30 pm–6.30 pm on Tuesday evening and for those aged 12–15 between 4 and 6 pm on Wednesday evening … and for those 16 and above it's 6–8 pm on Friday evening.

M: Is there anything at the weekends?

D: Yes. We also have workshops on Saturdays from 10 am–1 pm, but they're usually for older members, <u>18</u> and above. We also have social outings to theatres, at discount rates. So it's possible for whole families to come. We even get free theatre tickets at times, which we announce on our website.

M: Oh that's good to know. And what about school holidays?

D: Well, during the holidays, we run <u>summer camps</u> for young people up to the age of 16. These usually run from 10 am–1 pm and 2 pm–5 pm Monday to Friday. They are combined with the youth club activities and run during August.

M: And what about performances?

D: For each level, we aim to have at least <u>one show</u> a year in the summer. There is no pressure for anyone to perform, but we do encourage everyone to get involved one way or another, either acting or behind the scenes. Usually everyone is really enthusiastic to take part.

M: Is it possible to have a look around?

D: Yes, sure. The building's used by other groups. … We have no changing facilities, just a large room with lockers where people can put their things, if necessary. But we advise people to come dressed for the workshops … in loose clothing and trainers.

· · · · · · · · · · · · · · · · · · · · · · · · · · · · · · · · · · · · · · · · ·

M: Can my kids join immediately?

D: Yes they can. We always ask people to come and have a go first of all. Children usually come to meet new people and then want to come back, even the shy ones.

M: That's a good sign. Is there a fee?

D: There's a joining fee of <u>£14</u> a year, per person, and then there's a separate fee for the Saturday workshops, but they're usually very cheap. It's just to pay the workshop trainer, as we survive on small grants and gifts.

M: OK. I think I'd like to bring the children along.

D: Great! What's your full name and address?

M: My name's Maggie Campbell.

D: Is that C–A–M–P–B–E–L–L?

M: Yes.

D: And the address?

M: It's 133 Arbuthnot Drive. I'll spell it. It's A–R–B–U–T–H–N–O–T.

D: And the postcode?

M: It's RV27 8PB

D: And the children's names again?

M: Terry, he'll come for the Tuesday class, so that's the 17 March. And Andrea, she'll come for the class on the 18th March. And Jasmine on the 20th.

D: Can I take a mobile number?

M: It's <u>07700336601</u>.

D: And your email address?

M: It's M-A- …

**ANSWERS**

| | | |
|---|---|---|
| **1** 5.30 (pm) | **2** 4 (pm) | **3** Friday |
| **4** (older members) 18/eighteen | | |
| **5** summer camps | **6** 1/one show | **7** (£)14 |
| **8** Arbuthnot | **9** RV27 8PB | **10** 07700336601 |

**5** Encourage students to develop their answers by giving at least one example and reason. Follow up with the whole class, checking both these elements. To round off this section, have a brief global discussion on content, and a review of the listening section from the organisational point of view, e.g., *the types of questions, the number in each set, what they test, the purpose of such testing,* etc.

# Language focus 1: Likes and dislikes
page 9

**1** Look at the sentences with the class and elicit the answer. Go through the Grammar reference on page 219 of the Student's Book to refresh students' knowledge if necessary. Highlight the essential difference between the use of the *–ing* form and *to*.

**ANSWERS**

She uses the *–ing* form after love as she is emphasising what her children love from past experience of doing it. This is different from *would like* followed by the infinitive with *to*, which indicates future action, routine, habit or duty, as opposed to enjoyment from past experience. Compare: *I'd love to go to the cinema/I want to go to the cinema* with *I love to go to the cinema*.

**2** Ask students to work in pairs. Make sure students are clear about why the sentences are correct and incorrect.

**ANSWERS**

| | | |
|---|---|---|
| **1** Correct | **2** Correct | **3** Incorrect – 'to join' |
| **4** Correct | **5** Correct | **6** Correct |
| **7** Incorrect – 'doing' | | |

**3–4** Students can do the exercises in pairs, checking the answers to exercise 3 before moving on to exercise 4. Check comprehension by asking one or two questions about reasons for the answers or suggesting other answers for each exercise.

**ANSWERS**

**3**

| | |
|---|---|
| **1** playing | **2** to live |
| **3** being/to be | **4** keeping/to keep |
| **5** taking | **6** to be |
| **7** socialising/to socialise, staying/stay | **8** playing |
| **9** to see/seeing | |

**4**

**1** I'd like to live in the country.

**2** Nowadays people dislike doing certain sports.

**3** I like playing tennis.

4 She enjoys shopping enormously.

5 He likes people he knows to be honest.

6 She would prefer to see the film on DVD at home rather than at the cinema.

7 He really loves mingling/to mingle with other people at parties.

## Further practice

Before students do exercises 5 and 6, you can ask them to do some further practice in the Review section, online or using the photocopiable material in the Teacher's Book on page 128.

5 (CD) Before students discuss different ways of communicating, write the phrase *ways of communicating* in a box at the top of the board, in the middle. In a row below this box draw four or five boxes. Elicit different ways of communicating, e.g., email, letter, instant messages, video-messaging, social media such as Facebook, landline, smartphone, video calling such as Skype or Facetime, and other communication apps. Write examples and draw additional boxes, if necessary. Ask students what the relationship is between the first box and the row of boxes beneath, i.e. general/specific (examples); hyperordinate/subordinate. Use whichever terms you think are suitable. Point out that they are classifying information and elicit the term *classification*. Elicit and point out features like *classification of information* and refer students to this and other features in IELTS essentials on page 205 of the Teacher's Book throughout the course.

6 (CD) Students can discuss the questions either in small groups or pairs, followed by whole-class feedback.

## Speaking PART 2 page 9

Ask students to go through the *What to expect in the exam* box. To emphasise certain important points, elicit and/or stress that they only have one minute to make notes of 10–12 words in total. Ask what the effect of reading sentences or long notes aloud would have on their fluency. Note that making and taking notes are essential skills that need to be practised in academic settings.

1–3 (CD) Ask students to work in pairs and follow the instructions. You can allow students to follow the three stages through themselves or stop them after each exercise. Before you start the sequence, check that they understand what they are doing.

### POSSIBLE ANSWERS

1 supportive, helpful, patient

4 Refer students to the *How to go about it* box and the Task Card. After they have looked at the box, ask them a few content questions. Read through the prompts on the Task Card, eliciting which part of

the task is the most important, i.e. *and explain why*, and explain why – the first prompts are description, setting the scene for the reasoning required in the last prompt. Ask students to complete the exercise in pairs and then check their answers.

> ### ANSWERS
>
> who this person is – present simple/future with *going to*
> what this person does – present simple
> what qualities this person has – present simple
> explain why you would like to be similar to this person – conditional

5 Before students start, go through the example, eliciting the types of words in the list, e.g., *nouns, adjectives,* etc., and tell them to write only 10–12 words as notes in order. Elicit which prompt they should write more words for. Students should do this first on their own and then compare their notes in pairs. You can ask one or two students to read out their notes.

   Remind them that each point must be covered. Ask students to discuss the best way for them to write their notes, horizontally or vertically (like the prompts or notes in a PowerPoint presentation).

6 Monitor students as they roleplay, encouraging them to be responsible for timing themselves. Allow 1–2 minutes each, permitting them to use their mobiles for this, if it is permissible. Time permitting, and depending on your students, ask a student to talk about the prompt card and/or answer it yourself.

   If time allows, ask students to adapt the card or write their own cards, e.g., *a family member/celebrity,* etc. *they admire/would not like,* etc. Some students may want to do this, as they may not want to do the same card as their partner.

## Reading Passage page 10

1 Introduce the IELTS Reading test to students. Go through the *What to expect in the exam* box and refer students to the Ready for Reading on page 84. Clarify and/or elicit information about the Reading test from the students. Ask students to do the exercise in pairs or groups. Point out the importance of the following reading skills in IELTS: *surveying, predicting, skimming and scanning* – see IELTS strategies page 203. Point out that each of the three passages are a minimum of 750 words and approximately 2,700 words in total. Elicit the importance of initially surveying the title and sub-headings, then going on to look at the questions before skimming the text.

2–3 (CD) Students do these exercises in pairs or groups.

### Questions 1–13

Ask students to answer Questions 1–13 on their own or do the three sets of questions in stages.

Once you are satisfied students are preparing effectively, let them do the reading. Time them for 20 minutes, but give extra time if necessary. At this stage, confidence-building is important, and the extra time allowed for a correct answer can be slowly reduced over the duration of the course.

When going over the answers, it's helpful to project the text onto the board so you can underline and indicate where to find answers. You can prepare this before class so you are sure of the answers yourself.

*True/False/Not Given* questions are one of the main areas of difficulty for students in the IELTS Reading test, so take time to go over and discuss answers. The distinction between *False* and *Not Given* must be carefully explained to students from the outset so that care can be taken in future units.

Make a grid with numbers 1–13 on the left. Each time the students do a reading exercise, get them to write their answers in the grid and keep it as a record. They should tick the questions that are right, and leave the ones that are wrong blank. This will help them analyse their reading performance and identify what areas to focus on in their self-study. As in the exam, the reading passages vary in difficulty. As a rough guide, if students are aiming for a score of 6/6.5 in Reading, they should aim to have at least 9 out of 13 correct answers.

## Questions 1–6

Ask students to go through the *How to go about it* box. Then check they have understood the contents by asking them questions to help them analyse the form of the headings, e.g., *What are general nouns? Where do they occur in the headings here? What is the importance of general nouns? How do they help you?* Refer students to IELTS essentials on page 205. Point out that paragraph and section headings are often made up of general nouns like *benefit*, *effect*, *solution*, etc. preceded by an adjective and/or followed by a prepositional phrase like *of … .* These general nouns are usually paraphrases of words in the passage, but not always. The nouns summarise the content and the meaning or function of the sections in relation to the rest of the text. It is useful to train students to notice different section and paragraph types and where they would expect them to appear in a text.

Many of your students are used to a *bottom-up* approach where they read every word. Gradually, however, encourage them to employ a *top-down* approach as well, where they *skim* and *scan*. In the IELTS exam, students need to *skim* the Reading Passage to get the gist and *scan* to locate information. They use close reading when they stop to analyse specific information in the Reading Passage to answer a question.

It is essential that you do not over analyse a text and the questions. Gradually wean students off this as you go through the course, as detailed analysis slows them down in the exam.

## Questions 7–10

Encourage students to use the headings to help locate the answers. As Question 7 is the first specific question, tell students that they will probably find it near the beginning of the text. Check if any of the questions relate in any way to the section headings. Use the scanning techniques described in Ready for Reading on page 84.

## Questions 11–13

Introduce students to *True/False/Not Given* statements. As students find *False* and *Not Given* statements particularly difficult, spend time analysing the questions before they answer them. Look at examples of some common sentence types in Ready for Reading on page 84. Read the explanation there with the whole class for the difference between *False* and *Not Given*. Once again, students should use the headings to help locate the answers.

**4** 💬 Students discuss the question in pairs or in small groups.

### Extension

Encourage students to notice and keep a record of general nouns they meet with an example of context, especially noting where they occur in a text, e.g., at the beginning of paragraphs in introductions, in topic sentences, etc. You can also keep a class record for revision purposes as the course progresses. See the Wordlist on page 211.

## Language focus 2: Present simple, present continuous and past simple
page 13

**1–3** Students do exercises 1–3 in pairs. Then go through the examples and explanations with the whole class and refer students to the Grammar reference on page 219 of the Student's Book, or display it on an interactive whiteboard using the Presentation Kit. Elicit the form and function of the three tenses with examples from students' own experiences by asking questions, e.g., *How do you get to school/college, etc?. What are you doing now? What did you do … ?.*

ANSWERS

**1**

1 Paragraph G   2 Paragraph A   3 Paragraph F

**2**

1 noted – past simple
2 are making, is changing – present continuous
3 help – present simple

**3**

a present simple
b present continuous
c past simple
d present simple

**4** Students do the exercise in pairs followed by whole-class feedback.

ANSWERS

| | |
|---|---|
| 1 helps | 2 participated |
| 3 affected | 4 influenced |
| 5 are recruiting | 6 feel |

**5** Ask students to do this in pairs. Check general comprehension by eliciting several examples from the class.

### Further practice

Ask students to do the exercise from the Review on page 16.

### Extension

Time permitting, and as a future revision exercise, ask students to work in pairs/groups. Give them a text on any subject of no more than a page. Ask them to underline examples of the present simple, present continuous and past simple only (ignoring all other tenses). This will help them notice the verbs and the tenses in the sentences and the frequency of certain tenses. Choose non-academic, and general academic texts. Follow up with a brief discussion.

## Writing  TASK 1   page 13

### Verbs of movement

**1** Briefly introduce Writing Task 1, pointing out that one of the things students have to do is describe line graphs. Mention that this section is an introduction to the writing task on page 206. Ask students to do the exercise in pairs. If possible, show the image of the lines on the whiteboard, and check their answers carefully. You can then show how each movement works on the page. Make sure students understand all of these verbs so they can accurately describe line graphs. You might want to check comprehension by giving true/false phrases for A–B, etc. and asking students to decide if they are correct or not.

ANSWERS

1 h   2 d   3 b   4 g   5 j   6 i   7 a   8 e
9 c   10 f

**2** Students follow the instructions in the Student's Book.

ANSWERS

| | |
|---|---|
| 1 fell and then levelled off | 2 hit a peak |
| 3 dipped | 4 plummeted |
| 5 rose gradually | 6 remained flat |
| 7 declined steadily | 8 fluctuated |
| 9 hit a low | 10 soared |

**3–4** Students do the exercises in pairs. Emphasise the importance of using nouns where possible instead of verbs as they help to summarise information. Elicit where they have already seen this in Unit 1, i.e. section headings in the Reading section.

Go through the example in exercise 4 carefully and stress the preposition after the noun and encourage students to learn the nouns with their prepositions, e.g., *decrease/drop/increase/rise in*, etc. To help build students' vocabulary and their confidence, encourage them to keep a written/electronic record of verbs and their nouns for use in Task 1 along with the appropriate preposition (also for Task 2 and Speaking). Point out that this process is called *nominalisation* and is an essential part of IELTS. Refer students to *Nominalisation* in IELTS strategies on page 203. Introduce students to this here and reiterate where appropriate throughout the course.

ANSWERS

**3**

The following verbs can be nouns: dip, decline, decrease, drop, fall, increase, rise
Note: recover/recovery, stabilise/stability/stabilisation, fluctuate/fluctuations

**4**

Possible answers

2 There was a peak in numbers in the year 2009.
3 There was slight fall followed by a quick recovery in the amount of money spent.
5 There was a steady increase in book purchases over the year.
7 There was a gradual decrease in attendance at the conference last year.
8 There were (some) fluctuations in the growth rate during the previous year.
9 There was a low in member numbers in March.

**5** Ask students to do the exercise in pairs and elicit several examples from the class.

## Analysing main trends and purpose

Give more details about Task 1, as you go through the *What to expect in the exam* box. Elicit from students how much they know about this part of the exam and whether they have analysed and then written about data before. This may be the first time for many of them. Refer students to Ready for Writing on page 128 for more information. When you do exercises related to Task 1, give students time to look at and absorb the information and gradually encourage them to see patterns, i.e. *trends, both similar and contrasting*. Emphasise here the distinction between general, e.g., *the overview*, and specific, e.g., *the data*, information when they analyse and write. For the importance of the relationship between general and specific information, see IELTS essentials on page 205.

For Task 1, encourage students to self-correct where possible. Use a set marking scheme that suits you, e.g., use one based on symbols that indicate the type of error in the piece of writing for the student to correct, e.g., verb/subject agreement (v/s) or preposition (prep). After correction, encourage students to fill out a grid indicating the three most commonly occurring errors for each piece of writing and to work on them.

Encourage students always to paraphrase the rubric in the task where possible – if it can't be paraphrased, then they should not paraphrase, as they might change the topic of the task. Each answer has to contain an overview to obtain a good score. The answer has to be written in paragraphs and be no less that 150 words. Point out that each number counts as a word. Students are not penalised for writing too many words, but they are penalised for not summarising and listing information. Encourage students to aim for 180–185 words maximum and for a minimum of about 160 words. Refer students to *Summarising* in IELTS strategies on page 204. Highlight the word *summarise*, which is the first word in the generic rubric.

In the exam, students should always do Task 1 first as it helps to get them started with writing in preparation for the longer Task 2. They should aim to spend the suggested 20 minutes writing about the task in the exam and during exam practice sessions. For homework and in class preparation they should spend longer and gradually increase their speed during the course.

Encourage students to use a range of generic vocabulary applicable to the task, a range of complex sentences and to avoid repetition.

## Steps for students to analyse data

Encourage students to:
- Look at the topic of the graph/diagram in the title, axes (if a graph), headings or labels (depending on chart type).
- Analyse the data by circling significant points only – contrasts, sudden movement, start and finish.

- Write brief notes on the data; write adjectives, e.g., *gradual/significant*, *dramatic* and nouns, e.g., *rise/fall/fluctuations* next to the appropriate lines.
- Look for general trends and patterns and whether they can group data together.
- Write the answer, paraphrasing the instructions in the introduction, with two body paragraphs showing major trends and examples of specific data.
- Write an overview which can be in the first paragraph, at the beginning of the second paragraph or at the end like a conclusion.

It is very important that students do not try to describe everything in the chart or diagram in a linear fashion, as this does not demonstrate their ability to summarise the data.

Refer students to:
a the Task 1 Writing checklist on page 139 to help them write.
b Ready for Writing page 128.
c the Writing Task 1 band descriptors for bands 5–7 on the Student's Resource Centre. Go through the marking criteria headings so students are aware of what they are aiming for. Focus on only one or two boxes on the criteria table, e.g., task completion, and gradually increase awareness throughout the course.

**1–2** Students follow the instructions in the Student's Book.

ANSWERS

1
1 yes
2 Facebook slight; Pinterest – dramatic (more than double); Instagram – dramatic (more than double); LinkedIn – noticeable (up by a quarter); Twitter – dramatic (nearly 50% increase)
3 a

2
1 d  2 a  3 g  4 c  5 f  6 b  7 e

**3** When students have completed the exercise and you have checked their answers, go through the completed model, eliciting features such as: the paraphrases in the introduction, the overview, noun phrases following the pattern *there is/was* + (adjective) noun + prepositional phrase, linking devices and examples of data. Gauge the number of words. Encourage students to keep a record of phrases/chunks of language for recycling in the future.

ANSWERS
a there was an upward trend in the proportion of adult users of the websites
b enjoyed a 25% rise in the proportion of adult users
c the proportion of adults using Instagram more than doubled.
d the graph depicts
e remained stable
f a similar pattern was apparent
g the proportion of ... increased slightly

**4** Students write their own answer for homework or in class, time permitting. Encourage them to spend longer than the 20 minutes at this stage. You might want to accept a collaborative answer from students (in class and/or for homework) earlier on in the course to build their confidence, but each student should submit a copy. This will depend on your students. Encourage students to look at the checklist on page 139 even though they won't have covered all the points on the list. Remind them to check their work for errors.

Select a few errors anonymously from students' work for class discussion after checking their work.

---

*Model answer*

The chart shows the proportion of users of Twitter by age group from November 2010 to May 2013 in the USA.

Overall, it is clear that there is an upward trend in Twitter use with the greatest increase seen among those aged 18–29. For example, there was a substantial rise in the proportion of 18–29 year-olds using Twitter with a more than twofold increase from approximately 14% in November 2010 to 30% in May 2013. By contrast, while the use of Twitter among those aged 65+ was slightly upward with some noticeable fluctuations and a peak of about 6% in May 2011, their use constituted about 4% in November 2010 compared to 5% at the end of the period.

The rise in Twitter use among 30–49 year olds was dramatic, with an increase of more than 150% from about 7% to 17% in November 2010 and May 2013, respectively. Similarly, there was an increase among those in the 50–64 year-old age group, with those in November 2010 accounting for 6% of users in this age group against approximately 13% in May 2013.

*Word count: 183 words*

**COMMENTS**

*The response fulfils the requirements of the task. There is a clear overview which is supported by reference to the data in the graph. The summarising and comparison mean the information is not just listed but combined into an integrated whole. There is a range of vocabulary and different structures are used.*

---

**Extension**

Encourage students to take an interest in national and international affairs by looking at news channels on the internet to increase their world knowledge. If you have internet access in the classroom, show them an example of the BBC news website, if it is available. Also encourage students to look at websites showing data, such as Eurostat and Office for National Statistics (ONS), so they become familiar with looking at the presentation of data/ statistics.

---

**REVIEW 1 ANSWERS** pages 16–17

## Vocabulary: Describing people

| | | |
|---|---|---|
| **1** humorous | **2** talkative | **3** punctual |
| **4** reliable | **5** talented | **6** conscientious |
| **7** ambitious | **8** sporty | |

## Language focus 1: Likes and dislikes

**1** c **2** f **3** e **4** a **5** h **6** b **7** d **8** i **9** g

## Language focus 2: Present simple, present continuous and past simple

1 enjoy, is causing
2 use, did you first use
3 have, contact
4 want, is, lives, is studying, started
5 spend, was
6 are having, communicate
7 think, it, became, runs
8 was, liked, told, made, is
9 helped, started, support
10 appeal, understand.

## Writing Task 1

1 Club membership increased dramatically between January and March.
2 There was a steady fall in visits to the museum in 2016.
3 There were noticeable fluctuations in online sales.
4 The number of people joining the social website reached a peak in 2015.
5 There was a gradual increase in spectator numbers over the football season.
6 Overall, it is clear that the numbers rose erratically throughout the period.
7 There was a slight decline in the number of visitors to the leisure centre.
8 Ticket sales to the concert rose significantly.

**ACCURACY IN IELTS**

**1**
1 rose **dramatically** (spelling mistake)
2 users in **the** (spelling mistake) morning.
3 He enjoys **being** (wrong verb form)
4 people prefer **to spend** (wrong word) time
5 **rocketed** (wrong tense)
6 My best **friend** (spelling mistake)
7 really **talented** (wrong word form)?
8 so **I don't go** (wrong tense)
9 He **loves** (wrong verb form)
10 Attendances at the conference **fluctuated significantly** (word order)

# 2  Technology – now and then

Photocopiable activity: Group game (groups of 4) – Don't say it page 129

Workbook pages 12–19

## Content overview

This unit focuses on the past, technology and making things.

**Listening** SECTION 2

Museum competition

Question types: Multiple-choice; Matching

**Reading**

The Chinese Bronze Age

Question types: Identification of information in the text – *True/False/Not Given*; Classification; Multiple-choice

**Writing** TASK 2

Discussing both views and giving own opinion

**Speaking** PART 2

Describing an electronic device you have bought/received

**Vocabulary:** Verbs of cause and effect

**Word building:** Evaluating adjectives

**Language focus 1:** Past simple and present perfect

**Language focus 2:** Habit in the past; Adverbs of frequency

## Digital overview

**Presentation Kit**

Interactive versions of Student's Book exam tasks

Embedded audio and answer key for all activities

**Teacher's Resource Centre**

Communicative activity: Group game (groups of 4) – Don't say it

Workbook audio, answer key and wordlists

**Student's Resource Centre**

Class audio

Wordlist

Speaking Part 2 video and video worksheet

## Vocabulary: Verbs of cause and effect

page 18

### Lead-in

Elicit from students as many examples of technology as they can think of in two minutes. This can be done as a whole-class activity with the examples being written directly on the board or students writing examples on their own first, before whole-class feedback. Encourage them to think of the past, e.g., the wheel, as well as the present and current developments. Then ask them to classify their examples accordingly or elicit from the students themselves how they should be classified. Ask them what several of the examples of technology are called in the language(s) they know.

1 💬 Ask students to discuss the questions in pairs, giving them 5–8 minutes. Monitor the discussion, giving hints where necessary, but try not to interfere. As part of whole-class feedback, ask several pairs to justify their choices for the most important inventions of all time and narrow the whole class's choices down to two items. Alternatively, time permitting, elicit the feedback above for students' choices and write their answers on the board in tabular form with the headings *Items* and *Reason*. If applicable, encourage students to do the writing on the board.

2 Make sure students understand what a suffix is. Go through the rubric and check that they understand what they are doing. Remind students of the verbs of movement for Writing Task 1 in Unit 1 where the noun and verb form were the same for *rise*, *drop*, etc. Point out how important this is for fluency, flexibility and general competence in language use, especially as it helps to build their use of vocabulary and increases confidence. Point out *shape/shape* here and ask the students to keep a vocabulary record of similar verbs and nouns, as well as nouns made from the suffixes here. Students complete the exercise. When they have finished, and checked their answers, elicit answers at random from several students. For further practice you might want to elicit other verbs and nouns, as often students will want to supply them.

**ANSWERS**

1 improvement  2 destruction  3 production
4 effect (does not follow the patterns mentioned)
5 harm        6 enhancement  7 promotion
8 damage      9 ruin/ruination  10 result
11 advance/advancement           12 deterioration

**3** Students complete the activity in pairs and feedback as a whole class. Write the three adjectives (positive, negative and neutral) on the board and indicate the headings as students call out their answers. Randomly check comprehension afterwards by saying a verb or noun and asking students to classify it.

**ANSWERS**

| | | |
|---|---|---|
| 1 Positive | 2 Negative | 3 Neutral |
| 4 Neutral | 5 Negative | 6 Positive |
| 7 Positive | 8 Negative | 9 Negative |
| 10 Neutral | 11 Positive | 12 Negative |

**4** Students can do this exercise in pairs or individually followed by whole-class feedback.

**ANSWERS**

1 promotion      2 destruction
3 Advancements/Improvements
4 production      5 deterioration

**5** Ask students to read the rubric and example. Encourage one or more students to explain the example and elicit reasons as to why it is important to be able to transform sentences in this way, e.g. competence, flexibility, etc. When you have gone through the answers with students, introduce the idea, and importance of, paraphrasing. Refer students to *Paraphrasing* in IELTS strategies on page 203 and seek to elicit paraphrases covertly and overtly throughout the rest of the course.

**ANSWERS**

1 People constantly debate whether television has positively or negatively influenced society.
2 The use of mobile phones is dramatically affecting the way we communicate.
3 Climate change has destroyed many crops.
4 Did the invention of the internet really harm the way people live and work?
5 The sales of certain mobile telephones deteriorated sharply as a result of a series of new software inventions.
6 The use of technology meant that the archaeologists hardly damaged the site.
7 Many people like Einstein and Newton have shaped science.

**6** After the student discussion, have a whole-class discussion.

**Round up**

Point out the importance of nouns and remind them of the focus on nouns in Unit 1. Elicit whether the nouns in exercise 2 are general or specific nouns. For further practice, elicit from students the adjectives and phrases that were used in exercise 5 to build meaning around the general noun, e.g., *a dramatic effect on the way we communicate*. And as a further noticing exercise, point out the relevance of these words for paragraph and section headings in the Reading test, and for working out the meaning of Writing Task 2 questions.

## Listening SECTION 2 page 20

**1** Ask students to go through the *What to expect in the exam* box. Check they understand by asking them questions about this section. Then tell them to read through the questions, and elicit differences between the questions in this section and Section 1, e.g., less personal, longer questions so more reading; different types of questions, especially the matching questions. Ask them to read the *How to go about it* box and discuss it in pairs. Then discuss as a whole class clarifying any points.

Make sure they understand the importance of the pre-listening preparation in the exam. Remind them that in the exam itself they hear the recording once only. Stress that if they miss an answer they should predict, answer and move on, as dwelling on it can cause them to miss the next couple of answers.

Ask selected students to give and explain any words they circled/underlined in Questions 11–15. Go over the synonyms suggested. Take any questions about the Listening test and then play it. Ask students to transfer their answers to a grid or sheet of paper and then check their answers in pairs. If necessary, play the test again. Allow students to change answers. Check the answers as a whole class and play Section 2 again, asking the students either to follow the script or look at the questions and answers as they listen. Discuss any questions that were generally problematic for the class as a whole.

An alternative confidence building pre-listening activity is to ask the students to work in groups and use the questions to describe as much information as they can about what they will hear. This information can then be discussed as a whole class.

**POSSIBLE ANSWERS**

yearly: every/each year; on a yearly basis
is held together: happens/takes place/is organised in conjunction with/along with/as part of
subject: topic/theme
during the preparation for: while the …. is being prepared
influence: have an effect/impact on

**Listening script 02**

Welcome. My name's Darren Timpson, and I'm the Director of the Penwood Museum and I'm here to announce the winners of our annual competition, which as usual runs <u>in conjunction with our summer exhibition</u>. Each year the competition has a specific theme. And the theme we chose for this year's competition is 'the use of technology <u>to improve links between the local community and the museum</u>'. Entrants could choose from a selection of the museum's artefacts to create exhibits on this topic. We've had loads of entries from secondary schools, which is important as more local teenagers are getting involved.

I just want to give you some background information about this year's competition. The competition was open to groups of young people from institutions like schools and youth clubs, who were aged between <u>15 and 19</u> on the final entry date for the competition, which was 13 May. While preparing their competition entry, <u>the competitors were allowed to use the educational facilities at the museum</u> and to look for help from local sponsors, but were not allowed to buy any equipment. We then had seven shortlisted exhibits, which visitors to the museum of all ages were allowed to vote on for the first three places.

<u>The prize-winning exhibits are having a big impact on Penwood Museum attendances, which have risen by up to 45 per cent since the summer show opened.</u> The first prize in this year's competition has been won by a group of seven young people, who chose various exhibits from the museum's collection of equipment from the 1950s to the 1970s. They arranged them with modern versions and then recorded their own reactions and comments to the exhibits. They then did the same with the comments made by visitors aged 65 and over. And so can we have a round of applause for the winners from Tigers Community Centre, who called their entry *Technology – now and then*?

And the second prize winners are Tabard High …

...........................................................

Before we have some refreshments, I'd like to draw your attention to some of the video commentaries on the winning exhibit which have been left by members of the public, and which are very moving … and some very funny. I particularly liked seeing the recording of the reaction of several people when they talked about an early wooden-framed TV from their childhood. <u>They remembered their first TV, which they thought still fitted in with today's trends.</u> They remembered how they would sometimes all go round to someone's house to watch TV as a special treat. But they thought the modern TV screen with the remote was much easier to watch.

As for the collection of old radios, it has to be seen. They are really huge old wooden-framed radios in perfect working order and in perfect condition. Some teenagers' reactions to the radios were very funny; they couldn't believe how big they were.

And the older visitors, all of whom used to have one, said they liked them. <u>But they also thought they</u> <u>were too big to fit into living rooms these days.</u> A few more items worth looking at from the display are old kitchen items. Young people thought the cooker from the 1950s looked funny alongside the latest microwaves.

Nearly all interviewees who were aged 65 and over used microwave ovens, <u>which they thought were much handier</u>. Seeing old typewriters on display next to slim laptops made them look weird and cumbersome. <u>All those who were 65 and over preferred the laptops, which they thought were thrilling.</u> The other electronic items on display were a collection of old and fairly recent cameras. <u>They also thought the older cameras were 'well made</u>, and better than the newer ones'.

I'd like to thank you all for coming and please give a round of applause for all the entrants to the competition.

**ANSWERS QUESTIONS 11–15**

**11** C  **12** B  **13** C  **14** A  **15** C

**ANSWERS QUESTIONS 16–20**

**16** F  **17** A  **18** C  **19** D  **20** E

**2** Students discuss the question in pairs or small groups followed by whole-class feedback.

## Word building: Evaluating adjectives page 21

Elicit the meaning of the title of the section. Ask the students how they normally evaluate something, e.g., probably by saying *I think*, etc. Point out that they can evaluate and give their opinion by using adjectives, both positive and negative. Ask them to look briefly at the list in the exercise. Then elicit the concept of prefixes and suffixes, referring back to the suffixes in Vocabulary: Verbs of cause and effect at the beginning of the unit. Ask students to compare this with language they know. Point out that as in the Vocabulary section, the use of prefixes and suffixes is a good way of expanding their vocabulary.

**1–4** Follow the instructions in the Student's Book and check the answers. Explain why other alternatives are incorrect, if necessary.

**ANSWERS**

**1**
unimportant: insignificant, trivial, irrelevant, minor
useless: ineffective, worthless, inadequate
valueless: insignificant, worthless, useless
harmless: safe

**2**
Possible answers
important: crucial, vital, essential, key
useful: practical, helpful, effective
valuable: invaluable, worthwhile, useful
harmful: damaging, destructive, detrimental

ANSWERS

**3**

| | | | | | |
|---|---|---|---|---|---|
| 1 | useless | 2 | impractical | 3 | unimportant |
| 4 | unnecessary | 5 | insignificant | 6 | harmless |
| 7 | valueless | 8 | inconvenient | 9 | ineffective |
| 10 | unappealing | 11 | worthless | 12 | uninspiring |

**4**

| | | | |
|---|---|---|---|
| 1 | impractical | 2 | (an) effective (solution) |
| 3 | convenient | 4 | worthwhile |
| 5 | (a) harmless (activity) | 6 | inspiring |

## Round up

Elicit the importance of these adjectives as a preparation for the next section.

## Speaking PART 2 page 22

**1** Introduce the Speaking Part 2 Task Cards by eliciting some brief exam information on timing, writing notes, etc. Remind students that they only have one minute so notes must be brief (refer them back to the practice in Unit 1). Use a stopwatch to time them. Ask students to read the task cards, choose a task and make notes.

POSSIBLE ANSWERS

An electronic device you have bought: smart watch, online, last week, to track fitness
An electronic present you have received: tablet, friend, last month, attractive, modern, convenient, practical

**2** Monitor students as they discuss their notes with another pair. Ensure each point on the card is covered.

**3** Go through the checklist before students start speaking with a new partner. At this stage, ask them to choose two or three items that they would like feedback on. Encourage them to keep within the time limit for the task and, in order to create awareness, ask them to monitor their own time as good time management is an essential skill in the IELTS exam. Ask students to check their notes before they speak to see if they have used evaluating adjectives. Allow them to change any adjectives if they haven't. Give whole-class feedback, especially as regards the use of evaluating adjectives.

## Language focus 1: Past simple and present perfect page 22

**1** Do this as a whole-class activity. Elicit the reasons for the tense choices from the Listening test. If there is still confusion, revise the differences between the past simple and the present perfect, and active and passive voices, eliciting as much as possible from the students. Refer students to the Grammar reference on page 220.

ANSWERS

1  a  won – present perfect, chose – past simple;
   b  arranged – past simple, recorded – past simple;
   c  allowed to use – past simple

2  the present perfect introduces the news about the winner. It describes an event which has a connection to the present. The past simple is used to describe completed actions, events or states in the past.

3  a and c. In a the passive is used as the prize is the focus of the sentence. In c the passive is used because the agent is not important.

**2** Ask students to do exercise 2 in pairs or groups and check their answers at the end of the exercise.

ANSWERS

1  began
2  were, didn't have, have become
3  have started
4  went, have never visited
5  Have you ever seen
6  have improved
7  did, have not done, spent

**3** Students discuss their answers in pairs.

ANSWERS

1  active; revolutionised
2  active; contributed
3  active; led
4  passive; was first played
5  passive; was invented
6  active; created, shaped, lived
7  active; travelled
8  active; influenced

**4** Give students a time limit to write the five sentences and monitor for accuracy. Make sure they use some time phrases.

**5** Encourage students to develop their answers for the *wh-* questions. Monitor for accuracy as they work together. Give them a time limit before they change roles. Question forms are often demanding for students and they may need extra practice. Also ensure that answers are given as fully as possible.

## Reading Passage page 23

By way of a reading review, elicit reading skills from Unit 1. See Teacher's Book page 13. Review the reading skills: prediction, time management, skimming and scanning. Refer students to the list of IELTS strategies on page 203.

### Questions 1–13

Ask the students to read Questions 1–13 in pairs/ groups and discuss the content of the Reading Passage. During whole-class feedback, elicit whether the passage is the same as or different from the passage in Unit 1, e.g., ask if it's *historical, descriptive, argumentative* or *problem and solution*. Discuss which features the task has, e. g., *classification, description* and how important it is to notice all this before reading the passage and elicit reasons. Point out the importance of noticing and refer students to IELTS Strategies on page 203.

Go through the *How to go about it* box. Check students' predictions and underlining/circling choices carefully. Students do the test on their own. Encourage them to be responsible for their own time management, but give them time 'warnings' at 10 and 15 minutes. Go round the class checking where they are in the test at these stages so you can gauge their competence throughout the course. Give them an extra 5–10 minutes, but tell them to put a mark against the question they were on after the initial 20 minutes. This way they can see how much they need to speed up by the time of the actual exam.

Ask students to compare answers, and, justify their answers.

Go over the answers, projecting the digital text onto the board, if possible. Focus on one or more sections carefully, e.g., classification and/or *True/False/Not Given* answers. Avoid overworking the Reading Passage, as this puts students off reading. At this stage, you can go over any difficult words in the text, pointing out that there is no glossary in the exam except for one or two words. Tell them it should be possible to predict the meanings from the context, and that precise dictionary definitions are not necessary in order to answer the questions.

**ANSWERS**

**1** TRUE   **2** FALSE   **3** FALSE   **4** NOT GIVEN
**5** FALSE   **6** FALSE
**7** B   **8** B   **9** A   **10** C   **11** A   **12** C   **13** B

**1** Discuss the question as a whole class.

### Language focus 2: Habit in the past

page 25

**1** Go through the examples, making any necessary clarifications. Elicit examples from the students for concept checking by asking students about things they used to/would do. Go through the Grammar reference on page 220 and point out the structure of questions and negatives with *used to*.

**ANSWERS**

**1** a   **2** a   **3** b

**2** In pairs, students discuss in detail what is wrong with some of the sentences and correct them. Discuss as a whole class.

**ANSWERS**

**1** Correct
**2** Correct
**3** *Used to* is used to talk about states (e.g. occupations), not *would*.
**4** Correct
**5** You don't say *would build* or *used to build* his own car, but *built*
**6** *Didn't go* to is needed, not *didn't use to*. The action is neither repeated nor a state.
**7** Correct
**8** Correct

Students make sentences about their own childhoods. Each student says one to the rest of the class and explains the sentence. Peer correct here where possible.

### Adverbs of frequency   page 25

**1–3** Go through exercises 1–3 as a whole class. Elicit the answers from students and go through the Grammar reference on page 220.

**ANSWERS**

**1**
sometimes, position 4
**2**
usually, normally, commonly
**3**
position 2: usually
position 3: commonly, regularly, often
position 4: occasionally, not often
position 5: not often, hardly ever, rarely

**4** Ask students to do the exercise individually, followed by whole-class feedback.

**ANSWERS**

**1** never   **2** usually/normally   **3** correct
**4** rarely   **5** correct   **6** correct

**5** Ask students to discuss the following questions in pairs:
1 What would people do in the past without technology?
2 What kinds of electronic devices did people use to have in your secondary school?
3 How did people use to find information before the arrival of the Internet?

During whole-class feedback, elicit examples and reasons from students. If possible, ask students to ask you the same questions.

# Writing TASK 2 page 26

**1** Introduce Writing Task 2, going through the *What to expect in the exam* box. Refer students to the checklist on page 139 and Ready for Writing on page 128.

Give students time to work in pairs and analyse the writing task. When they have done this go through their answers as a whole class, pointing out the different elements of the task: the generic aspects of the rubric, e.g., *time, word length* and *Give reasons and examples,* and the topic for discussion in a statement (in italics) followed by the focus of the task (again in italics). Emphasise that the statement contains two views and the task then asks students to discuss each view (two body paragraphs) and then write about their own view (one body paragraph). With an introduction and conclusion, this is five paragraphs in all. Reiterate this again as they go through the *How to go about it* box.

Students can do exercise 1 in pairs followed by whole-class feedback.

### ANSWERS

**1** Positive: the first part (*Some people believe* …)
   Negative: the second part (… *while others think* …)
**2** **a** positive **b** negative **c** negative **d** positive

**2–3** Students can do these exercises in pairs. Ask them to discuss the ways suggested and give reasons for their own preferences.

### ANSWERS

**2**
**a** more inconvenient/less convenient/greater inconvenience
**b** harmless for society
**c** affecting production at work positively
**d** (more) impractical

**3**
Brainstorming: where you write down as many ideas associated with the topic as you can, often in a limited time.
Word association: where you write down words that you associate with a word or idea; using perspectives such as educational, social, financial, environmental, economical, technological.

You can give examples of the different methods, trying and comparing the use of opposites, word association, and generating ideas. Different pairs or groups can try different techniques and compare answers.

**4** Point out that introductions should be short, perhaps no more than two or three sentences with a maximum of about 30 words. Point out that as the conclusion should also be short, about 20–30

words, this leaves about 190 words to achieve the minimum word limit, so about 65 words for each body paragraph. Students should, however, aim for about 75–80 words for each body paragraph. When it is broken up like this it is more reassuring for students.

When students have made their choices, elicit reasons from the whole class.

### ANSWERS

Introductions 2 and 3: They cover all three elements of the question: both points of view and the writer's own opinion. Introduction 1 is quite short and covers only the two points of view and does not state the writer's position/stance/opinion.

**5** Students can do this exercise in pairs or groups. Point out the features of an introduction: a general statement (a hook) followed by a statement, which says what is going to be discussed in the body paragraphs. Point out the general-specific relationship between the two sentences, with the first sentence giving general background related to the topic and the second sentence highlighting the particular aspect of the topic the answer will focus on.

### ANSWERS

Add another sentence: e.g., Personally, I think it is a mixture of both./Personally, I think that technology is largely beneficial.

**6–7** These can be done in pairs or groups with students giving their reasons for their answers. It is important now to point out the generic rubric relating to giving reasons and examples, which students tend to ignore because they see it all the time and do not notice it. Point out that each paragraph should contain reasons and examples to back up any statement that they make. Tell them to think of 'State and prove' (making a statement and backing it up with evidence) as a feature of organisation in writing a paragraph. (Compare writing an overview and proving it in Writing Task 1 with paragraph headings and paragraph development in reading, e.g., topic/general statements followed by supporting evidence in reading passages.)

### ANSWERS

|  | Example | Reason | Result | Additional Information | Purpose | Contrast |
|---|---|---|---|---|---|---|
| **Adverb** | for example |  | As a result | Moreover |  | However |
| **Conjunction** |  | because |  |  | in order to |  |
| **Other** | like, such as |  |  |  |  |  |

**8–9** These exercises can be done in pairs with whole-class feedback. It is essential that students are able to distinguish between adverbs and conjunctions. Point out that part of the writing criteria tests their ability to develop ideas using complex sentences, i.e. sentences that have two or more ideas/clauses linked using conjunctions.

ANSWERS

**8**
for instance/Take, for example, …

**9**
Conjunction/contrast: but, although
Conjunction/reason: since, as
Conjunction/result: so, and so
Adverb/additional information: similarly, furthermore, also
Adverb/result: consequently, so, therefore
Other/purpose: to

**10** This can be done as a group exercise with answers being collated on the board. Time and resources permitting, students can rewrite the text on a large sheet of paper to display to the whole class. This is a good way to raise awareness of paraphrasing for all levels.

**11** Students do this for homework or in class as a timed essay. Encourage students to look at the checklist on page 139 and to think about the content of this writing section.

*Model answer*

Technology is seen by some people as the key to success for young students. Others, however, argue that it has a negative impact, but I think technology is a positive force for the young as they study.

 Some are of the opinion that the role played by technology in the studying process for the young is very important, because, compared to the past, studying is now much more efficient and convenient. For example, recent advances in areas such as mobile technology mean that information can now be accessed at any time and anywhere, thus reducing the effort students need to devote to researching for essays and studies in general.

Others, however, believe that the negative effect technology can have on young people's studies is not insignificant. They argue that far from improving the way young people deal with knowledge as they study, technology is, in effect, harming the thinking process. Their argument is that students' thinking is being done by laptops and tablets. As a result, they are unable to analyse and use the information they encounter, which can damage their education.

Personally, I feel that technology is useful for young students nowadays. As well as improving the studying process, technology allows young people to manipulate the vast amounts of knowledge they

encounter via the internet and in libraries. Without technology, in fact, preparing for exams and studying would both be impractical, because they would not be able to look at, process and examine the vast amounts of information at their fingertips.

As we have seen, while the effect of technology on young people's studies is seen as both positive and negative, on balance I think it is a valuable tool.

*Word count: 281 words*

COMMENTS

The response to the task clearly follows the organisation required in the task. There is an introduction and each of the two views has a separate paragraph with supporting ideas. The third paragraph explains the writer's opinion against the background of the first two body paragraphs with the conclusion connecting the former to the introduction and the task.

**Round up**

Review what students have learnt in the writing section.

**REVIEW 2 ANSWERS** pages 28–29

# Vocabulary: Verbs of cause and effect

**1**
1 improvements  2 damaged  3 led to
4 improvements  5 effect  6 make easier
7 resulted in  8 changed shape

**2–3**
1 In the last 10 years, health care has been <u>improved</u> considerably by technology. / Considerable <u>improvements</u> in health care have been brought about by technology.
2 There has been serious <u>damage</u> to the environment as a result of/due to computer waste. / The environment has been seriously <u>damaged</u> by computer waste.
3 Some startling technical <u>advances</u> such as driverless cars have resulted from scientific research.
4 Global communication has been <u>improved</u> by smartphone technology.
5 Air travel has been profoundly <u>affected</u> by certain inventions such as the jet engine.
6 In future, industrial production will be <u>made easier</u> by inventions such as 3D printing.
7 Greater stress among workers compared to the past has <u>resulted from/is the result of/due to</u> the rapid pace of advances in technology.
8 The automobile world has changed shape <u>as a result of</u> new techniques in design.

# Word building: Evaluating adjectives

1 Having advanced computer skills is unnecessary for all workers.
2 Travelling daily to an office is inconvenient for modern workers.
3 Inventions like the radio and TV are often seen as unimportant by some people.
4 Using computers for long periods of time is definitely harmful.
5 I think having a knowledge of computer programming is invaluable.
6 The changes in the sales figures were insignificant.
7 In my opinion, the software training was ineffective.
8 Doing the language games on the computer was certainly worthwhile.
9 It is impractical to have everyone studying the same subjects at university.
10 The lecture on technology in the workplace was uninspiring.

# Language focus 1: Past simple and present perfect

1 has transformed, came
2 visited, have been
3 installed, have helped
4 received, shaped
5 have rarely ever used, downloaded
6 happened, influenced
7 needed, have built
8 have risen, dipped
9 was, has been
10 has definitely been, became

# Language focus 2: Habit in the past

1 haven't visited
3 knew
6 used to
11 it never seemed
12 just carried on

**1**

New technology has changed student life forever, **because** with the internet students can access information for essays and do research from anywhere. **For example**, they can work at home or in cafés or on trains without going to a library. Students can now use resources **such as** articles, books, videos and lectures online and watch lectures that they have missed. **Furthermore**, the books students need at the library can often be reserved online or they can go on the internet **in order to** buy books and have them delivered next day. **As a result,** considerable amounts of time can be saved. **Though**, technology **may** make the studying process much more convenient, it can cut students off from each other **and so** it is important for them to meet face to face in seminars and lectures.

**2**
moreover: furthermore
like: such as
to: in order to
consequently: as a result
since: because

# 3 Thrill seekers

Photocopiable activity: Group game (groups of 4) – Grammar grab page 130

Workbook pages 20–27

## Content overview

This unit focuses on seeking thrills, sports and the benefits of sports.

### Listening SECTION 3

BA sports centre

Question types: Note completion; Table completion

### Reading

Thrill seekers

Question type: Matching information; Identification of information in the text – *True/False/Not Given*; Multiple-choice

### Writing TASK 1

Describing a table; Analysing and comparing data

### Speaking PARTS 1 AND 3

**Part 1** Discussing sport

**Part 3** Discussing physical activity/the benefits of sport

**Vocabulary:** Sports

**Word building:** Adjectives ending in *-ing/-ed*

**Language focus 1:** Adjectives with prepositions

**Language focus 2:** Comparison

## Digital overview

**Presentation Kit**

Interactive versions of Student's Book exam tasks

Embedded audio and answer key for all activities

**Teacher's Resource Centre**

Progress Test 1

Communicative activity: Group game (groups of 4) – Grammar grab

Workbook audio, answer key and wordlists

**Student's Resource Centre**

Class audio

Wordlist

Speaking Part 1 videos (3) and video worksheet

Speaking Part 3 videos (4) and video worksheet

## Vocabulary: Sports  page 30

### Lead-in

Elicit from students what they think the title of the unit means. Elicit the meaning of extreme sports and the connection with the unit title.

**1** 💬 Ask students to work in pairs and describe what is happening in the photographs. Students then discuss the questions as a whole class followed by whole-class feedback. Write any new vocabulary on the board and encourage students to add words to their vocabulary records.

> **ANSWERS**
> 1 Coasteering
> 2 Kite buggying
> 3 Snowmobiling
> 4 Highlining, slacklining, tightrope walking

**2** Students can do the exercise in pairs or individually and check their answers in pairs. If students want to, elicit more sports places and equipment. (Tell them that they may see *racquet* as *racket* in US spelling.)

> **ANSWERS**
> | | | | |
> |---|---|---|---|
> | 1 | football, rugby | 2 | boxing |
> | 3 | running | 4 | bodybuilding, weightlifting |
> | 5 | swimming | 6 | water-skiing |
> | 7 | tennis, squash | 8 | golf |

**3** Once students have done the exercise in pairs, again ask them to update their vocabulary record. Encourage students to organise their records systematically as per the table in exercise 2, classifying the sports by name, equipment and place. Remind them of the importance of classification in the IELTS and elicit why it is important. Encourage them to date the entries so they can look back and see what they have learnt.

> **POSSIBLE ANSWERS**
> 1 Formula 1 racing, motocross
> 2 water-skiing, swimming, wind surfing, water polo, sailing, surfing
> 3 tennis, squash, badminton
> 4 skiing, snowboarding
> 5 rugby, running, cricket
> 6 table tennis, table football
> 7 judo, fencing, boxing
> 8 show-jumping, horse-riding
> 9 squash, basketball
> 10 football, basketball, hockey, cricket

**4** This exercise can be done in pairs or groups for variation, followed by whole-class feedback. Encourage students to evaluate the sports, etc. as per the previous unit e.g., *appealing/unappealing*, *practical/impractical*, etc. and also to use the verbs and nouns related to cause and effect e.g., *effect*, *improve*, *damage*, etc. It is important that students activate and recycle vocabulary at every opportunity. Allow students to ask what you think. Refer students to *Evaluation* on page 205 in IELTS essentials.

# Listening SECTION 3 page 31

## Lead-in

Ask students to read the *What to expect in the exam* box and check they understand by asking questions. Stress the main difference here between Section 3 and the first two sections of the Listening test: the focus is more academic, usually interchanges between students about an academic topic or between students and tutors; there can be up to four speakers; and Section 3 is more difficult than the previous sections. You may want to point out that to achieve a good band score of say 6/7, students would need to get about 7/8 out of 10 correct in Section 3.

**1** Ask students to skim the questions and tell you what the Listening test is about, focusing especially on headings in both sets of questions. You can ask them to do this in pairs/groups, expanding the notes and the information in the tables in sentences. Remind them that the questions are a summary of the content of the Listening test. Go over the strategies for these types of questions, emphasising the number of words required in the instructions. Point out that they need to check the part of speech that is required for questions 21–30. See if they can predict any of the answers and whether the answer is likely to have a plural or singular noun. Remind them that spelling is important.

Then ask the students to decide what words show that the answer is about to be given. Discuss student choices as a whole class.

As this is the first time the students have done this section, you may prefer to stop and check their answers after each group of questions. If necessary, go over how to read the table left to right while looking at the headings as they go across the rows.

**ANSWERS**

| | |
|---|---|
| 21 successful | 22 freelance trainers |
| 23 39 members | 24 more details |
| 25 representatives | 26 leadership development |
| 27 confidence | 28 (the) coaching |
| 29 full potential | 30 adventure opportunities |

**2–3** Play the test again while students listen without looking at the questions or script for pure comprehension purposes only. Once students have checked their answers and discussed the question, briefly review Section 3 as a Listening test and compare it with Sections 1 and 2. Encourage students to listen to the test again on their own, following the script and/or the questions/questions and answers.

## Listening script 03

**(T = tutor; M = Marco; K = Kelly)**

**T:** OK Kelly and Marco. We arranged this tutorial so you could give me an update of your joint project, the, mmm … case study on the work you've been doing at the Janson … Adventure Sports Centre. Is that right?

**M:** Yes. That's it. Mmm … it's won quite a few awards lately … it's not that far from the university campus.

**T:** Right … . Yes, I have it here. Fire away.

**M:** Well, at first we were going to look only at the management structure of the Centre, but, mmm … we decided to examine the reasons that have made it more <u>successful</u> than other centres. The Centre's success has not just come from its many achievements; it's also attracting people of all ages from a wide range of backgrounds. Mm … we talked to staff and members and …

**T:** How many people did you talk to?

**K:** There are just over 600 members overall and 43 staff, including <u>freelance trainers</u>. So far we've talked to mm … oh, about <u>39 members</u>.

**T:** Didn't you think of giving a questionnaire to everyone?

**K:** We decided against it.

**T:** Why was that?

**K:** Well, we thought that face-to-face interviews, however brief, would be better as we'd be able to probe people gently to give us <u>more details</u>, if need be.

**T:** And your findings so far?

**M:** The members we've spoken to all think that the centre's very well-run. The site and event managers're very focused and work well together. And the management team includes <u>representatives</u> from the Centre users.

**K:** This means that when decisions are made, they're not taken in isolation of the members, as so often happens in other organisations. The management team's then in touch with the members and vice versa.

**T:** You seem to have learnt a lot so far.

**M:** I agree. It's been a really challenging, but exhilarating experience being there. I can't wait to go in every day.

· · · · · · · · · · · · · · · · · · · · · · · · · · · · · · · · · · · · · · ·

**T:** OK. Would you like to tell me a bit about the reasons behind the success of the Centre? Kelly, would you like to go first?

**K:** OK. Mmm … well … when we questioned the people we asked what they thought … the most important reasons for the Centre's success were. There were three factors that stood out from all the others …

**T:** Can you say something more about each of these specific points, Marco? Would you like to go on?

**M:** Well, as Kelly said, we isolated three main factors that were clearly more important than others. We found that, for most people and organisations like businesses, having award-winning courses that encouraged team-building and <u>leadership development</u> were absolutely crucial to the success of the Centre. They felt that the quality of the courses, which had been validated by external assessors, were important to … having <u>confidence</u> in the Centre.

**T:** Yes. That doesn't sound surprising considering how many centres and clubs are not as professional as this centre appears to be. We can't expect them all to be perfect, but … . And the next factor?

**M:** Mmm … I personally thought the quality of facilities would come next, but a close second was the quality of <u>the coaching</u>, which is more professional than most places the respondents have come across.

**K:** Like Marco, I expected facilities to come next, and …

**M:** … most people said the Centre managed to attract some really top quality people working as coaches. They see their job as pushing participants to realise their <u>full potential</u>. They are really good … the most experienced coaches are those running courses in team-building in management. They are also very motivating leaders, who are passionate about what they do.

**T:** And the third factor? … Kelly?

**K:** Mmm … the next factor is the range of courses and <u>adventure opportunities</u>. There are outdoor endurance courses covering trekking, mountain climbing, obstacle courses and the Centre also offers to design specific courses for companies. It was really thrilling to see all this in action as the staff worked to become the best in their field.

**T:** It sounds as if you've got a lot out of this experience.

**M:** It's the sort of place I'd like to work after I've graduated.

**K:** Me too.

## Language focus 1: Adjectives with prepositions  page 32

**1–4** Follow the instructions in the Student's Book. Students do the exercises in pairs and check as a whole class. Ask them to keep a record of *adjectives + prepositions* in their vocabulary records. Encourage students to learn adjectives with prepositions where applicable. Refer them to the Grammar reference on page 220.

**ANSWERS**

**1**
**1** on  **2** to  **3** about  **4** in  **5** with  **6** to
**7** about  **8** of  **9** about  **10** of, about

**2**
**1** b/f  **2** c  **3** e  **4** d  **5** b/f  **6** g  **7** a

## Speaking  PART 1  page 32

**1** Do the first question as an example on the board. Ask students to write the others in their books. Stress the nature of the questions: personal, including questions about their country and family. Point out the topic range can be very wide, but no specialist knowledge is required. Emphasise the length of time of this part of the test (4–5 minutes) and also stress that they only have to give one or two sentences in answer, but not just a few words.

**ANSWERS**

1 What kinds of sports are popular in your country?
2 Do you do/play the same sports now as you did in the past?
3 Are the same games as popular as in the past where you live?
4 Do young people do more physical activities like extreme sports now than in the past?
5 What makes these games interesting to people?
6 Are sports more challenging now than they were in the past?
7 Are young people challenged more nowadays than in the past?

**2** Before students do the exercise, elicit *adjectives + prepositions* that could be used with each question. Monitor the pairwork to ensure accuracy and the use of the *adjectives + prepositions*. To check use, ask several students questions from exercise 1. If students don't use *adjectives + prepositions* in their answers, ask them and/or the class how they can paraphrase their answers to do so.

## Word building: Adjectives ending in *-ing/-ed*  page 33

### Lead-in

As a lead-in, you could ask students to describe what is happening in the photographs, or tell them if necessary. Elicit an evaluation of the activities in the photographs from the point of view of the participants and the students' perspective.

**1** The adjective endings *-ing* and *-ed* are a common cause of confusion for students. Go through the example and first question with the students. Point out or elicit that the adjective with *-ing* (*challenging*) tells you what the experience is doing to you – i.e. *it challenges you* – and that the adjective with *-ed* (*challenged*) tells you how you feel if you have a challenging experience: i.e. *I was challenged*. Stress the use of such adjectives in evaluation and refer students to *Evaluation* in IELTS essentials on page 205. Ask students to do the second question on their own and compare their answers in pairs, followed by whole-class feedback.

**ANSWERS**

If something is challenging it means that it *makes people challenged*. It is an *active adjective*. If somebody is challenged by something it is having an effect on the person to make them feel challenged. It is a passive adjective.

**2** The students do this exercise in pairs, followed by whole-class feedback.

**ANSWERS**

1 thrilling  2 irritated  3 interested  4 inspiring
5 exciting  6 annoying, annoyed  7 challenging
8 invigorated

**3** This exercise helps students to activate the vocabulary. Students ask and answer the questions in pairs. Monitor the pairwork to ensure they develop their answers, explaining and expanding where possible by giving reasons and examples for their answers (which is good practice for both Speaking Part 3 and Writing Task 2). Monitor accuracy. Elicit responses from several students and allow them to ask you questions.

**4** Students do this in pairs, followed by whole-class feedback.

**ANSWERS**

1 excited       2 challenged    3 interesting
4 fascinating   5 motivated     6 exciting
7 refreshed     8 excitement

**5** As students do this in pairs, monitor and provide support.

**Round up**

Elicit the distinction between the two types of adjectives and encourage students to use them where possible. Point out how they are not just word building but expanding their vocabulary/ lexical range. Ask them to keep a record of these and other adjectives they come across. Point these out during the course, where possible.

## Speaking PART 3 page 34

**1** Students can do this in pairs/groups adding their own reasons. Get whole-class feedback. Point out and go through the *What to expect in the exam* and *How to go about it* boxes.

**2** After students do the exercise in pairs/groups, elicit what the grammar structures are in the phrases, e.g., they are all expressed as purposes, *to/in order to*, etc. Ask students to give other examples.

**ANSWERS**

1 to  2 so  3 so that  4 in order to  5 so as to
6 in order to

**3** Stress the importance of this for paraphrasing *reasons* in all parts of the exam. Students can again do this in pairs/groups. Write examples of students' sentences on the board.

**POSSIBLE ANSWERS**

1 because they want/like to keep fit
2 because they would like/want to lose weight
3 because they would like/want to make friends
4 because they like/want to relax
5 because they want an adrenaline rush
6 because they want/would like to improve their performance

**4** Students do this exercise in pairs, giving reasons and examples. As an introduction to the questions, you can select one or two and go through them checking student comprehension of the questions and what they are being asked. They can be asked to explain or paraphrase the questions, as far as possible. Remind them about adjectives ending in -*ing* and -*ed* and also adjectives with prepositions. Monitor students as they discuss and give whole-class feedback

**Round up**

Compare the three parts of the Speaking test. Stress that in Part 3 they are expected to develop their ideas more and use abstract rather than personal examples, etc.

## Reading Passage page 35

Go through the *What to expect in the exam* and the *Don't forget!* boxes with students. Emphasise the patterns in texts, and give examples of what is meant by cause and effect, etc. You might want to introduce the idea of elements in texts, like cause/effect, problem/solution and past/present/future, going together within paragraphs and across paragraphs. Refer students to IELTS essentials on page 205. Start students noticing cause and effect relationships at this stage and then develop it as it comes up across the course. This is very important as understanding this concept can help students to use the lexical cues given in the text to indicate these patterns. Give students hints about paragraphs, e.g.:
- Does paragraph D contain any causes? *As a roller coaster …*
- Does it contain any effects? *… the body through weightlessness, high gravitational forces and acceleration, the brain struggles to make sense of conflicting and changing signals from the senses.*
- Are *the body through weightlessness, high gravitational forces and acceleration* also causes?
- Are there any other effects in the paragraph?
- Can you analyse the next paragraph in the same way?

Encourage students to make a habit of first looking at the multiple-choice question with the alternative headings before reading the text. This encourages them away from the vertical-linear approach to texts and questions.

**1** As a pre-reading exercise, ask students to work in pairs and look at the picture and talk about various rides. Time permitting, you might want to ask students to skim the questions and tell you what the passage is about. Give the students a time limit, e.g., two minutes. Ask students to answer the questions, writing their answers on a grid or a sheet of paper. Give the students a 20-minute time limit, just as they will need to allocate in the exam. Remind them of the technique of underlining key words in the questions.

> **ANSWERS**
>
> **1** B **2** F **3** H **4** I **5** D **6** H
> **7** NOT GIVEN **8** FALSE **9** NOT GIVEN **10** TRUE
> **11** NOT GIVEN **12** TRUE **13** B

Alternatively, you may also want to break up the Reading Passage, focusing on the two main sets of Questions 1–6 and 7–12 and then doing Question 13 as a whole class, as follows:

## Questions 1–6

Ask students to read Questions 1–6 focusing on the words and/or phrases that will help them to scan for the information, bearing in mind that they may be scanning for synonyms/paraphrases. Ask them to read the rubric carefully especially the *NB*.

To help with text navigation by using predictions about organisation, ask students to analyse the phrases in 1–6 looking at any general nouns, e.g., *types*, and to consider where the answers are likely to be in the passage: beginning, middle or end of the text. For example, for phrase 1, do you need to give examples of the types of the rides in an experiment before the experiment is explained? Is this likely to be right at the beginning, right at the end or somewhere in the middle?; and for phrase 4, is this likely to come before or after the experiment is described? And again, where is this likely to be in the Reading Passage? Such skills can help students develop their ability to navigate reading passages and are an essential technique to acquire. Refer students to IELTS strategies on page 204.

## Extension

After students have finished the Reading test, ask them to focus on the phrases in Questions 1–6 and decide whether they refer to part of or the whole of the paragraph. Ask them to write the general nouns in their (electronic) vocabulary lists and add to the list as they go through the course. Point out that they will meet these words again and again in all components of the IELTS exam.

## Questions 7–12

After students have checked their answers for Questions 1–6, they can analyse the *True/False/Not Given* statements, eliciting the differences.

## Question 13

Do Question 13 with the class. After doing Questions 1–12 they should be able to answer this without further reference to the text.

**2** Students discuss the questions in small groups.

## Round up

Ask students to list what they have learnt. Leave it up to them initially, giving hints if necessary, about text navigation and predicting organisation.

# Language focus 2: Comparison
page 37

**1** This will be a basic review for many students. Go through this with the whole class and then refer students to the Grammar reference on page 221.

> **ANSWERS**
>
> **1** gentler: 'r' is added. Yes 'more' is possible as the adjective 'gentle' has two syllables.
> **2** more immersive: 'more' is added. No, you cannot add an ending as the adjective 'immersive' has more than one syllable.

**2** Students can complete the table individually and check their answers with the whole class. Review any spelling changes, e.g., *-y* to *-ier/-iest*, and doubling the final consonant on single-syllable adjectives such as *wet*.

**ANSWERS**

| Adjective | Comparative | Superlative |
|---|---|---|
| bad | worse | the worst |
| good | better | the best |
| noisy | noisier/more noisy | the noisiest |
| wet | wetter | the wettest |
| tasty | tastier | the tastiest |
| cheap | cheaper | the cheapest |
| lively | livelier | the liveliest |
| appetising | more/less appetising | the most/least appetising |

**3** Ask students to do the exercise in pairs and check in whole-class feedback.

> **ANSWERS**
>
> **1** happier     **2** easier
> **3** more popular     **4** the most energetic
> **5** more difficult     **6** the least/most stressful
> **7** more/less important     **8** the fittest

**4–5** Ask students to do these exercises in pairs. You might want to write some student answers on the board.

ANSWERS

**4**
1 happiness
2 ease
3 popularity
4 energy
5 difficulty
6 stress
7 importance
8 fitness

have: happiness, difficulty, importance
need/require: energy, fitness
enjoy: happiness, popularity
experience: difficulty, happiness, stress

**5**
1 People who do some physical activity are supposed to enjoy/have greater happiness than less active people.
2 Places to do specialist sports can be found with more ease outside cities and towns.
3 With more people taking it up, bowling enjoys/has more popularity than it used to.
4 Which sport do you think requires/needs the most energy (of all)?
5 People have greater difficulty/more difficulties organising their lives around work nowadays.
6 Is work the aspect of modern life that causes the greatest stress?
7 Does mental activity have less/more importance than physical activity? / Is mental activity of lesser/greater importance than physical activity?
8 People don't realise that racing drivers are the individuals with the greatest fitness in sport. / People don't realise that racing drivers are the individuals that have the greatest fitness in sport.

**6** Ask students to do this in pairs and check the answers as a whole class

ANSWERS
1 … more exciting than …
2 Correct
3 … more dangerous than …
4 … fitter …
5 … the most exciting …
6 Correct
7 … the fittest …
8 Correct
9 Correct
10 … more tiring than …

**7** Depending on the size of your class, do the questionnaire as a whole class or in two groups. Make sure students actually ask the questions and don't just point at them or say the number. If you have time, you may like to collate their answers on the board.

**Round up**

Point out to students the function and importance of comparatives/superlatives in IELTS: specifically, in comparing data in Writing Task 1, giving opinions and making evaluations in Speaking and Writing (e.g., *more important/challenging than*) and noticing the same in Reading and Listening.

## Writing TASK 1 page 38

### Lead-in

Ask students to work in pairs and look at the table. Ask them to discuss which sports they participate in or like/dislike.

**1** Elicit the main points to note in the table, e.g., topic, subjects, sports. Ask students to do the exercise in pairs and check their answers globally, eliciting where they found the information.

**2** Pair work is followed by whole-class feedback.

ANSWERS
Sentence 4, because we do not know numbers only proportions.
1 True  2 False  3 True  4 No information
5 True  6 False  7 False  8 True

**3–4** Students work in pairs. Elicit feedback with reasons for their answers.

ANSWERS
**3**
2 … a far smaller proportion of men than women … or … a far greater proportion of women than men …
4 Proportionately, nearly twice as many men as women went cycling/BMXing.
6 … played basketball, …
7 Basketball was the least …

**4**
a 5  b 8  c all of the others.

**5–6** Students can compare their answers with other students before whole-class feedback.

POSSIBLE ANSWERS
It is clear that the proportion of both genders participating in selected activities varies noticeably.

**7** This can be done as a whole-class exercise.

ANSWERS
1 a smaller percentage … than
2 a far greater proportion of … than
3 … less likely than …
4 twice as many … as …
5 … compares data about …
6 … while …
7 … the least popular …
8 … there are … differences in …

**8** Ask students to do the exercise individually, followed by checking in pairs and then with the whole class.

> **ANSWERS**
> 1 The rugby match was attended by a third of the number of spectators as the football match.
> 2 The sports department was visited by five times the number of shoppers in February 2008 when compared to February 2009.
> 3 More than 40% of the competitors were from the main city.
> 4 A smaller proportion of players were home-grown rather than from overseas.
> 5 Three-quarters of the members of the sports club paid by credit card rather than cash.
> 6 The team won just over 50%/half of the games they played last season.

**9** Ask students to write an answer for Writing Task 1 on page 206. Encourage them to focus on making comparisons.

> *Model answer*
>
> The data provides information about the engagement of men and women in various sports in the UK from 2005/06 to 2008/09. Overall, it is clear that participation of both genders in the selected sports varied with jogging experiencing a significant increase. It is noticeable that whereas jogging, cross-county and road-running, had the lowest level of participation among both genders, there was a significant increase in involvement. In 2008/09, participation among men was higher with a rise to 7.6% from 6.9% in 2005/06. By contrast, the rise among women was much larger, to 4.8% in 2008/09 from 3.5% at the beginning of the period.
>
> For indoor swimming or diving, while there was a slight decline in the proportion of male participation from 2005/06 to 2008/09, 13.3% to 13.0%, the drop in female engagement was greater, from 18.0% to 16.5% over the period. By comparison, in cycling for various purposes a greater proportion of men than women took part, with male involvement increasing slightly from 12.7% to 14.4% compared to a fall among women from 7.0% to 6.4%.
>
> *Word count: 177 words*
>
> **COMMENTS**
>
> The response fulfils the requirements of the task, summarising, including an overview in the second sentence of the first paragraph, and exemplifying using appropriate data. There is a range of vocabulary and structures and there is also clear paragraphing.

**REVIEW 3 ANSWERS** pages 40–41

## Vocabulary: Sports

1 winter
2 baseball
3 track-and-field
4 car-racing
5 water
6 Outdoor
7 table tennis
8 racket
9 boxing

## Word building: Adjectives ending in -ing/-ed

1 thrilled, thrilling.
2 motivated
3 exciting, excited
4 fascinating, fascinated
5 invigorating, irritating
6 annoying, challenging
7 interested, interesting

## Language focus 1: Adjectives with prepositions

The sport that I am most enthusiastic about is gymnastics.
As a keen motorist, I'm not interested in walking holidays.
She's very fit and capable of playing tennis for a long time.
It's my sister that's mad about football, not me.
I'm addicted to all kinds of video games.
As my grandfather's very active, he's the sort of person who rarely gets bored with life.
I'm a cyclist and keen on fitness.

## Language focus 2: Comparison

**1**
1 livelier, the dullest
2 quieter, noisier
3 the most energetic, lazier
4 the most difficult, easier

**2**
1 popular
2 important
3 fitter
4 better
5 sadder
6 expensive

**ACCURACY IN IELTS**
1 compared
2 involved
3 Generally
4 likely
5 men
6 compares
7 males
8 larger
9 least

# Ready for Listening

## IELTS Listening test

**SECTION 1**
Form completion
Sentence completion
Labelling a map

**SECTION 2**
Matching
Multiple-choice

**SECTION 3**
Multiple-choice
Selecting items from a list
Table completion

**SECTION 4**
Multiple-choice
Labelling a diagram

## Introduction  page 42

This is the first of the four *Ready for* units. You can use these units in the order they occur. Alternatively, you can use parts of the units for revision purposes or for further practice at any time during the course. You can also use the units as an introduction to the IELTS examination.

Elicit information about:
- the length of the Listening test
- the number of questions
- the difference between the four sections from a content point of view, i.e. the first two sections are of a more social nature, and Sections 3 and 4 are of an academic nature
- the nature of the questions
- the strategies required, including honing concentration skills
- the speed of the dialogue and the level of difficulty.

For the latter, point out that the test and questions become more difficult as the test progresses, and that the questions also vary in difficulty throughout the test. Encourage students to ask you questions.

It is important that students always keep in mind the number of questions they should be aiming for in each section to achieve a good score. For example, to obtain a band score 7, ideally students should aim for at least: 10/10 in Section 1; 8 or 9/10 in Section 2; 8/10 in Section 3; and 6 or 7/10 in Section 4.

Point out that as in the Reading test, the number of correct answers required to achieve a particular band score varies from exam to exam, but that the standard in each exam is the same. Refer students to the band descriptors on the Student's Resource Centre for information on the scores in the Listening test.

## Optional lead-in

Before students start, ask them the questions below or ask them to discuss the questions in pairs.
1 How long does the Listening test last?
2 How many sections are there?
3 What sorts of situations are Sections 1 and 2 related to?
4 What sorts of situations are Sections 3 and 4 related to?
5 How many times do you hear the recording?
6 Where do you write your answers during the test?
7 How long do you have to transfer your answers?
8 Why do you have to be careful when you transfer your answers?

**ANSWERS**
1  40 minutes (30 minutes for the test and 10 minutes to transfer answers)
2  Four        3  (More) general/social situations
4  Academic    5  Once
6  In the question booklet and then transfer to an answer sheet
7  10 minutes
8  Because it's easy to make mistakes, especially spelling mistakes, and leaving off the s at the end of words.

You can also ask students to create their own infogram/poster/class webpage for the Listening test on the computer. Alternatively, the infogram can be paper-based for classroom display. Check any display items for accuracy and visual impact.

## SECTION 1  page 42

1 (🔊) Ask students to work in pairs predicting a) the word type, e.g., noun, verb, adjective, adverb or number; b) possible answers, where they can, and the type of information that is needed. You can also ask students to use the questions in the test to expand the information to create as full a picture as possible of the dialogue. Students can also think about who is supplying the information in each case.

Note, all four listening sections can be done individually or as a full test. You might want to repeat the individual sections or the four sections as a full test, pointing out that in the exam the students may hear the same recordings in different exams if they take the exam more than once. In this case, it is important to point out that students need *to do* the test rather than *try to do it from memory*.

Remind students of the range of possible question types for Section 1, highlighting the fact that the questions may not just be note/form completion as here.

Ask students to answer the questions as a Listening test.

## Ready for Listening

### 🎧 Listening script 04

**(R = receptionist; C = Clara)**

R: Good morning. How can I help you?

C: Hi. Mmm … I'm not registered as a patient here at the moment as I moved to the north of the city, and I was wondering if it was possible to register again now and make an appointment as well.

R: Yes, I can register you today, but all the appointments for today are taken, unless it's an emergency.

C: No, I can't say it's an emergency.

R: OK, so I can register you. Is it just for yourself?

C: No, it's for the whole <u>family</u>, myself, my husband and my daughter as well.

R: I can check on the system to see if your details are still on here.

C: I moved to another doctor about four and a half years ago, so …

R: Well, I can have a look.

C: OK.

R: Can you tell me your name and date of birth? And I can check using both.

C: My name's Clara Wight.

R: Is that W–H–I–T–E?

C: No. It's <u>W–I–G–H–T</u>.

R: Right. Mmm and your date of birth?

C: <u>23rd October</u> 1990.

R: OK … let's see. … Was your address before 72 Crocket Street?

C: Yes. That's it! That was my old address.

R: We have basic details, but no records. They were all transferred to the other health centre you registered at when you moved. Mmm … and your present address?

C: It's <u>88 Palace Avenue</u>.

R: And the postcode?

C: It's <u>ZE24 2TP</u>.

R: If you fill in this form for yourself and your family, then we can input the details.

C: OK. But do I need to bring any proof of identity?

R: I need proof of your address from a utility bill etc.

C: I've not got any bills, but I've got letters saying we're connected for the gas and electricity and, of course, I've got a letter showing the tenancy <u>agreement</u> with our name and the address on it.

R: That should be OK.

························································

R: The first available appointment I have is on Thursday at 3.00 with Dr Jackson.

C: Mmm that's a bit awkward as I've got to <u>pick up</u> my daughter from school. Have you got anything later?

R: I've got an appointment with Dr Barker at 4 pm on <u>Friday</u> …

C: Yeah that's OK.

R: But it's at our other health centre.

C: Where's that?

R: It's not that far. It's less than 10 minutes' walk from here on North Street. Do you know where the cinema is on North Street?

C: Yes.

R: Well it's on the same side of the road between the cinema and the pharmacy on the opposite side of the road from the bank.

C: Yes …. I know it. There's a small park just further along on the same side of the road on the other side of New Street, where the bus stops.

R: Yes. That's it. We will send you a text to confirm – can I just confirm your mobile number's 07700 900807?

C: Yes, that's correct. Thanks for your help.

R: Bye bye.

**2–3** Students do the exercises in pairs. During whole-class feedback, discuss any issues re strategies, etc.
Remind students of the ten-minute transfer time at the end, the need for accuracy, and writing the answers in the correct boxes.

## SECTION 2    page 43
Briefly elicit any information specific to Section 2, e.g., whether it is usually a monologue or not, level of difficulty, etc.

**1–3** Students do the exercises in pairs, checking with another pair before whole-class feedback.

**4** 🎧 Ask students to answer the questions as a Listening test. Watch students as they do the test, gauging which questions or sections students find easy or difficult. Discuss this during feedback when the answers are reviewed. You may want to play parts of the test again, e.g., the part of the test relating to Questions 11–16, and discuss the processing of information involved in such questions, e.g., preparing for paraphrases and predicting the answers, and predicting possible matches.

**ANSWERS**

**11** D  **12** E  **13** A  **14** B  **15** C  **16** G  **17** B
**18** B  **19** B  **20** C

After students have done the test, ask them to transfer their answers to a separate sheet of paper. They can then check their answers, written before and after transfer, with other students, followed by whole-class feedback.

 **Listening script 05**

Good evening, everyone, and welcome to the official opening of the Glitz Theatre, an exciting new development on this side of the city – the renovation of the theatre has taken nearly three years of painstaking restoration work and the results of the effort that has gone into it all are clearly visible.

Before we proceed to the opening ceremony, I'd like to say a few words about the transformation of the theatre.

The venue has changed from being a rundown building to what can only be described as a modern theatrical experience, and for me it's wonderful to see so many of the original features of the building still intact, especially on the façade, where all the dirt has been removed. There is now multi-coloured glass panelling on the façade, so the entrance looks really welcoming.

The auditorium, which was not particularly welcoming in the past, has had a complete makeover to create something modern and up-to date. And we now have a concert venue for a wide range of uses, where we can hold not just plays, but concerts for pop and classical music and conferences. For the latter, we also have a new extension with rooms for meetings and educational purposes all fitted out with the latest technology along with an area for mingling and entertaining.

The foyer of the theatre here, as you can see, has been made bigger with a much larger ticket office and machines for collecting tickets that have been booked in advance. And where there was only a machine serving coffee and cold drinks and a few stools and high tables there's now a proper coffee shop selling a wide range of light refreshments, which looks rather inviting. The roof terrace, which used to be closed, is now accessible, with a landscaped garden and a restaurant open to the public all year round.

The basement, which leads out into a garden at the back, has been converted into a members' room with a café for light refreshments and an area for art

displays or stalls. The theatre shop is no longer beside the ticket office; it is now next to the entrance to the basement cafe. It doesn't just sell sweets, as it did before, but theatre-related memorabilia, including programmes and books, DVDs, CDs, posters …

● ● ● ● ● ● ● ● ● ● ● ● ● ● ● ● ● ● ● ● ● ● ● ● ● ● ● ● ● ● ● ● ●

And in the information pack you all have you may notice that there is a programme of events for the summer months, mmm … . As it's during the school holidays, there'll be a wide range of special events aimed at children. For the matinee performance each day, the theatre is offering free tickets to 200 children up to 16 years of age. And there'll be special rates for theatre-goers who book a meal in the roof-terrace restaurant as well. And there'll be special evenings where there'll be concerts and plays by local groups. And also every Wednesday, tickets will be half-price for members of the theatre. The membership is only £70 a year and gives members and a guest access to member-only events and to previews and access to the members' restaurant in the basement.

And another innovation at the cinema is the monthly programme of lectures and master classes delivered by actors, producers and writers, on various aspects of the theatre. This is certainly a major development which will definitely pull in many cinema enthusiasts, and hopefully revitalise the area.

I'd now like the Mayor to say a few words before opening …

## SECTION 3  page 45

Discuss Section 3 briefly from the perspective of the content, the nature of the dialogue, and the complexity compared to Sections 1 and 2, e.g., the information is of an academic nature, and the fact that there may be more than two speakers.

**1–3** Ask students to do the exercises in pairs, checking their answers after each exercise with other pairs of students, and then as part of whole-class feedback.

**ANSWERS**

**1**
talk: lecture/seminar/paper/presentation

**2**
Nearly all of them could be undecided.
Possible answers:
A  number of questions
B  photographs/photos/illustrations/drawings
C  amount of data/information/facts/figures
D  length of questioning
E  period of research: investigation/study
F  people to be/asked questions/participants
G  objectives

**3**
Numbers: Questions 27 and 30
Plural: Question 26 and 28

**4**  Ask students to answer the questions as a Listening test. Watch students as they do the test, gauging which questions or sections students find easy or difficult, especially reading and completing the table. Discuss this during feedback when the answers are reviewed.

| ANSWERS | |
| --- | --- |
| **21** C | **22–24** A, F, G in any order |
| **25** everything | **26** lectures |
| **27** 9 | **28** shows |
| **29** home life | **30** 8 |

**5** Referring to the Listening script on page 229 of the Student's Book, students work in pairs to check if any of the words and phrases they used when they were thinking of paraphrases in exercise 2 came up in the Listening test.

---

### Listening script 06

**(Z = Zahra; T = Thomas)**

**Z:** Hi Thomas.

**T:** Zahra, hi. So, have you decided yet what you're going to do your seminar paper on?

**Z:** Yes, I have. Mmm … it's all at an early stage so far, but it's on <u>the impact of smartphone technology on our lives</u>, but I'll probably restrict it to just the field of studying at university.

**T:** Well, that sounds very topical. If you think of it, smartphones only started to become popular around 2008 and look how quickly they've changed everything.

**Z:** Yes, of course. Things're happening so fast, … I love new technology, but it's all too much at times. It'll be interesting to research. At least, I think it will.

**T:** Yes, I do, too. And how're you going to do the research for your seminar paper?

**Z:** Well, mmm, I thought of interviewing people in the student body and members of the public – <u>I want a wide range of ages and backgrounds, but I haven't narrowed it down yet.</u>

**T:** Any minimum age?

**Z:** 16/17 minimum perhaps, but as for an upper age limit, not really.

**T:** Mmm … and <u>what're you setting out to show?</u>

**Z:** <u>I'm not sure at this stage either</u>, but something along the lines of … mmm … the idea that we are allowing smartphone technology to control the way we do things too much, but I haven't made up my mind yet. I'm just thinking on my feet here. I haven't really thought it right through to the end, to be honest.

**T:** What about your questionnaire?

**Z:** Mmm … , yes that's another thing. <u>What I'm not really decided about is the length the questionnaire should be.</u>

**T:** The best thing is to keep it short.

**Z:** Maybe. But I'll finalise the length when I sit down to type it up.

---

**Z:** I need to find someone to try out my questions on. I've got some already written.

**T:** I can be your guinea pig if you want.

**Z:** Great!

**T:** Fire away!

**Z:** Let's see, … . Let's start with this one … which electronic device do you use most frequently?

**T:** Mm, I love my tablet, but actually, I'd have to say it's probably my smartphone.

**Z:** What do you use it for generally?

**T:** Mmm … apart from communication like video-phoning my family and friends at home and social media, and listening to and downloading music, I use it for practically <u>everything</u>, but probably less and less for texting.

**Z:** On a scale of 1–10, where 1 is least useful and 10 most useful, how useful do you find your smartphone is for communication?

**T:** Very useful, so 8. Without it, I'd be totally lost.

**Z:** And what about studying? Do you use it in your studying?

**T:** All the time. I use it for mmm … for searching on the net, and I also use it for downloading documents and for writing or dictating notes or bits of assignments on my mobile …

**Z:** Mhmm …

**T:** … and recording <u>lectures</u> or parts of them when I can't be bothered taking notes on my mobile and then it transfers to my laptop automatically when I switch it on.

**Z:** And I thought I used my mobile a lot!

**T:** … but in the main I use it for studying more and more, rather than just browsing the internet.

**Z:** Using the same scale, what about using the mobile for studying then?

**T:** Well, let's see … . It's more essential than communicating for me, but it's a score of … <u>9</u>.

**Z:** What about entertainment?

**T:** I can use it for music and music videos and films and TV <u>shows</u>.

**Z:** What score would you give it for usefulness?

**T:** Mmm … well, for that, I'd give a score of 7.

**Z:** What else do you use it for?

**T:** For many different things like the news, the weather, health checks, as my wallet, train tickets and as a TV remote control. I can't wait to get it connected up to more things at home. I think I'll end up using it for organising my entire <u>home life</u>.

**Z:** Do you think so? And the score for these other things?

**T:** A definite <u>8</u>.

**Z:** OK thanks, that's really helpful …

## SECTION 4 page 46

Elicit information about Section 4 as per the previous sections, making sure that students are aware that there is only a brief pause during the Listening test. So they have to read as many questions as possible at the beginning and always read several questions ahead, if possible.

Discuss the transfer of the answers, reminding students of the importance of accuracy, and of putting the answers in the correct box in the exam answer sheet. Stress that in the exam only answers in the answer sheet are marked.

**1–2** Ask students to do the exercises, and to check their answers with other students, followed by whole-class feedback. As diagrams can cause some students difficulty, ask one or more students to describe the diagram on page 47 in their own words and predict answers.

**ANSWERS**

**1**
**31** boreholes/provide    **32** in the past/induce rain
**33** proof/increases rainfall    **34** not support
**35** agriculture/weather control

**2**
Possible answers
**31**
A employed/utilised in factories    B on farms
C drinking and washing/use in the home
**32**
A mystical/magical methods/ ways
B burning (something)    C ritual (dancing)
**33**
A between 10 and 20%    B just over half
C a quarter
**34**
A not many advantages
B price of the equipment/equipment is expensive/
   costly/not cheap
C impact/outcome/result
**35**
A needs extra money/funds    B needs attention
C an astonishing tale

**3**  Ask students to answer the questions as a Listening test. Again, watch students as they do the test, gauging which questions or sections students find easy or difficult. Discuss this during feedback when the answers are reviewed.

**ANSWERS**

**31** B  **32** A  **33** A  **34** C  **35** B  **36** chemical
**37** freeze  **38** generator  **39** fuel tank
**40** cloud level

### Listening script 07

Good morning everyone. The topic of my talk this week is a rather unusual method of bringing water to drought-ridden regions of the world. The methods people most think of, or read about in newspapers and/or see on TV, er … are preventing deforestation and encouraging reforestation to prevent water run-off from barren land, and hence to stop flooding. Another method is … mmm … drilling bore holes to bring water from aquifers deep in the ground to irrigate the land.

But the method I'd like to talk about today is the production of rain through seeding clouds. For those of you who are not familiar with this practice, it is basically a process where nature is coaxed, as it were, to produce rain. In many places in the world, attempts have been made throughout history to produce rain in times of drought through magic, but from the latter part of the last century scientists've been endeavouring to come to the rescue by chemical means.

And at times they've been trying not just to produce rain, but also to divert it so that it does not rain on special days, such as national or international ceremonies. Cloud seeding has been carried out since the middle of the last century, but no scientist can confirm that the practice is actually responsible for rain, and not nature itself. Because who can confirm that the clouds would not let loose a deluge anyway?

Having said that, I am aware there is some evidence that seeding clouds to produce rain can lead to a 15% increase in rainfall. But what would happen, for example, if the actions of cloud seeding in one place led to a disastrous deluge in another? It would also be tricky to prove that any damage was the responsibility of cloud seeders. Some people are understandably against the practice of cloud seeding, as we don't really know the consequences of interfering with nature.

Cloud seeding has apparently been used by Californian officials to replenish reservoirs. In other parts of the US, electricity utility companies are especially fond of seeding to bring more water to hydroelectric plants.

With national budgets devoted to agriculture running into the tens of millions, if not billions of dollars in some cases, the interest in attempts to control the weather is not surprising and deserves attention.

Last year the agricultural and meteorology departments at the university were given a 20 million dollar grant, funded in part by the government and various companies in the food and agricultural industry, to conduct research into cloud seeding to increase precipitation. While the research is aimed primarily at the US, it is hoped that the benefits accrued will have far-reaching consequences for other drought-ridden regions of the planet.

Now … let's see, mmm … if we look at this diagram here, we can see how cloud seeding works. There are two basic methods: from the air and from the ground. Looking first at seeding from the air, we can see that an aeroplane flies above the clouds from where it fires silver iodide into clouds by dropping chemical flares in order to increase precipitation. Silver iodide crystals then attach themselves to water droplets, which makes the water freeze and fall as rain or snow over high ground. If we now look at the diagram showing cloud seeding from the ground, we can see that there is a ground seeding generator here on the right, which has a tall chimney, and er … next to this is on the left is, … mmm … a fuel tank containing propane. Heat generated from the burning of the propane lifts the silver iodide crystals up to cloud level again leading to precipitation.

So let's now …

Photocopiable activity: Collocations board game (groups of 4) – World problems pages 131 and 142

Workbook pages 28–35

## Content overview

This unit focuses on world issues and opportunities.

### Listening SECTION 4

The development of railways

Question types: Note completion; Multiple-choice

### Reading

Skills shortage in the engineering industry

Question types: Summary completion; Identification of writer's views/claims – *Yes/No/ Not Given*

### Writing TASK 2

Suggesting causes and solutions; Developing a topic sentence

### Speaking PARTS 1 AND 3

**Part 1** Talking about products

**Part 3** Discussing problems

**Vocabulary 1:** General nouns

**Vocabulary 2:** Developing ideas

**Language focus:** Countable and uncountable nouns

## Digital overview

**Presentation Kit**

Interactive versions of Student's Book exam tasks

Embedded audio and answer key for all activities

**Teacher's Resource Centre**

Collocations board game (groups of 4) – World problems

Workbook audio, answer key and wordlists

**Student's Resource Centre**

Speaking Part 1 videos (3) and video worksheet

Speaking Part 3 videos (4) and video worksheet

## Vocabulary 1: General nouns page 48

### Lead-in

Elicit from students the possible contents of the unit from the title and the photographs on page 48. Ask students for synonyms for the words *global* and

*issues*. Check if students think the word *issues* is positive, negative or neutral, and then do the same for the word *opportunities*.

1 🗣 Students discuss the questions in pairs and then as a whole-class exercise. Ask them to describe the photographs and answer the questions. Point out the general nouns like *issues* and *opportunities* from the questions. Ask students to give you other similar nouns from the questions, e.g., *problems*, *situations*, *reasons*, and *examples*. Tell them to compare these nouns with the noun *photograph* – the latter refers to something specific: we have an idea of what it is. The other nouns need a context. Adjective and prepositional phrases help us know what the words *issues*, *problems* and *opportunities* refer to, because these words change according to context, e.g., *the problem of overfishing/ overcrowding, countless opportunities for work*. Check students' answers to the questions and ask them for reasons for their choices.

2 Ask students to do the exercise with the same partner, checking the answers with another pair before whole-class feedback.

> **ANSWERS**
> **1** f  **2** e  **3** g  **4** b  **5** c  **6** a  **7** d  **8** h

3 Ask students to do this exercise in pairs or as a whole class. Remind them of the distinction between words like *issues and opportunities*, and *photographs* in exercise 1.

> **ANSWERS**
> opportunity, situation, problem, possibilities, crisis, occasion, incident, circumstances, outcome

4 Ask students to do the exercise in pairs, or if necessary, as a whole class.

> **ANSWERS**
> *problem* can be used in both gaps.

5 Students complete the exercise in pairs. Many, if not all, of these adjectives and nouns will be familiar to students, but they may not use them a lot in their speaking and writing. If necessary, by way of example, do the first item with the class. When the rest of the answers have been checked in whole-class feedback, point out the need to use a wide range of vocabulary in speaking and writing. At this point, it may be a good idea to show students the band descriptors for Speaking and Writing Task 2 on the Student's Resource Centre.

Focus only on the Lexical Resource column, i.e. the column dealing with vocabulary range for Score Bands 5–7. Encourage students to study the band descriptors during the course.

ANSWERS

1 b   2 c   3 a   4 g   5 h   6 f   7 d   8 j
9 e   10 i

**6** Ask students to complete the exercise individually and then check the answers in pairs before global checking.

ANSWERS

| 1 | incident | 2 | possibility | 3 | cause |
|---|----------|---|-------------|---|-------|
| 4 | events | 5 | problem | 6 | issue |
| 7 | impression | 8 | outcome | | |

**7** 🗪 Before students do the exercise, encourage them to use the nouns and adjectives from the section so far, where possible. While checking their answers globally, ask two or more pairs which nouns and adjectives they used. If possible, describe an imaginary or real situation of your own.

### Round up

Emphasise the use of general nouns, the adjectives that are used to describe such nouns, and hence the collocations. Ask students to keep a record in their (electronic) vocabulary lists. It is worthwhile asking students to dictate the words onto their phones, making sure the spellings and pronunciation are correct. Throughout the rest of the course, they can add other words they encounter.

## Listening  SECTION 4  Page 50

Ask students to read the *What to expect in the exam* and *How to go about it* boxes. Check understanding by asking specific questions about the content of the boxes and/or asking them to summarise the information in their own words. Quickly review Listening Sections 1–3 and point out the differences between the different sections. Point out, or elicit from the students themselves, the strategies they will need to employ while listening: concentration; processing the text in the questions; hearing; listening and writing, especially if answers come together; looking at headings and markers to prepare for the answers, etc.

Point out that:
- they should look at several questions together, if they can, in case the answers come close together
- the words in the text may not always be exactly in the order that they occur in the recording. E.g., *the train arrived slightly later than scheduled – the arrival of the train was later than scheduled*
- reassure them that the answers are always in order, i.e. in the recording the answer to the first question will be before the answer to the second question and so on.

Elicit from students a list of steps they should follow in approaching Section 4: skim the questions; make sure the rubrics are being followed, especially as regards the number of words; make sure the spelling is correct; work out what types of words are needed for each gap; predict answers where possible – predicting something general for something specific, such as a more general noun for a specific noun, e.g., *furniture* for *chair*; make sure to transfer words to answer sheet correctly. For the steps in prediction see, IELTS strategies on page 203.

### Discussion

**1** 🗪 Ask students to discuss the two questions.

### Questions 31–37

As a pre-listening task, ask students to work in pairs/groups and *examine,* not just look at, the questions. For example, for question 31, students read the two headings in bold and decide the type of word (noun, verb, adjective or adverb) needed to fill the blank; whether the answer is singular or plural, if it is a noun; read the whole line and do not stop at the blank space; try to think what the word is to do with – something related to history/background, change, things that have happened. These can also be turned into questions that students can use for examining all questions in the IELTS exam.

Depending on the level of the students in your class, you may want to play the recording in sections e.g., Questions 31–35, 36–37 focusing students' attention on the headings.

ANSWERS

| 31 | events | 32 | timetable |
|----|--------|----|-----------|
| 33 | developments | 34 | Money |
| 35 | industrialisation | 36 | cotton |
| 37 | costs/charges | | |

### Questions 38–40

Point out, or elicit, the steps to be followed for answering these questions: underlining key words in the rubric (*improvement/modern railways*); predicting what students think the main improvements from the list are (this will also help students to engage with the items); thinking about the social/economic aspect of the previous headings. Elicit if any of the items A–F relate to this section.

Remind students that the questions in the Listening, and likewise in the Reading test:
- are a summary of the contents of the recording
- have a discourse and fit together, so questions and answers must logically fit together.

Everything in IELTS is logical and predictable.

ANSWERS

IN ANY ORDER: B, C, F

## Discussion

**2** Ask students to discuss the question in pairs and/or groups followed by whole-class discussion. As in all discussions, emphasise the need to back up the main points made with reasons and examples, using *like*, *such as*, *for instance*, *for example* and *if*, etc. Also, remind students of the use of countable nouns to give examples of uncountable nouns, as well the use of general nouns .

## General note

Point out to students that at the end of the exam they are given 10 minutes to transfer their answers onto an answer sheet. It is essential to practise this during the course, as frequently students introduce mistakes during the transfer, either through spelling mistakes or by putting letters in the wrong box. Students can check their answers, especially spelling, in pairs before whole-class checking. Point out that even one spelling mistake, or one letter in the wrong box can affect their score band.

Encourage students to keep a dated record of their Listening test results for revision purposes later.

---

 **Listening script 08**

Good morning, I'm going to talk to you today about the importance of infrastructure developments such as railway systems in helping solve some of society's problems and I'll also highlight some social and economic opportunities these have provided.

First of all, I'd like to give a brief overview of the history of the railway system and its effect on the world. The timeline given here shows the most significant <u>events</u> in the expansion of the railways in the UK in the early 19th century. Let's start with probably the most important year on the timeline, the year 1831, which saw the opening of the successful Liverpool to Manchester railway. This was powered by the locomotive, *The Rocket*, which was created by engineer Robert Stephenson. This is generally thought of as the first modern railway, because both goods and passenger traffic were carried on trains according to a scheduled <u>timetable</u>.

The success of the railway would not have been possible without previous <u>developments</u> to which Stephenson is indebted. As you see in 1803, the first horse-drawn railway was opened in south London by an engineer called William Jessop. The first railway steam locomotive was built in 1804 by an English engineer Richard Trevithick and in the year 1812, the first commercially successful steam locomotive, *the Salamanca* appeared on the scene at Middleton in Yorkshire in the north-east of England. After the success of the Stockton to Darlington railway in 1825 with the engine *Locomotion*, <u>money</u> flooded into the north-west of England as the region went through a period of rapid <u>industrialisation</u>, with the railway linking the rich town of Manchester and the thriving Port of Liverpool.

---

And the social and economic effect of the opening of the Liverpool and Manchester Railway on the commercial world? It was quite dramatic. By 1834, the number of passengers using the railway had risen to nearly half a million. Also more merchandise, including coal and <u>cotton</u> was transported between the two cities using the railway. The age of the railway as a means of carrying people from one place to another had arrived. The increase in rail passenger numbers and in the movement of goods led to a drop in other <u>costs</u> such as those for road and canal use.

Just as the inventions of these earlier pioneers opened up travel, between towns and cities in the UK, railways around the world are still creating trade links within countries and across borders, bringing communities and nations together.

Railway systems worldwide are responsible <u>for improving people's living standards by bringing jobs to people and people to jobs</u>. In India, for example, millions have access to work though the railways. The country comes top as regards the number of passenger-kilometres yearly, a staggering one billion passenger kilometres a year accounting for about one third of the total number of passenger-kilometres travelled globally in 2006. But the Swiss are the top rail travellers individually with about 2,500 kilometres each year according to the Switzerland Office for Statistics.

There are now many examples of modern high-speed links around the world, which provide business and tourist opportunities <u>generating jobs and trade links</u>. We have the Eurostar, with passenger statistics showing the increasing popularity of the line, and the Sapsan, the high speed link between Moscow and St Petersburg in Russia, and also the Bullet train in Japan and the high-speed rail link in China.

Now let's look at some of the business opportunities created in India in greater detail.

## Language focus: Countable and uncountable nouns Page 51

### Lead-in

Give a review of countable and uncountable nouns. Elicit some examples of nouns from the class, especially any that they might have problems with, e.g., *information*. Ask students about countable and uncountable nouns in their mother tongue.

**1** Go through the example as a whole class and ask students to look at the picture of the train and elicit examples of nouns that are countable, e.g., *trains, carriages, trees, arches, bricks, leaves, people*, and uncountable nouns, e.g., *transport, infrastructure, architecture, nature, steam, grass*, or examples of nouns from the classroom. Or ask students questions about the picture: Look at the … Is the word *steam* countable or uncountable? Refer students to the Grammar reference on page 221.

**2** Ask students to do the exercise in pairs. After checking the answers, point out one aspect of the relationship between countable and uncountable nouns: countable nouns, e.g., *chairs,* are examples of uncountable nouns, e.g., *furniture.*

ANSWERS

**1** b **2** a **3** j **4** f **5** c **6** d **7** h **8** e
**9** g **10** i

**3** Once students have done the exercise in pairs and checked their answers, check understanding by eliciting reasons for some of the answers. Also, as in exercise 1, highlight the use of the countable nouns in relation to the uncountable nouns, i.e. the specific countable nouns are examples of the uncountable nouns.

ANSWERS

1 equipment, computers
2 weather, storms
3 information, details
4 Business, businesses
5 Accommodation, flats
6 Furniture, wood, trees
7 Rubbish
8 jobs, work, money

**4** Make sure students understand the rubric by asking a student to explain what they need to do. Go through the words in the box, asking students to categorise the nouns as countable and uncountable. As the answers are being checked globally, elicit the reason for any verb changes, and non-changes.

ANSWERS

1 … machines are    2 behaviour …
3 Information    4 Robberies are …
5 opportunities    6 Suggestions … are
7 Language … follows    8 litter

**5** After going through the example(s) with the whole class, ask students to do the exercise in pairs.

ANSWERS

1 Useful information is available nowadays on the internet.
2 Social media help people make new friends.
3 Transport such as buses and trains leads to the development of communities.
4 Accommodation is becoming very expensive in many major cities.

5 Technological waste, such as computers and phones, is now a growing problem.
6 Leisure activities help people relax.
7 Electronic goods like refrigerators cause considerable harm to the planet.

**6** Go through the examples with students. Then allow them time to ask and answer in pairs.

## Speaking PART 1 Page 52

Point out to students that they may be asked questions about a wide range of subjects in Part 1. For example, they might be asked about flowers, transport, weather, etc., not just about their hobbies and their family. However, reassure students that subjects do not require any depth of knowledge and they are of a personal nature. They are only required to give short answers of one or two clauses (not just *yes/no* answers).

**1** Ask the students to complete the exercise individually and then compare their answers with another student, before checking as a whole class.

ANSWERS
**Food**
1 Countable: types/country
  Uncountable: food
2 Countable: products
  Uncountable: food
3 Countable: people
  Uncountable: food
4 Countable: people
  Uncountable: food

**Manufactured goods**
1 Countable: types, country
  Uncountable: equipment
2 Countable: goods, country
3 Countable: country, goods
4 Countable: shops, country, countries
  Uncountable: merchandise
5 Countable: clothes
  Uncountable: furniture

**2** Ask students to work in pairs, reminding them to use nouns and verbs from the previous section. Allow students to ask you some questions and/or ask individual students several of the questions by way of checking. If your students feel comfortable talking in front of each other, ask pairs to roleplay asking and answering a set of questions, and give feedback. Doing this can help build student confidence.

## Reading Passage Page 52

**1** Prior to completing the reading section, students discuss the questions in pairs/groups, followed by whole-class feedback.

As with the Listening test, go over the *How to go about it* box for Questions 1–9. Ask students to explain in their own words the procedure for completing the summary using the wordlist. Elicit questions or comments from students relating to this type of question and address any concerns they might have, e.g., the amount of reading involved in the questions as well as the Reading Passage and how to answer the questions effectively and efficiently in the time given.

For Questions 10–14, make sure students are clear about the difference between *True/False/Not Given* statements and *Yes/No/Not Given* statements for claims. It is crucial that students are able to see the difference. If necessary, point out the information in Ready for Reading on Student's Book page 84.

## Questions 1–9

Ask students to look at the title of the summary and the title of the Reading Passage. Ask them to explain the title and predict what information they expect to find in the passage. Then ask them to skim the passage itself in no more than two minutes. Students work in pairs and compare their predictions, and then describe the contents of the passage, generally.

Tell them to complete the summary following the steps above. Give about 12 minutes. Ask them to write the answers on a sheet of paper. When they have finished, ask them to compare their answers with a partner, checking spelling, etc.

**ANSWERS**

1 H   2 C   3 D   4 Q   5 P   6 I   7 A
8 B   9 O

## Questions 10–14

For Questions 10–14, ask students to analyse the questions in pairs, checking, for example, for positive or negative adjectives, and comparisons. Alternatively, ask students to explain the sentences in their own words as a whole-class exercise. Then tell them to answer the questions individually and then compare them with a partner.

**ANSWERS**

| 10 NOT GIVEN | 11 NO | 12 YES |
| 13 NOT GIVEN | 14 YES | |

## Discussion

**2** Ask the students to discuss the question in pairs, reminding them to give reasons and examples for their answers. Elicit some opinions from individual students.

## Vocabulary 2: Developing ideas
page 55

**1–2** Ask students to read the rubric and check they understand what they are required to do. Ask them to do the exercises individually and then compare their answers with a partner.

**ANSWERS**

**1**
| 1 encourage | 2 stunned | 3 pleases |
| 4 fascinated | 5 attracts | |

**2**
| 1 It | 2 It | 3 them |
| 4 It | 5 them | |

**3** Ask students to work in pairs or groups. When they have finished, ask them to compare their answers with another pair or group. Write several sentences on the board for each of the four sentences in the exercise. Ask students to choose the best alternative.

**POSSIBLE ANSWERS**

1 It is spreading at an alarming rate.
2 It makes people anxious and frightens them.
3 They frightened the government/schools/parents.
4 They attract them because many people like the thrill of being scared.

## Speaking  PART 3  Page 55

Ask students to read the *How to go about it* box and then ask questions about the contents. Answer any questions students may have.

**1** Students answer the questions in pairs and then give feedback to the class.

**ANSWERS**

solve: tackle, remedy, deal with, cope with
issue: problems, situations, matters of concern
rising: growing, increasing, spreading, on the rise
main: major, most important
facing: confronting, challenging
opportunities: chances, openings, prospects
problems: issues

**2** Ask students to do the exercise in pairs. You could also allocate one question to each pair, followed by feedback to the whole class.

**ANSWERS**

The first question: link with vocabulary – individuals/people; issues/problems; solve/tackle

**3** Ask students to work with a different partner. Students can take turns asking and answering the questions and giving feedback between each roleplay. Remind them to develop their answers as per the *How to go about it* box. If necessary, for weaker students, elicit ideas to help them answer the questions on world problems.

## Writing TASK 2 page 56

**1** Students first answer the questions 1–3 in pairs and then check their answers with the whole class.

ANSWERS
1 Negative
2 causes, measures
3 Give reasons and examples.

**2** Once students have completed the exercise in pairs, check the answers as a whole class.

ANSWERS
**A**
causes: cost of accommodation, shortage of land, migration of people to cities
solutions: subsidise accommodation, more tower blocks with flats, economies in rural areas improved/ revitalised

**B**
causes: cost of accommodation, shortage of land
solutions: provide cheaper accommodation, revitalise the economies in rural areas

**3** Students can do this exercise in conjunction with exercise 2. Alternatively, the exercise can be done with the whole class and the answers collated on the board.

ANSWERS
The solutions and causes are similar.
**A** has three causes and three solutions with a cause and solution in each paragraph.
**B** has two causes in one paragraph followed by paragraphs with one solution in each.
The organisation is a matter of preference.

### Suggesting causes and solutions

**1** After students have completed the exercise, write samples of the causes and solutions on the board using the following sequence:

Cause → Problem → Solution

Emphasise the importance of this sequence in Academic English. Refer students to IELTS essentials on page 205.

POSSIBLE ANSWERS
1 man-made pollution/(natural) climate change
2 human actions
3 population increases, fewer resources, greater life expectancy
4 pressure from agriculture/population increases/ climate change

**2** Students do this exercise on their own before comparing their answers with the whole class. It

is important to emphasise paraphrasing and to develop it where possible throughout the course.

ANSWERS
**a** Governments ought to encourage people to …
**b** Protection orders can be put on …
**c** Water desalination plants might work in …
**d** I think that more trees should be planted

**3** This can be done as a whole-class exercise.

ANSWERS
**1** d **2** b **3** a **4** c

### Developing a topic sentence

**1** Read through the rubric with the students and make sure that they understand what a topic sentence is. Elicit what the relationship is between the topic sentence and the other stages in the writing of a paragraph, i.e. effectively a summary/ overview of the paragraph contents followed by specific proof (reasons and examples). Refer students to IELTS essentials on page 205.
   Ask students to check their answers in pairs. As a whole class, elicit reasons for their answers.

ANSWERS
1 reason        2 contrast        3 result
4 example       5 purpose         6 result
7 concession

**2** This can be done as a whole-class exercise, or in pairs, following on from exercise 1.

ANSWERS
1 because        2 Yet             3 therefore
4 For example    5 in order to     6 then
7 Although

**3** This can be done as a whole-class exercise or in pairs.

ANSWERS
Adverbs: however, nevertheless, though, nonetheless, still, even so
Conjunctions: though, although, but, while, even if, much as
Both: yet

**4** This can be done as a pairwork exercise.

ANSWERS
1 However
2 but/although
3 While/Although
4 Even if/tThough
5 Even so/Nonetheless

**5** Students work in pairs to complete the Task 2 writing.

*Model answer*

Towns and cities around the world are much less healthy for their inhabitants compared to the past. This situation is the direct result of several factors, but many approaches exist to address the issue.

One reason for the problem is greater population density combined with increased traffic, which, in turn, causes pollution, like air and noise, as well as stress. For example, many countries worldwide, not just in Europe, are becoming more urbanised as people move to cities because of the entertainment and education facilities available, along with greater work opportunities. As a result, city life is considerably less wholesome now both physically and mentally than for previous generations.

To make city environments healthier, however, several important steps can be taken. For example, urban areas can be made greener by introducing more green spaces, even if they are only micro-gardens with a few trees, shrubs and seats. This can lead to both cleaner air and reduced stress. The problem can also be addressed by public and private buildings being made greener with the creation of roof gardens for people to relax in.

Having transport systems that are efficient, cheap and comfortable is another way of ensuring that cities are healthy places. Such a measure will also enhance the quality of city life by reducing air pollution and stress on the roads as people are drawn to using the transport system. Attractive buildings that integrate work and living conditions as well as facilities like leisure, health and education set in attractive open spaces, can also lead to improvements in the health of the urban environment.

Thus, despite cities being less healthy than in the past, the root causes can be tackled with several simple strategies.

*Word Count: 284 words*

**COMMENTS**

The response meets the requirements of the task, because it is more than 250 words; it is divided into five clear paragraphs with an introduction linked to the task; the first body paragraph deals with causes and the next two paragraphs with solutions; each body paragraph is connected to the introduction with the use of a topic sentence. The conclusion then summarises the response.

---

**REVIEW 4 ANSWERS** pages 58–59

## Vocabulary 1: General nouns

**1**
| | |
|---|---|
| 1 a burning issue | 2 a serious problem |
| 3 a golden opportunity | 4 a state occasion |
| 5 trying circumstances | 6 an imaginative solution |
| 7 a difficult situation | 8 a major cause |
| 9 a faint possibility | 10 a profound impression |
| 11 an unexpected outcome | |

**2**
| | |
|---|---|
| 1 outcome, unexpected | 2 faint, possibility |
| 3 cause | 4 situation, difficult |
| 5 problem | 6 impression, profound |
| 7 solutions, effective | |

## Vocabulary 2: Developing ideas

**1**
1 dangerous   2 motivated   3 alarming
4 appealing

**2**
1 People sometimes feel motivated enough by health adverts to change their lifestyle. They can encourage people to exercise.
2 Certain situations such as flooding can be very alarming. They are very frightening for people.
3 The volume of electronic waste in the world is now dangerous. Throwing away your old computer endangers the environment.
4 Action video games are appealing to people of all ages. The characters, story and graphics are attractive to many people.

## Language focus: Countable and uncountable nouns

**1**
| | |
|---|---|
| 1 fruit | 2 accommodation |
| 3 rubbish/packaging | 4 clothes/clothing |
| 5 media | 6 information |
| 7 furniture | 8 language |

**2**
POSSIBLE ANSWERS
1 I like fruit such as/like apples and oranges.
2 I have lived in an apartment and a house.
3 People throw away things like bottles and lots of paper.
4 I mainly buy work clothes like trousers and shirts.
5 I like to read the newspaper every day to keep me up to date on world events.
6 The internet contains lots of news, facts and data relating to many different topics.
7 I have a really comfortable sofa and chairs at home.
8 I keep a notebook with me so I can write down any new words or phrases.

ACCURACY IN IELTS
1 ~~trying~~ major issue
2 such ~~details~~ incidents
3 ~~However,~~ Although I agree that this is a major issue, I think …
4 contributing ~~measure~~ factor
5 ~~As~~ For example, …
6 makes the ~~event~~ situation worse
7 As regards ~~actions~~ solutions, …
8 positive stories ~~for~~ in order to
9 negative and positive ~~occasions~~ events

# 5 The future

Photocopiable activity: Whole class – Find someone who … page 132

Workbook pages 36–43

## Content overview

This unit focuses on the future, predictions and robotics.

**Listening** SECTION 1

Booking an exhibition

Question types: Note completion; Table completion

**Reading**

Future predictions

Question types: Summary completion; Multiple-choice; Short-answer questions

**Writing** TASK 1

Describing a pie chart

**Speaking** PART 3

Discussing the future

**Vocabulary:** Adjective/Noun collocations
**Vocabulary 2:** Verbs of prediction
**Word building:** Forming adjectives from nouns
**Language focus:** Ways of looking at the future

## Digital overview

**Presentation Kit**

Interactive versions of Student's Book exam tasks

Embedded audio and answer key for all activities

**Teacher's Resource Centre**

Communicative activity: Whole class – Find someone who …

Workbook audio, answer key and wordlists

**Student's Resource Centre**

Class audio

Wordlist

Speaking Part 3 videos (4) and video worksheet

## Language focus: Ways of looking at the future  page 60

### Lead-in

Ask students to look at the title of the unit and predict what the unit is about.

**1–2** Ask students to look at exercises 1 and 2 in groups. Tell them to appoint someone as a secretary to take notes for each question. To help develop students' organisational skills, ask them to classify their notes under headings using the general nouns *impact, ways, reasons (why)* for each question, and/or (sub)divide/code the changes according to the near future, five years ahead, and the distant future. The secretary can give brief feedback for the respective questions during whole-class feedback about the questions. These are the skills students need for all components of the IELTS exam.

Monitor the groupwork and, after eliciting answers, give feedback on students' language and organisational skills.

**3–4** Students can do these exercises as a whole class or as pairwork followed by whole-class discussion. Ensure that students can see the differences between the different ways of expressing the future in English, referring students to and/or going through the Grammar reference on page 222.

ANSWERS

**3**
1 Plan
2 Fixed schedule
3 Prediction
4 Prediction
5 Prediction
6 Fixed schedule

**4**
a the present continuous – 2
b *going to* – 1
c *will* – 5
d future continuous – 3
e future perfect – 4
f present simple – 6

**5–6** Tell students to do these exercises on their own and then check their answers in pairs. Follow up with whole-class feedback.

It is important that students understand the differences in usage of future forms. A good score in Speaking Part 3 can depend on the correct manipulation of these forms. They may also be required in Writing Task 2 and the Listening test.

**7** Before students do this exercise, you can check their comprehension of the ways of talking about the future by asking them how to make predictions, fixed arrangements, etc. Ask students to do the exercise in pairs, and then compare their answers with another pair before checking their answers during whole-class feedback.

**8** After the pairwork, elicit examples from students, encouraging them to give reasons and examples.

## Round up

Invite students to clarify any issues they have about ways of expressing the future; where possible, invite students to suggest the answers before giving them yourself. You could also summarise the future by going over the different ways in the Grammar reference using the Presentation Kit.

## Speaking PART 3 page 62

**1** Students work in pairs using the *Useful expressions* and picture to talk about the world in the future. If necessary, elicit example sentences from the students prior to the discussion. Remind students that there are no photographs in any part of the IELTS Speaking test. Ask students to give feedback as a whole class, focusing on the use of tenses and the *Useful expressions*.

Elicit from students the purpose of the useful expressions, reminding them of the organisation exercise at the beginning of the previous section. Such constant reminding will help students 'notice' more.

**2** It is important that students understand what is being asked in the questions in Part 3. Sometimes, the questions are long and the students focus on the last thing they hear. For example, they might hear *city life/2030* and not the *ways/have changed*. Remind students again about the classification exercise they did in speaking at the beginning of the unit. Prior to roleplay, ask them to do the same, noticing and analysing the task for the next two questions; time permitting do the same for the next set of questions.

Go through the ideas briefly and also the checklist criteria on page 181 to make sure students understand what each question is looking for. Remind them that they should be focusing on abstract ideas. Monitor the student discussion.

## Round up

Finish the section by giving feedback on question comprehension and/or the development of student ideas (including examples of good practice from students). Select four or five language points for discussion. Include examples of good practice.

## Vocabulary: Adjective/Noun collocations page 63

**1** Ensure students have chosen the correct adjectives, by eliciting the answers from the class, before moving onto exercise 2.

**2** Students work in pairs. Then check their answers during whole-class feedback.

**3** Ask students to discuss the questions in groups. You might want to ask them to appoint someone to take notes and be the group spokesperson during whole-class feedback. Or you can wait and see if they do it themselves. If they don't, encourage them to appoint someone next time they have a group discussion.

## Listening SECTION 1 page 63

### Lead-in

Before students do the pre-listening activity, elicit the features of Section 1 in the exam using the word *features* in your question. Remind them of anything they might have left out, e.g., the example, the number they need to get correct for a good score. Give them hints rather than the answers, e.g., *What about the number of correct answers needed?*

**1** Ask students to do the exercise in pairs. During whole-class feedback, discuss what other contexts the words and phrases might be used in.

> **ANSWERS**
>
> **1** a chance to see a show, film or play before it opens to the general public
> **2** two weeks from now  **3** limitations
> **4** register  **5** appear
> **6** enrol/join  **7** variety/scope

### Questions 1–10

Ask students to read through the questions and then describe the content of the conversation in as much detail as possible. Check if they have any questions/concerns about any of the question types. Play the listening test all the way through and ask students to write their answers as they listen.

Ask students to check their own answers and then again with a partner. Play the test again allowing students to change their answers and tell them to highlight the new answer. Mistakes are often made during the transfer of answers to the answer sheet in the exam. You might want to ask students to write their answers into a grid for practice. Monitor this stage yourself.

Consider doing a quick recap of the pronunciation of numbers and letters.

> **ANSWERS**
>
> **1** Monday  **2** day passes
> **3** Tuesday, Friday  **4** SF6799
> **5–6** IN EITHER ORDER: B and E
> **7** 17  **8** marina
> **9** 5/five  **10** 3.95

---

## Listening script 09

**(M = Marcus; C = customer)**

**M:** Good morning, Fair booking office. Marcus speaking. Can I help you?
**C:** Is that the booking office for the Fair on Futuristic Home Design?
**M:** Yes sir, that's correct. How can I help you?
**C:** Well, mmm … I'm attending the Fair and I'd just like to check a few things if that's OK?
**M:** Yes, sure.
**C:** OK. I understand the Fair opens the week after next on the Tuesday, and … the preview is on <u>Monday</u>.
**M:** Yes, that's right. There is a preview on Monday, but the Fair's not open to the general public on that day. But for the rest of the week it is.
**C:** OK, I see. That's fine. I've got two complimentary <u>day passes</u>; can you tell me if I can use them on any day?
**M:** Well, I'm not sure if there are any restrictions, … let's see … yes, here we are.
**C:** Yes?
**M:** You can use them on any day including the preview day, except Saturday. But you need to sign up for the workshops and seminars you want to attend in advance.
**C:** Oh, I see. I haven't decided which workshops or seminars to attend yet.
**M:** Mmm … well … Saturday you can't attend any with the passes you have, and Thursday they're already completely booked. I think the other days'll book up fairly quickly now, as there's a lot of interest from the general public and retailers.
**C:** You mean I won't be able to attend any workshops on Saturday even with my free pass?
**M:** I'm afraid not. It's better to register for the other days now.
**C:** OK. I suppose, mmm … I'll attend all the seminars on <u>Tuesday</u> and <u>Friday</u>. Do you need my name?
**M:** No, I just need to take your reference number from the day passes. Your name will come up with the number; it'll be the same number on each one. I'll register one for Tuesday and one for Friday, and then when you use one it'll automatically cancel.
**C:** OK, the number is <u>S–F–6–7–99</u>.
**M:** … 99. Thank you, I've got that.
**C:** What about services like places to eat and so on?
**M:** Oh, there are 15 restaurants in all.
**C:** That's a lot.
**M:** There'll be lots of people … there are <u>three sandwich bars</u> and the others are different types of dining areas around the Fair. Some <u>restaurants from the area around the Fair venue</u> will be there doing special promotions at the Fair itself, so you won't go hungry.

........................................................

**C:** Is there somewhere nice to stay nearby?
**M:** Oh yes. There're rooms at the nearby halls of

residence, which are part of the university. They're just across the road from here.

**C:** How much are they?

**M:** A single room is £65 per night, which includes breakfast in the cafeteria. And there are some very pleasant family-run hotels in the area. They range from around £70 to about £90. It depends how much you want to spend really.

**C:** What about getting there? Are there good transport links?

**M:** Yes. We're very well located – about a 30-minute walk at most from the train and bus station, and about 45 minutes from the airport. There are lots of buses; the best one, which stops just by the main entrance, is bus 70. No, sorry, it's bus 17. I keep getting them mixed up. You want the bus going in the direction of Brookfields. The buses run every 12 minutes and you catch it from Stop W close to the station.

**C:** OK. How much does it cost?

**M:** It only costs £3.20 from the station. But you can also buy a weekly ticket for £15.

**C:** How long does it take?

**M:** Ten minutes, but there may be lots of traffic.

**C:** OK.

**M:** And there's also a river bus.

**C:** A river bus?

**M:** Yes. You can take Route A to the marina. It runs every 20 minutes. You can catch it on the river front, which is five minutes' walk from the station.

**C:** Is it more expensive?

**M:** Not much. It's £3.95 and there's no weekly pass. But the journey only takes 5 minutes and it's probably more pleasant and comfortable.

**C:** And taxis? Just in case.

**M:** Mmm, for a taxi … you'll pay a maximum of £20.

**C:** Mmm … well that all sounds OK.

**2** Students can discuss the questions in groups. Ask each group to select one person to give feedback to the class.

### Round up

Check any difficulties and gauge whether reading and completing the table caused any problems.

## Word building: Forming adjectives from nouns  page 65

**1** Before students do the exercise in pairs, elicit and/ or point out why nouns are important in IELTS and why it is important to know adjectives they can make from nouns, and vice versa, (expands vocabulary and builds confidence).

Point out that when adding the suffix to the existing word, some letters need to be dropped, some added and others changed. Write three columns on the board, one for each suffix. When

students have finished, elicit the adjectives for the relevant columns on the board.

**ANSWERS**

| Adjectives ending –al | Adjectives ending -ous | Adjectives ending –ful |
|---|---|---|
| technological | luxurious | useful |
| agricultural | populous | successful |
| traditional | spacious | beautiful |
| national | dangerous | |
| industrial | industrious | |

**2** Ask students to do the exercise on their own, check the answers in pairs, followed by whole-class feedback.

**ANSWERS**

| | | |
|---|---|---|
| **1** spacious | **2** technological | **3** beautiful |
| **4** traditional | **5** national | **6** Luxurious |
| **7** populous | **8** successful | |

**3** Tell students to use the negative form as well if it is more appropriate. Monitor for accuracy of meaning and for logical examples.

## Reading Passage  page 65

### Lead-in

Before students do the Reading test, elicit a few of the skills that they need to use to complete the test in the time given. Remind them especially to be aware of time management and, if mobile phones are allowed in the classroom, to time themselves using the reverse clock. Try not to overburden them with skills by recycling and focusing on a section each time, referring students to the IELTS strategies on page 203.

**1** Ask students to do the exercise with a partner and then compare their answers with another pair. If you have time, write A–D with the phrases on the board and elicit suggestions and reasons for predictions.

Encourage students to skim the text, setting a time limit of about 2 minutes. Check how close their suggestions were and if they were surprised by any of the suggestions. Tell them you do not expect detailed analysis of the Reading Passage.

### Questions 1–13

Depending on your class, you might want to ask students to answer the questions on their own, just referring them to the *How to go about it* box, and gauging their reaction afterwards. Or, before students do the test, you can go through each set of questions analysing the skills needed. A third option is for students to answer the questions in three stages after analysing the questions.

## Questions 1–7

Review the strategies needed to complete summaries on page 54 of Unit 4. Ask what is different about the instructions for the task in Unit 5 and the one in Unit 4 (the words from Unit 4 are taken from a wordlist; in this question type the words are taken from the passage). Essentially, the skills are the same (predicting the types of words, etc.).

Go through the *How to go about it* advice carefully, step by step. The advice about checking to see if the summary is based on part of the passage or the whole passage is particularly relevant. Suggest they look at the first and last sentence and one in the middle to gauge this, but remind them that summaries without a heading can cover the whole reading passage. Point out the names in the summary and the text which will show them the extent of the summary – they can circle or box the names.

## Questions 8–11

Go through Question 8 with the students, analysing the stem and the options A–D. By way of encouraging engagement with the multiple-choice question, ask students to paraphrase where possible.

## Questions 12 and 13

Remind students that their answers should be taken from the Reading Passage and that they should use no more than three words.

As students do the test, tell them to write their answers on a sheet of paper, answer grid or in their books. Remind them there is no extra time to transfer their answers to the answer sheet as there is in the Listening test. Point out that correct spelling is essential – that even one wrong word can affect the score band. Also point out that once they locate answers in the passage, they need to do close reading around the part of the text where the answer is.

They should check answers in pairs before whole-class feedback, discussing any problem areas.

ANSWERS
1 high-quality emotions
2 ugly objects
3 distinction
4 digital, artificial
5 power themselves
6 feelings
7 emotional state
8 A    9 C    10 D    11 B
12 alternative power sources
13 negative emails

Students discuss their reaction to the text in small groups followed by whole-class feedback or as a whole class. Invite students to evaluate the predictions as *practical/impractical, realistic/unrealistic, fanciful,* etc. or as already beginning to happen.

## Extension

It is important not to overuse the Reading Passage in class so as not to demotivate the students when it comes to reading. However, this needs to be balanced with students learning vocabulary and chunks from the text. Put students into groups/pairs and ask them to select about seven words or expressions that they think might be useful to learn. As this is student-centred they are likely to engage with the process more. Be prepared for the selection of phrases/words which are of little value. Discuss choices as a whole class and give your own.

# Vocabulary 2: Verbs of prediction

page 67

**1–2** Do both these exercises as a whole class, eliciting which verbs students are (most) familiar with. Elicit the four verbs that cannot be used in this context and discuss context and appropriacy issues. Illustrate the differences if necessary. Go over the noun and verb forms and remind the students that using a variety of structures as well as a wide range of vocabulary helps to increase their chances of a better score.

ANSWERS
1
prophesy, assume, foretell, foresee
2
prediction, predicted/predictable
forecast, forecast(ed)
projection, projected
estimate, estimation, estimated
anticipation, anticipated
expectation, expected

**3** Go through the examples, even if the students are familiar with the structures. Point out that contractions aren't acceptable in Writing Task 1, e.g., ... *sales'll* ..., etc. Focus on the changes to the verbs. Ask the students to look out for similar necessary changes in the other sentences. Remind them also of the impersonal subject *it* here.

Point out that using a variety of structures like this will improve the style of their writing. Ask students to follow the instructions for doing the exercise.

ANSWERS
1 By the year 2030 it is estimated that the population will have increased to nearly 70 million.
2 Spectator numbers are forecast to rise dramatically towards the end of the year.
3 It is projected that sales next month will be lower than this month.
4 Sales are predicted to climb at the rate of 20 per cent a year.

5 Attendances are anticipated to decline gradually in the next two years.
6 It is expected that advances in technology will not slow down in the coming years.
7 Ticket purchases are estimated to recover in the third quarter.

## Extension

To help increase students' flexibility with these structures, ask them to work in pairs. One student reads out one of the sentences from the exercise, and the partner transforms the sentence without looking at the exercise. Encourage them to do the transformation both ways. When you see that the students are becoming faster, do a quick check around the class. Once you are happy that the students are able to do the transformations easily, ask them to close their books. Dictate some of the sentences, which the students then have to transform and write down. Check answers with the whole class. You can use this checking sequence with other transformation exercises.

## Writing TASK 1 page 68

### Lead-in

Before students look at this section, elicit a few skills/strategies that they need to use in Writing Task 1.

1 Give students time to look at the rubric and charts individually. Next, put them into pairs and ask them to describe the charts in their own words. Then go through the *What to expect in the exam* and *Don't forget!* boxes with the students, eliciting and/or clarifying information. Suggest students write short notes on the charts as they discuss, and mark significant similarities and differences between the pie charts. Emphasise that they should automatically do this with Task 1 questions.

Students can then look at the model and do the exercise in pairs, checking their answers followed by whole-class feedback. Allow them to consult other students during the pairwork.

Elicit students' reasons for their choice of tenses, comparing especially the introduction and overview with the rest of the model. Ask them to locate the overview at this stage and highlight the fact that it is at the end (compare this with the overview in Unit 1 – pointing out the different places for the overview). Point out the uses of paragraphs and elicit what information each contains. Ask which indicators in the charts show the most appropriate tense to use.

**ANSWERS**

| | | |
|---|---|---|
| 1 show | 2 is | 3 is expected |
| 4 is predicted | 5 will be | 6 is anticipated |
| 7 is estimated | 8 will account for | 9 will be |
| 10 will remain | | |

Ask students to work in groups and select about seven words or chunks they could learn and recycle in the future. Discuss the choices as a whole class.

2 Students choose the linkers. When the answers are discussed with the whole class, ensure they understand the difference in meanings if they chose the wrong answers. If they haven't already done so, ask students to add these linkers to their page of cohesive devices in their (electronic) vocabulary lists.

**ANSWERS**

1 In contrast/By comparison
2 By contrast/Meanwhile.
3 but/whereas
4 Meanwhile/In contrast
5 whereas/whilst

3 Follow the instructions in the Student's Book. Highlight the need to have at least one example of complex sentences in their own writing for Tasks 1 and 2.

**ANSWERS**

| | | |
|---|---|---|
| 1 64%, 44% | 2 12%, 5% | 3 64%, 44% |
| 4 1%, 6% | 5 2%, 18% | 6 64%, 44% |

4 Ask students to write their answer for Writing Task 1 on page 207, for homework or in class, time permitting. Encourage them to use the checklist on page 139 as they write.

---

*Model answer*

The charts show projections for global production by sector in 2030 and 2050. Generally speaking, there is little change in the projected proportion of production by the various sectors in the two years, with manufacturing and services being the most dominant.

It is forecast that the services and manufacturing sectors together will account for more than three quarters of global production in 2030 and 2050, 80.8% (50.2% and 30.6%) and 84.3% (51.2% and 33.1%) respectively. By contrast, the proportion of production from energy is expected to decline from 6.7% in 2030 to 4.3% in 2050, a drop of approximately one third. It is also anticipated that there will be a similar dramatic drop for agriculture production from 4% to 2% with production in materials, by contrast, comprising 3.5% in 2050 compared to 2.9% in 2030.

As regards info-communications and technology, there is expected to be little difference in the proportion of production the sector constitutes, with a slight rise from 5.6% to 5.9% over the period.

*Word count: 165 words*

---

COMMENTS

The response fulfills the requirements of the task, summarising all the information and supporting the overview with specific data. There is a range of vocabulary and structures relating to forecasts about the future.

## Extension

Internet access is needed for this extension. To encourage students to look at more data sets, ask them to work in pairs/small groups in class or as a homework project and select an example of data about the future. The data does not need to be presented as a pie chart. Students then prepare a short presentation lasting no more than two/three minutes using the data. They can elicit questions from other students. The presentation can be done by a spokesperson, in pairs or small groups.

## REVIEW 5 ANSWERS　pages 70–71

## Vocabulary: Adjective/Noun collocations

1　modern civilisation
2　agricultural societies
3　urban populations
4　dominant cultures
5　thriving communities
6　general public

## Word building: Forming adjectives from nouns

1　luxurious, spacious
2　dangerous, traditional
3　national, beautiful
4　technological, traditional
5　successful, industrial
6　useful, traditional
7　populous, agricultural
8　national, useful, technological

## Language focus: Ways of looking at the future

1
1　will land, will be living
2　will have changed, will be, will have access
3　are going to face/will face, will increase
4　We're meeting, will be, are going to do
5　will close, is opening

2
a 4　b 5　c 2　d 3　e 1

ACCURACY IN IELTS

1
1　By the year 2025, the proportion of **graduates** in the workforce will **have** risen significantly.
2　It **is** estimated that shopper **numbers** in the department store will increase next month.
3　Next year, there will **be** a noticeable **rise** in smart TV sales to 5,000 units a month.
4　The trend in energy consumption is predicted to **dramatically** increase during **the** next decade.
5　The projected **sales** figures for next year show that **there** will be a slight decline.
6　The use of industrial robots **is** anticipated to continue increasing **worldwide**.
7　In the last **quarter** of the year, it is expected that registrations at the gym will **begin** rising again gradually.
9　Overall, it **is** expected that a clear upward **trend** will be seen in the funding for space research.

2
1　By the year 2025, there will have been a significant rise in the proportion of graduates in the workplace.
2　Shopper numbers in the department store are estimated to increase next month.
3　Sales of smart TVs will rise noticeably next year to 5,000 units a month.
4　It is predicted that the trend in energy consumption will dramatically increase during the next decade.

# 6  The fruits of nature

Photocopiable activity: Whole class – Processes card ordering page 133

Workbook pages 44–51

## Content overview

This unit focuses on nature, conservation, and describing processes.

### Listening SECTION 2

Describing a place

Question types: Multiple-choice; Labelling a map; Sentence completion

### Reading

The fruit of the olive tree

Question types: Matching information; Identification of information in a text – *True/False/Not Given*; Flow-chart completion

### Writing TASK 1

Describing a process; Describing sequences

### Speaking PART 2

Describing a place

**Vocabulary 1:** Lifecycles and processes

**Vocabulary 2:** Conservation

**Language focus:** Transitive and intransitive verbs

## Digital overview

### Presentation Kit

Interactive versions of Student's Book exam tasks

Embedded audio and answer key for all activities

### Teacher's Resource Centre

Progress Test 2

Communicative activity: Whole class – Processes card ordering

Workbook audio, answer key and wordlists

### Student's Resource Centre

Class audio

Wordlist

Speaking Part 2 video and video worksheet

## Vocabulary 1: Lifecycles and processes  page 72

### Lead-in

As an awareness-raising exercise, elicit what students know about the lifecycle of plants and insects, and what part insects play in the former.

You could develop this into a brief discussion about the conservation of animals/plants in general, giving hints to get students started, for example, *What about …?/Are there any examples in …?/ Think about … .*

1　Look at the photographs and ask students to describe them to each other in pairs, pre-teaching and/or eliciting *lavender, germinate, bloom* (noun and verb), *pollinate* and *cocoon*. Invite students to ask you questions as they discuss, as well.

2–3　Discuss the vocabulary that helped students to match the photos with the texts and check for logical links. Tell students to enter new words under a heading in their (electronic) vocabulary lists. Elicit how they might record the words, especially the verbs, and see what they come up with (transitive and intransitive). If they don't notice the tense and voice in the texts, point them out and elicit the reason why they are used. How much you focus on them will depend on your students.

> **ANSWERS**
> **2**
> a 4　b 1　c 3　d 2
> **3**
> Any or all of the words listed below:
> a　flowered, fruit, produced, becomes, seeds, fall, carried, birds, animals, wind, drop, ground, spring, germinate, grow, process, repeats.
> b　blooms, crop, picked, hand, machine, collected, taken, factory, crushed, oil, extracted, plant, made, essence, used, perfumes, toiletries.
> c　lays, eggs, leaves, plants, hatch, caterpillars, eat, weave, form, cocoon, insect, emerges.
> d　plants, produce, flowers, open, attract, insects, pollinate, plant.

4　After students have described a lifecycle, using words from exercise 2 where possible, elicit a couple of examples from them, writing down words and phrases (as notes) on the board as they speak. Check that the words/phrases you have written are in the order of the lifecycle described.

### Extension

Elicit where possible synonyms/paraphrases of the information given and ask other students/the class to describe the same lifecycle using the original notes and paraphrases.

## Reading Passage   page 73

**1** Elicit as much information from students as possible from the title and picture, e.g., facts they might know and the types of elements or features they might expect to find in the passage, (like processing, uses, history, harvesting, description of the tree, oil production and so on). Do not necessarily elicit these in order as preparation for the next exercise. However, do elicit the concepts of whether these *should* be in an *expected* order in this text, and more importantly in other texts, as a way of reinforcing the generic and (fairly) predictable organisation of academic texts. Refer students to *Process* in IELTS essentials on page 205.

Elicit what type of passage it is and ask students for reasons.

ANSWERS
Descriptive/factual

**2** Students work on their own and discuss as a whole class.

ANSWERS
1 C   2 G   3 E

### Questions 1–14

Tell the students they should always skim the Reading Passage and the questions first. Remind them that when reading the passage, they should skim at high speed for gist, scan to locate information and read closely. Stress that the more efficient they are at the first two skills, the more time they have for the close reading.

Go through the *How to go about it* boxes. Check that students are using the right strategies to find the answers. For Questions 1–5, briefly analyse the questions, eliciting the general nouns in each phrase and the content/specific words relating to the text. Ask whether the pre-reading prediction exercise can help them locate the information generally in the passage before they look at it.

As preparation for the flow-chart in Questions 10–14, point out the significance of the title, the word limit and the fact that the text is in note form. Explain that sometimes the information in the flow-chart and the Reading Passage may not be in the same order. Elicit the grammatical form of most of the words in the flow-chart, and ask them to predict the form of the missing words. Relate this to the pre-reading exercise focus on nouns and verbs.

Allow students 20 minutes to do the Reading test. Ask them to write their answers on a separate sheet, and to note which question they've reached at the time limit. Allow extra time, if possible. Encourage them to be responsible for their own time management. Remind them of the advice in the *Don't forget!* box and the importance of spelling in the flow-chart.

Students check their answers in pairs and then as a whole class. Make sure they have located the correct answers in the text.

ANSWERS
1 E   2 I   3 F   4 J   5 H   6 FALSE
7 TRUE          8 NOT GIVEN
9 FALSE         10 shortly
11 production method   12 heat
13 leftover cake       14 feed, compost

**3** 👥 Students discuss the questions in small groups.

### Extension

To show students how they can increase their skimming speed, ask them to underline the nouns and verbs in the first paragraph. Then read the nouns and verbs to the students as they look at the text and ask them if they can understand generally what is being talked about. Get them to do the same in pairs for the next paragraph. Students can do the same with the texts on page 72. One student reads the noun/verbs and the other student, without looking at the text, listens and says what is being talked about.

## Language focus: Transitive and intransitive verbs   page 76

**1–2** Go through both exercises with the whole class. Check students understand the difference between the two types of verbs by eliciting what they know. Give them examples of transitive verbs, e.g. *build, raise,* etc. intransitive verbs from Task 1 in Unit 1, page 13, e.g. *rise, fall, climb,* etc. and verbs that are both, e.g. *increase, decrease,* etc. Depending on your students, you might want to look at why intransitive verbs and verbs that are both intransitive and transitive are common in Writing Task 1, i.e. processes, which generally don't have agents with *by*. It can be quite an eye-opener for students. Again, students may know all this, but sometimes may not notice exactly why the distinction between verbs is essential here. It is worth pointing out that without a grasp of this, of the part played by these types of verbs, a good score in Writing Task 1, especially, will elude them.

Remind students that intransitive verbs cannot be used in the passive. Remind them of the examples in Writing Task 1 in Unit 1 again and refer them to the Grammar reference on page 223.

ANSWERS
**1**
1 harvest(ing), occur(s)
2 is cleaned, is processed, is extracted
3 are grown

**2**
transitive: is cleaned, is processed, is extracted, are grown, harvest(ing)
intransitive: occur
both: grow

**3** Ask students to do the exercise on their own. Then check their answers in pairs and as a whole class.

ANSWERS

| Transitive | Intransitive | Both |
|---|---|---|
| make | look | decrease |
| produce | happen | weave |
| collect | rise | |
| sow | become | |
| process | flow | |
| pick | emerge | |
| crush | occur | |

Note: The verb *become* can be intransitive in certain circumstances: <u>That hairstyle becomes you.</u> Otherwise, it is a linking verb and functions like the verb *to be*.

**4** Ask students to work in pairs, followed by whole-class feedback.

ANSWERS
1 the sun
2 cereal, wheat, corn, spelt, rye
3 tea
4 cotton
5 a butterfly
6 flowers

**5** Elicit or point out that the focus of the exercise is on transitive verbs; hence, they are used here in the active and in the passive. Tell students to peer correct if necessary. Monitor this process and make a note of any consistent errors for whole-class feedback. At this point, stress the auxiliary verb in the passive. In an extended text, students might leave out the auxiliary because the passive without an agent occurs frequently, as do intransitive verbs.

POSSIBLE ANSWERS
1 The sun rises and goes down every day.
2 Cereal(s)/Wheat/Spelt/Corn/Rye is/are gathered/harvested to produce bread.
3 Tea leaves are cultivated to produce a hot drink from China.
4 Cotton is white and is utilised to create a very light cloth.
5 A butterfly comes out of a cocoon to become a flying insect.
6 Flowers are colourful, bloom in gardens and look and smell very nice.

**6** Do this exercise as a whole-class activity, giving examples where necessary. Point out the focus here is on intransitive verbs so they can compare the previous stage.

ANSWERS
grow (tall), become (bigger), sprout, appear, open up

**7** Students do this exercise in pairs, followed by whole-class feedback.

ANSWERS
seeds: grow
saplings: grow (tall)
branches: prune, bear
tree: grow (tall), become (bigger), bear
buds: appear
flowers: open up
fruit: harvest, ripen, cultivate

**8** Students can label the diagram with verbs and nouns and then describe in pairs. They might want to compare their answer with other students before whole class checking. Monitor students during the pairwork and give feedback. Elicit example answers from volunteers in the class.

**9** Ask students to complete the text individually. Get whole-class feedback.

ANSWERS
1 are planted/grown
2 are transplanted
3 pruned
4 grow
5 sprout
6 pollinate
7 ripen
8 harvested

**Round up**

Elicit a brief summary of transitive and intransitive verbs. Also ask about the importance of the use of these verb types, e.g., in processes and flow-charts, and in all parts of the exam for the expression and comprehension of abstract concepts.

**Speaking** PART 2 page 77

**1** Monitor students as they describe the photographs in their pairs, encouraging them in the use of the types of verbs in the previous section. Monitor the pairwork for the use of the verbs, and give whole-class feedback after eliciting examples from the class. Remind students that they will not have photographs in the exam.

**2** Ask students to study the Task Card and then listen to a student giving a possible response. Ask them to identify the prompts mentioned.

ANSWERS
All the stages

**3–4** Students listen again and complete the blank spaces as directed. Students then compare answers with a partner, matching the notes to the prompts. Allow students to compare their answers with other students.

**ANSWERS**

**3**

| 1 | mountain | 2 | Ireland | 3 | 14 |
|---|---|---|---|---|---|
| 4 | family | 5 | landscape | 6 | views |
| 7 | scenic | 8 | empty | 9 | peaceful |
| 10 | escape | 11 | relax | | |

**4**

Where: 1, 2          When: 3
Who: 4               Why: 5–11

---

🎧 **Listening script 10**

I'd like to describe a place that is really very beautiful. It is a picnic area on a mountain top on the north coast of Ireland. It is close to where my father was born and I went there for the first time when I was about 14 years old with my family on holiday. And I've been back many times since. The place is special to me, because the surrounding landscape is breathtaking. I also like it because the views of the countryside below the mountain are really spectacular. The area is very scenic, but it's usually empty, as you need a car to get there and there are no facilities, so few people go there. That makes it very peaceful and somewhere to escape from the world. It isn't quiet because of the wind, but it is a place to relax.

---

**5** 🎧 Students follow the usual process here described in the rubric, and visualise somewhere they are familiar with rather than creating somewhere on the spot. Ask them to use the checklist on page 181 for feedback. They can focus on one or more points chosen by the person who speaks. Or the person who roleplays the examiner can choose which criteria to give feedback on. At all times, encourage students to begin with constructive feedback.

Remind students of the advice in the *Don't forget!* box, and elicit example responses to the Task Card exercise from volunteers in the class.

## Vocabulary 2: Conservation  page 78

### Lead-in

Elicit the meaning of *conservation*, with local, national and international examples. Focus on extending student range beyond their local environment. If they cannot come up with examples of any of the three perspectives given, prompt them.

**1** Let the students do this exercise in pairs without any teacher input. Check the answers in pairs followed by whole-class feedback.

**ANSWERS**

| 1 | d, c | 2 | c, a | 3 | d, b |
|---|---|---|---|---|---|
| 4 | b, d | 5 | b, a | 6 | c, b |
| 7 | c, a | 8 | a, d | | |

**2** Students do this in pairs, joining up with another pair to check their answers. It is important to give students opportunities, however, brief, to articulate the language, whether it be grammar or vocabulary, as they are likely to remember it more. Check and discuss answers, eliciting reasons and examples. The discussion is effectively a prelude to exercise 3.

When students have finished, project the answers and discuss the choices they have made through peer correction.

**ANSWERS**

| 1 | views | 2 | lungs |
|---|---|---|---|
| 3 | stretches, spoilt | 4 | sights |
| 5 | safeguarded | 6 | conservation |

**3** 👥 Students discuss in pairs/groups, appointing a spokesperson to give feedback. Encourage students to form pairs/groups with students they don't normally work with. Point out the evaluative nature of the *Useful expressions*. Give them about 30 seconds to think about the questions before discussing.

## Listening SECTION 2  page 79

### Lead-in

Ask students to summarise the features of Listening Section 2 by way of revision. Then look at the questions and ask them to predict what they think the listening is about. You could discuss how conservation projects get funding in order to introduce the ideas of people paying to stay, making donations and a host country being self-sufficient through selling produce or crafts.

### Questions 11–20

You might want to focus on the map here and Questions 14–17 before students do the test. Go through the *How to go about it* advice. Students work in pairs. Ask them to locate the entrance first, then each of the letters, explaining to one another where each of the items (letters) is in relation to the others, using the points of the compass and prepositions of location, e.g., *opposite*. Ask students to describe the map as a whole class. Then check words like *lodge* and *nursery* in Questions 14–17. Look at any other buildings or features that are included in the map.

Point out that the places in 14–17 are in the order that they occur in the Listening test.

For Questions 18–20, remind students to be careful with singular and plural nouns. Ask students to listen and do the test, following the same procedure as in previous units. Check the answers as a whole class.

**ANSWERS**

**11** C  **12** B  **13** C  **14** G  **15** B  **16** J  **17** A
**18** views  **19** landscape  **20** seeds, flowers

**Listening script 11**

Good morning and welcome to the Moorland Countryside and Woodland Programme. I'd like to give you some information about the programme and the short courses we run for people on woodland awareness.

We're actually a programme run by volunteers, and we were set up 15 years ago to educate people of all ages and backgrounds about the wonders of our woodlands and, hence, nature itself. And for the past five years we've been taking groups of youngsters in their teens on educational trips on Fridays, Saturdays and Sundays, mmm … from schools mainly from around the area, … but some've come from much further afield. At first, some youngsters're not very impressed by the setting, because we discourage them from using any electronic devices, especially smartphones, so they can engage more with the surroundings … this throws them quite a bit. But almost without exception, by the end of the three days they're here the young people don't want to leave and want to come back again. In fact, two of the workers here came with student groups five years ago, and when they left school they came straight to work for us.

The programme is completely self-sufficient, due in part to the sales from the plant nursery and also to donations, but the bulk of our income's now from running the educational and awareness courses.

This is a basic map of our centre. We're here at the entrance, and you can see the cabins running along the east side of the path as you go north. The first cabin, Beech Lodge, is for students. It's quite large and can accommodate 10 students in bunk beds. Then the next four cabins're for families, and the cabin after that, Chestnut Lodge, is for teachers, which can hold up to four adults. On the west side of the path, directly opposite the family cabins, are the educational facilities. They're quite up-to-date with all the latest wizardry. And next to that's the cafeteria, which is shared with visitors to the centre. Just beside the cafeteria is a family area with climbing frames for children. We don't allow open-air cooking here, because of the trees.

The plant nursery's that area you can see that runs all the way along the north part of the map.

· · · · · · · · · · · · · · · · · · · · · · · · · · · · · · · · · · · · · · · · · · · · · ·

If you go over here, between the family area and the nursery, the path leads to the woodland itself. We're on a hill here and quite high up, … and as there's some spectacular scenery around here, we have breathtaking views of the countryside. You can see the river stretching for miles through rolling countryside. Fortunately, the whole woodland is protected by law, so nobody can chop down any trees.

The landscape here's not changed for hundreds of years. Some of the trees've been growing here rather a long time, and the aim of the scheme and the volunteers is to keep it that way. We advise people to stick to the paths, because it's very easy to get lost.

As you walk through the woodland, you'll see workers removing dead wood and trees. I'd ask everyone not to remove anything like seeds or flowers from the woodland so we can try and conserve it for future generations.

## Round up

Sometimes, students find questions relating to maps difficult. Play the section relating to the map once again and invite questions/discussion about any issues they might have.

## Writing TASK 1 page 80

**1** First, ask the students to match the vocabulary to the relevant parts of the process, annotating the diagram. Let them decide which linking words they will use and where, and elicit what tense they will use. They should then describe the process to each other in their groups. Monitor and check for accuracy and use of vocabulary. Go through the *How to go about it* box.

**2** Students can work individually and complete the text with linking words. They can then compare their answers with a partner and possibly another pair. You might want to see if they can recall the vocabulary without looking back at the section. Remind them to discuss the use of as many alternatives as possible. Check their answers and suggest any possibilities they may have forgotten. Elicit or point out the tense, and the active and passive forms.

> **ANSWERS**
> 1 Once, When, As soon as, After
> 2 Then, Next, After that
> 3 where
> 4 then, next, after that
> 5 then
> 6 where

**3** Elicit alternatives for the word *step*. Go over any other vocabulary they may not know. Remind them of general nouns like *steps*.

> **ANSWERS**
> phase, stage

**4** Students write the introduction and the overview for the text in exercise 2. Pay particular attention to the overview as students often leave this out when describing processes. Monitor and write good examples on the board.

> **POSSIBLE ANSWERS**
> Introduction: The pictures show how glass is recycled/ the recycling process for glass.
> Overview: It is clear that during recycling glass goes through a number of stages.

## Describing sequences

**1** Students identify the linking word or phrase which is not used to describe sequences. *Where* is used to describe what happens at a point in a sequence. The word *when* can also be used in this way.

**ANSWERS**

at first

**2** Once students have located the linking words and phrases, tell them to put the sentences in order. You could put the sentences on strips and give these to groups of students so they can see the text as a whole in front of them.

**ANSWERS**

**1** If  **2** and, then  **3** Once  **4** then  **5** First
**6** After that  **7** At the same time

The life cycle of a mobile phone.
Correct order: 5, 7, 4, 6, 3, 1, 2.

**3** Elicit the answer from the whole class. Ask students to identify the transitive verbs and count them for the comparison.

**ANSWERS**

The manufacturing process

**4** Students can do this exercise in pairs, checking their answers with another pair before whole-class feedback.

**ANSWERS**

**1** d  **2** a  **3** c  **4** f  **5** e  **6** b

**5–6** Emphasise the importance of the nouns here, e.g., for summarising the whole process economically, as per the requirements of the rubric in Writing Task 1. Point out how you can make noun phrases to introduce more detail: e.g., using noun phrases like *At the packaging stage,* etc., which is then followed by the specific detail. Stress how this also helps with cohesion and coherence as they write the process step by step.

**ANSWERS**

**5**
packaging – 2a, 4f, 5e
storage – 3c
delivery - 4f
pasteurisation – 6b
harvesting – 1d, 5e
assembly – 4f

**6**
packaging: package/pack
storage: store
delivery: deliver

pasteurisation: pasteurise
harvesting: harvest
assembly: assemble

**7** Students can do the exercise in class or for homework. Tell them what you will be looking for in particular, e.g., linking words, especially those indicating sequences and logical processes. If this is being done in class, give them two minutes to look at the rubric and the diagram and to make notes, including the vocabulary they will use; to familiarise themselves with the task, the tense and the verbs, whether transitive or intransitive, active or passive. Next, give them two minutes to write an introduction and an overview, and 14 minutes to write the process. They should spend another two minutes checking and correcting any 'silly' errors.

Ask the students to use the checklist on page 139 to check their answers. Also ask them to look at the marked sample answer.

---

*Model answer*

The illustration shows the process involved in the production of pencils.

Overall, it is clear that the process is efficient and eco-friendly, because all parts of the tree are used. At the first stage, seeds grow in nurseries before being transplanted after four months. Three years later, the trees in the plantation are thinned allowing them to grow and improving the quality of the wood. When the trees are fourteen years old, they are cut down to make logs. These are then cut into thin pieces, called slats, before being treated to help them dry.

After sixty days, the wood can be used for the production of pencils. At this stage, a groove is cut into the slat and a special glue is injected, with a black lead being put into the slat and then another empty slat on top to form a sandwich. This is heated and hard-pressed so that the two slats become one piece, which is then cut to produce individual pencils. These are finally decorated, sharpened and stamped before reaching the consumers.

*Word count: 179*

**COMMENT**

The response reflects the diagram in the task detailing the steps as they occur. There is a clear overview and a wide range of vocabulary and a range of structures, including active and passive verbs in the present simple to reflect the nature of the task.

---

**REVIEW 6 ANSWERS** pages 82–83

## Vocabulary 1: Lifecycles and processes

**1**

| | A | B |
|---|---|---|
| 1 | blossoms | appear |
| 2 | trees | produce |
| 3 | butterflies | emerge |
| 4 | harvest | fruit |
| 5 | plant | trees |
| 6 | weave | thread |
| 7 | prune | branches |
| 8 | leaves | sprout |

**2**
Possible answers
1 Blossoms appear on plants and trees in spring.
2 Trees produce oxygen as a result of removing carbon dioxide from the atmosphere.
3 When butterflies emerge from a chrysalis, they are at first unable to fly.
4 Farmers harvest fruit every year.
5 It is important to plant trees in order to preserve the environment.
6 Manufacturers weave thread to make cloth.
7 It is often best to prune branches towards the end of summer when the trees have a chance to recover quickly.
8 Leaves sprout on trees following long periods of cold weather.

## Vocabulary 2: Conservation

1 panoramic, stretching
2 spectacular, landscape
3 sights, spaces
4 views, scenery
5 environment, extinction
6 safeguard, disappear
7 spoilt, protection

## Following directions

1 We start off here <u>on</u> Theed Street.
2 The tour takes us past Wren House on the <u>left</u>.
3 Correct
4 We go past Brompton Palace which is on the north side of the street on our <u>right</u>.
5 Correct
6 We then turn <u>right</u> into Weston Avenue to look at the Old City Hall, which is on the north side of the street.
7 We continue to the end of Weston Avenue where we go <u>north</u>.
8 Correct

## Language focus: Transitive and intransitive verbs

1 sun: goes down/sets, evening
2 wheat: cultivate/harvest, bread
3 cotton: produce/utilise, cloth
4 flowers: bloom, garden/spring
5 butterflies: emerge, cocoon

**ACCURACY IN IELTS**
1 When the seed **germinates**, the plant begins to grow.
2 As soon as the wood is burnt, carbon dioxide is released into the **atmosphere**, which can then cause serious problems.
3 The diagram **shows** how the water is purified.
4 Trees are the **lungs** of the planet as they purify the air we breathe.
5 If the plant produces fruit, it releases the **seeds** which are either carried away by the wind or birds.
6 More conservation projects need to be organised if we are to save the **countryside**.
7 **Pomegranates** are now found in many countries in the world.
8 What are the most common fruits in your **part** of the country?
9 It is clear that there are seven **steps** in the process.

# Ready for Reading

## Introduction   page 84

This is the second of the four *Ready for* units. You can use these units in the order they occur. Alternatively, you can use parts of the units for revision purposes or for further practice at any time in the course. You can also use the units as an introduction to the IELTS examination.

Elicit information about:
- the length of the Reading test
- the number of questions
- the nature of the Reading Passages, i.e. factual vs. argumentative
- the fact the test becomes more difficult as it progresses
- the fact that Reading Passages 2 or 3 will have 14 questions, which can affect the time needed to answer the questions in these sections
- the range of question types; the strategies required, including honing concentration skills
- the speed and time management required to answer the questions.

Encourage students to ask you questions.

It is important that students always keep in mind the number of answers they should be aiming for, about 30 answers to obtain a good score. Point out that as in the Listening test, the number of correct answers required to achieve a particular band score varies from exam to exam, but that the standard in each exam is the same.

You can also ask students the questions in the optional lead-in below to find out what they know about the Reading test.

### Optional lead-in

Before the students open their books, ask the following questions:
1   How many sections are there in the Reading test?
2   What kinds of sources are used for the texts?
3   What kinds of skills do you need to employ to answer the questions?
4   Do you need knowledge of specialist vocabulary to do the Reading test?
5   Where should you write your answers as you do the test?
6   What should you do if there are any unknown words that you need to know to answer the question?

ANSWERS
1   three
2   books, magazines, journals, newspapers (any two)
3   skimming, scanning, reading for gist, predicting, reading for detail, (any three)
4   no
5   (the) answer sheet
6   guess (from context)

Go through the introduction in the Student's Book. Remind students that there is no time to study the Reading Passages closely, and refer to the list of IELTS strategies for reading on page 203, and the IELTS Reading checklist on page 91 of the Student's Book.

Referring to skimming and scanning in the IELTS strategies, elicit from the students the difference between skimming and scanning. Remind students of the need to skim the Reading Passages and questions throughout the course and to balance this with reading closely.

### Further practice

You can also ask students to create their own infogram/poster/class webpage for the Reading test on the computer. Alternatively, the infogram can be paper based for classroom display. Check any display items for accuracy and visual impact.

## Understanding True/False/Not Given statements   page 84

**1–3**   Ask students to do the exercises in pairs, followed by checking their answers with other students and whole-class feedback between exercises.

ANSWERS
2
1   more for weapons than (i)
2   only (b)
3   is said to (h)
4   ten (f)
5   destroyed (g)/at the end of each dynasty (k)
6   simpler (d, i)
7   all (c)
8   are connected (j)
9   had an impact on (a)

3
1   NOT GIVEN. There is no comparison of weapons and ritual objects.
2   FALSE. ... speak of a series of ancient rulers who invented agriculture, writing, and the arts of government.
3   TRUE. ... founding the Xia dynasty.
4   FALSE. ... Yu also cast nine sacred bronze vessels.

5 FALSE. ... these were passed on to subsequent dynasties.

6 FALSE. ... the archaeological record reveals a more complicated picture of Bronze Age China.

7 FALSE. Archaeological investigation has confirmed much of the legendary history of the dynasty following the Xia – the Shang.

8 TRUE. Chinese scholars generally identify Xia with the Erlitou culture, ...

9 TRUE. ... that greatly influenced material culture in the Shang and subsequent Zhou dynasties.

Students can collect examples of sentences that illustrate items a–k in exercise 2 and add other types they may encounter. They can create a whole-class checklist and share the list electronically. This can be done for any question type in the Reading test.

## Understanding *Yes/No/Not Given* statements page 86

Ask students to read and discuss the explanation in pairs. Elicit an explanation from several students, encouraging them to use their own words.

**1–2** Ask students to do both exercises in pairs, forming groups to do a further check before whole-class feedback.

ANSWERS

1
1 Generalisation/Probability
2 Comparison
3 Qualifying word
4 Recommendation
5 Comparison
6 Probability
7 Qualifying adjective

2
1 Yes
2 Not Given
3 No
4 Not Given
5 Not Given
6 Yes
7 Yes

Invite questions and/or explanations about *Yes/No/Not Given* statements.

Students can collect examples of sentences that are used for a) writer's opinions and b) claims. They can create a whole-class checklist of sentence types and share the list electronically. This can be done for any question type in the Reading test.

## Paragraph/Section headings page 87

Elicit information from students about the range of structures used in paragraph/section headings.

**1–3** Ask students to do the exercises in pairs, followed by checking their answers with other

students and whole-class feedback between exercises.

ANSWERS

1
The following are most likely: *cause, effect, problem (solution)*

2
cause: factors
effect: leading to
problem: coastal erosion

3
1 factors:
... *with enhanced rates of sea level rise and increasing storminess, both of which are associated with global warming.*
*Sea levels are expected to rise significantly over the next century, largely as a result of the melting of ice sheets and thermal expansion of the oceans. Global warming will also change ...*
*The increase in the frequency and size of the latter, which have an enormous influence on ...*
2 coastal erosion:
... *rates of coastal change will escalate ...*
... *coastal change and near-shore sediment transport ...*
... *the form of UK coasts.*

**4** Students can do this exercise on their own. Allow them to check their answers with a partner before whole-class feedback.

ANSWERS
2; monitoring, techniques

**5–6** Ask students to do the exercises in pairs, followed by checking their answers with other students and whole-class feedback.

ANSWERS
5
i complexity
ii contrast
iii methods
iv need
v factors

6
i of making decisions about coastal defences
ii between engineered and natural defence techniques
iii employed to check coastal change
iv for an integrated approach to coastal management
v leading to coastal erosion

Students can collect examples of headings they may encounter. They can create a whole-class checklist and share the list electronically. This can be done for any question type in the Reading test.

## Summary completion  page 89

**1–2** Elicit information about summaries from students. Emphasise the importance/usefulness of questioning the exam questions as per the yes/no questions for each blank space. Such questions are part of a basic analytical process. The questions are hints to encourage students to think.

Students can create such questions for every question type in all aspects of the exam. You can do this as further practice for any part of the IELTS test.

**ANSWERS**

10 widespread consultation
11 Coastal managers
12 traditional constructions
13 isolation

## Sentence completion  page 90

**1–3** Students do the exercises in groups checking their answers with other students. Give students other exam questions such as *True/False/Not Given* statements to examine by questioning.

**ANSWERS**

the whole picture
Geoscientists

Photocopiable activity: Group game (groups of 3) – Collocations dominoes page 134

Workbook pages 52–59

## Content overview

This unit focuses on work, training and educational assessment.

**Listening** SECTION 3

A presentation

Question types: Multiple-choice; Sentence completion; Short-answer questions

**Reading**

Co-working

Question types: Matching information; Matching names; Multiple-choice

**Writing** TASK 2

Comparing advantages and disadvantages

**Speaking** PARTS 2 AND 3

Part 2 Describing a job/an achievement

Part 3 Discussing goals and career

**Vocabulary 1:** Work
**Vocabulary 2:** Collocations
**Language focus:** Conditionals 1

## Digital overview

**Presentation Kit**

Interactive versions of Student's Book exam tasks

Embedded audio and answer key for all activities

**Teacher's Resource Centre**

Communicative activity: Group game (groups of 3) – Collocations dominoes

Workbook audio, answer key and wordlists

**Student's Resource Centre**

Class audio

Wordlist

Speaking Part 3 videos (4) and video worksheet

Speaking Part 2 video and video worksheet

## Vocabulary 1: Work  page 92

### Lead-in

Write the title on the board and encourage students to predict what the unit is about. Elicit nouns and verbs related to the title. You could have a general discussion as to whether the students think the work and education environments are changing. Elicit how and why.

**1**  Ask students to describe the photographs to their partner, giving reasons for their answers. In the whole-class discussion, expand the discussion eliciting more evaluative comments, e.g., *They seem very supportive, because* … .

**2** Check answers as a whole class. These are commonly confused words and students may need time to assimilate the nuances of meaning in context here. If they're still having problems, refer them to a good learner's dictionary such as the Macmillan (online) Dictionary.

ANSWERS
a paid work people do on a regular basis
b what people do or the place they do something to achieve some kind of result
c the job or profession people have
d the job people follow, usually after gaining some kind of qualification
e a profession or occupation over a period of time
f what work people do to earn money
g what people gain at the end of a course, e.g., a degree

**3** Students do the exercise, followed by whole-class feedback. Elicit reasons for students' answers during whole-class feedback, also eliciting why certain words are not possible.

ANSWERS
1 livelihood
2 work
3 job/career/profession
4 job
5 work
6 profession
7 job, career
8 job/career

**4** Ask students to discuss in pairs and compare their answers with another pair, and then justify their choices. During whole-class feedback, elicit reasons and examples for each answer, and invite counterarguments.

## Speaking PART 3 page 93

### Lead-in

Ask students to summarise briefly what is expected in Speaking Part 3. You might want to show students the Band descriptors relating to Speaking for bands 6 and 7 on the Student's Resource Centre.

Ask students to read through the four criteria, and explain what they mean, or concentrate on two of the criteria.

1 Put students in pairs and ask them to read the rubric, and check that they understand what they are going to do. In whole-class feedback, elicit as full answers as possible and discuss the answers.

2 Before students change partners to ask and answer the questions, check they understand the focus of the questions by drawing their attention to the following general nouns in the questions: *aims and goals, benefits* and *sign*. Ask students to explain the questions in their own words, as far as possible – a paraphrasing exercise in preparation for answering without repeating the question, which will improve their score. Remind them of the *Don't Forget!* Box. Monitor the discussions. When students have given each other feedback, give your own feedback and discuss the questions as a whole class, looking at good ways to begin the answers and develop them using reasons, examples, causes and effects, etc.

## Reading Passage page 94

### Lead-in

Elicit from students techniques for skimming quickly e.g., looking at the nouns and verbs. Take this a step further by pointing out they can train themselves to skim faster by looking at only one word class. You can demonstrate this by showing them how they can activate schemata by looking at the nouns only. First, give them a list of function words like *at, by, from, to, with, for,* that will not give them the gist of a text, and then a list of words like *work, daily commuting, train, city, office, years.* Ask them what 'picture' the words conjure up for them and elicit whether it matters in which order the nouns are given. You might want to select a part of the Reading Passage to illustrate this.

1 Students do the exercise in small groups. Then, ask them to skim the heading, the Reading Passage and questions – they should be responsible for their own time management here and throughout the Reading test. Draw their attention to the *Don't forget!* box. Discourage them from reading the text in detail at this stage. However, encourage them to read the Reading Passage slowly at the end of the test to see how much they have been able to extract by skimming, scanning and using the questions.

### Questions 8–12

Advise students to put a box around the names of specific people in the text so they can limit their search to the part of the text relating to each name. Stress that the names are in the order they first appear in the text, but that the statements are jumbled. Tell them to look at the statements and underline key words, and then scan the text to find synonyms/paraphrases.

### Question 13

Encourage students to underline key words. They should be able to answer the question using the information they have collected about the Reading Passage.

Suggest they write their answers on a piece of paper or on an answer sheet as they do the test. Point out that they should pay particular attention to spelling, especially singular and plural. Remind students after 15 minutes that they have five minutes left. Allow extra time if the students have not finished.

Tell the students to go over the answers in pairs, and mark any changes they make during their discussion in another colour. Check as a whole class. Let them mark any problem areas on their reading grid.

**ANSWERS**

| | | | |
|---|---|---|---|
| 1 | communal setting | 2 | traditional office |
| 3 | work persona | 4 | work identity |
| 5 | norm | 6 | source |
| 7 | movement | 8 | D |
| 9 | C | 10 | B |
| 11 | A | 12 | A |
| 13 | C | | |

2 Students can discuss the questions in pairs or groups of four, followed by whole-class feedback. Tell them to add any new vocabulary to their (electronic) vocabulary lists.

### Round up

Discuss briefly issues and questions relating to the completion of the Reading test, e.g., strategies to use and/to refine, etc.

## Vocabulary 2: Collocations page 96

1 Direct students to the instructions in the Student's Book. Encourage them to put the nouns and their collocates into their (electronic) vocabulary lists. Note that the collocates may come immediately before or after the noun, or later in the sentence. Suggest students use the online Macmillan Dictionary, or a dictionary like the Macmillan Collocations Dictionary, to check collocations.

ANSWERS

1 considerable, enjoy, derive, accrue
2 huge, gain, outweigh, take
3 once-in-a-lifetime, career, seize, waste
4 enormous, achieve, guarantee, depends on
5 excellent, offer, boost, career
6 distinct, obvious, suffer, have
7 total, result in, ensue
8 outstanding, impressive, represent, a lack of
9 huge, show, make, room
10 good, deserve, throw away, arise

**2** Students should do this in pairs so they can discuss the options. Suggest they identify the main noun first and then look through the alternatives from exercise 1 to decide on the other choices. Go over the exercise with the class when they have finished, discussing any issues.

ANSWERS

1 success, guaranteed
2 failure, prospects
3 deserves, chance
4 improvement, room
5 disadvantages, benefit
6 benefits, accrue
7 represented, achievement
8 once-in-a-lifetime opportunity, seized

**3**  This can be done as pair or groupwork. Encourage students to look at the positive aspects of failure during their discussion, e.g., *motivation*, *perseverance*, etc., and to think of personal and abstract examples. If necessary, give students a personal, or fictional, example.

**Extension**

If you have access to the Macmillan Collocations Dictionary, choose the entry relating to one of the nouns on the list, like *benefit*, and show students the range of words it can collocate with. Students will know most of the words, but they will not have actively used them. Do this merely as a noticing exercise and remind students during the rest of the course to check collocations, especially as they write.

## Listening SECTION 3 page 97

**Lead-in**

As a brief lead-in, ask students to look at the photograph in pairs and describe what is happening.

**1** Follow the instructions in the Student's Book, and follow up with a brief discussion with the whole class.

**Questions 21–30**

Go over the *Don't forget!* box and ask students to read the questions. At this stage of the course, you can either ask them to describe the content of the dialogue using the questions as a summary before they do the test, or you can go straight to the test.

Play the recording once and let students check their answers with a partner, followed by whole-class feedback. Ask for justification for their answers and then play the recording again.

Remind them that they should pay particular attention to spelling, especially singular and plural nouns.

ANSWERS

Questions **21–25**
IN ANY ORDER: B D E F H
**26** information          **27** foolish
**28** nerves               **29** enjoyable
**30** questionnaires

**2** Students can discuss the questions in groups or as a whole class. Stress the need to justify their arguments. Repeat this when eliciting feedback from the class.

---

**Listening script 12**

(T = tutor; J = Jack; F = Francesca)

**T:** OK, if you want, we've got some time left for some feedback on your joint presentation today.

**J:** Yeah, we can do it now while it's fresh in our minds, if it's OK with Francesca.

**F:** It's OK with me.

**T:** So, Francesca, how do you think it went?

**F:** Well, mmm … I was really happy with it actually, but I'm glad it's over. I think the main advantage of doing the presentation was that we both learnt quite a lot about training and skills development for the workplace and how they improve people's opportunities in life, especially their job prospects.

**J:** And we learnt a lot from actually delivering the presentation as well, which is really useful for the future.

**F:** Yeah, that was important too. Mmm … as I said, I was pleased with it, but if I had to do it all over again, I'd change a few things.

**T:** Like what, for instance?

**F:** Well, mmm the <u>first thing I'd do is work on the pace of the talk and make the delivery slower</u>. And I'd keep a clock in front of me so that I was aware of the speed and … <u>and the next thing is mmm … the length of the talk … I'd make the presentation time 15 minutes for each of us</u>, because I think ten minutes each was much too short. If we'd given ourselves more time, it would have flowed better.

**J:** Yes, I agree. I thought the timing was a bit tight. I'd say maybe even 30 minutes each.

**T:** Mmm … 30 minutes might've been a bit long for both you and the audience.

**J:** Maybe you're right; 15 minutes each would probably have been better.

**F:** And the next thing is the order of the data. I thought the sequence was bad – it could've been a lot better.

**T:** Yes. If I had to give some particular advice, I'd say you needed to give yourselves a run through once or twice using the equipment, just to see what it's like. Doing it without preparation like that's not that easy.

**F:** No definitely not. And another thing for me is that we forgot to give out the handouts with the copies of our slides on them for people to take notes. I should've given them out before we started. And one final thing I'd do is … I'd check that everyone could see the screen properly, … mmm … I'd make sure the arrangement of the chairs in the room made it easy for everyone to see.

**T:** And Jack? What about you? How did you feel about it all?

**J:** Well, er … I agree with Francesca. Yeah … in everything she said. It's very difficult to make the delivery smooth. If … when I do it again, I'll definitely spend more time practising to make it run more smoothly.

..........................................................

**T:** But would you add anything to what Francesca said?

**J:** Mmm … perhaps I'd try to pack less information into the time given. Er … I thought at first it would be the opposite. Er … I was afraid that we'd end up looking foolish. And also I think I'd spend less time on the information gathering phase because, unless time is devoted to practising, it'll not be possible to give a good performance.

**T:** Yeah, I think I'd agree. Anything else?

**J:** Yeah. I get very nervous when I speak in front of people. If I did it again, I'd make sure I practised speaking out loud and projecting my voice. I think the key for me is learning to steady my nerves.

**F:** But you were very calm!

**J:** Not inside I wasn't!

**T:** Well, it didn't show.

**F:** I think you need the nerves to keep you going, but maybe try to take your mind off it beforehand by exercising or something.

**T:** Is that everything?

**J:** Yeah.

**T:** OK. Well, you'll be pleased to know the feedback from the class questionnaires was that the presentation was enjoyable, so well done. I have to say that I agree with them.

**J:** Oh, thanks.

**T:** I'll make a copy for both of you of the questionnaires, if you want. And if and when you do give a talk again, you can keep them to refer to.

## Round up

Discuss the nature of the questions themselves and review any question or strategy issues. You might want to focus on one question type and/or one they have difficulty with, e.g., selection from a list as in Questions 21–25.

## Language focus: Conditionals 1

page 98

**1** Go through this with the whole class and ask students to identify the tenses in the sentences. Make sure that they understand the relationship between the two parts of the sentences and that they can name the different types of conditionals. Review the conditionals, and refer the students to the Grammar reference on page 223.

> **ANSWERS**
> 3, 2, 1, 1

**2** Students do the exercise individually, check their answers in pairs and then as a whole class. Make sure students understand the grammar before moving on, to ensure they don't become confused as they move to the freer activities that follow.

> **ANSWERS**
> 1 will turn out        2 would succeed
> 3 will find            4 had worked
> 5 had been devoted     6 are given
> 7 had

**3** 🔊 Monitor students to ensure they are giving explanations. Tell them to use words like *because, for example, so, but,* and *like* in their explanations.

**4** Students do this exercise as a written activity on their own, checking their answers for accuracy, before pairwork checking and then whole-class feedback. For the pairwork checking, tell them to prepare justification for their answers for the whole-class feedback. Such justifications makes them look more closely at what they are doing and prepares them for close reading and noticing generally.

> **ANSWERS**
> 1 **Unless** the educational process …
> 2 Had there **not** been …
> 3 … I **would** have been born …
> 4 If people did**n't** have …
> 5 **If** some adults had …
> 6 Had universities **been** permitted …

**5** Follow the instructions in the Student's Book.

**6** 🔊 Ask students to choose two of the questions to ask their partner. Each should ask and answer the questions, swapping roles as they go on. Monitor and check the use of the structures and their relevance to the questions. Ask students to discuss their answers to the questions with the whole class. As an alternative, you can ask the students to work in groups. Encourage them to use conditional sentences as part of their explanations.

### Extension

Ask students to review their latest essays in pairs/groups and notice how frequently (and infrequently) they used conditionals, and suggest why.

### Round up

Review the conditional and elicit its different functions, e.g., speculation, persuasion in arguments and explanation and where they think they might underuse it, e.g., in writing for explaining (*if, for example, …*) and in speaking. For the rest of the course, elicit the purpose and function of conditionals for vocabulary and grammar input, so that students can see why they are learning it.

## Speaking PART 2 page 99

**1** Go through the exercise with the students. Remind them that in the exam they have one minute to write notes, but relax this here as they write the notes individually or in pairs. Before students proceed to the next exercise, go through the range of phrases, stressing why it is important to incorporate chunks like this into their speaking. Point out specifically the introductory *chunk/phrase* in each list and discuss the differences between them.

**2** 👥 Put students into pairs and ask them to practise timing each other (one to two minutes) taking about the topic.

Students should give feedback using the checklist on page 181. As before, the students can choose one or more criteria they would like to be assessed on. Emphasise the need to use conditionals where possible. Monitor the students for this specifically, and make notes of good phrases you hear and phrases to correct at the end.

### Round up

Go over the frames and ask students to choose which ones they would like to select for recycling. Discuss the importance of using chunks/phrases and point out that academic discourse/texts, spoken and written, use a wide range of generic language like this.

## Writing TASK 2 page 100

**1** 👥 Ask students to do the exercise in groups, and to select a member to discuss any interesting answers with the class. Remind them to justify their answers. Then, elicit the answers from the whole class and discuss the differences between this and previous Writing Task 2s. Elicit specifically what is required of them as regards the question (*Do you think …?*) in the rubric.

**ANSWERS**

1 education
2 streaming, i.e. teaching children in classes according to ability, with teaching children in mixed-ability classes
3 Yes: 'Do you think … ?'

**2** Ask students to read the text and complete it on their own, followed by pairwork checking and whole-class feedback.

**ANSWERS**

1 c: an example (condition, result)
2 a: a reason
3 b: a perspective, a claim/opinion, a contrast, conclusion

**3** Go through the exercise with students and check that they are fully aware of what is required of them in the exercise. Ask them to do the exercise in pairs, and to justify their answers to their partner before checking with another pair. Go through the exercise as a whole class. If possible, project the text of the model answer onto a smartboard or a white board. If you are able to, colour the relevant parts of the text that relate to items 1–5 so that students can clearly notice the position of the various elements in the development of the text. Take your time to elicit student comments and explanations, but, obviously, this will depend on your students.

**ANSWERS**

1 Having said that however, I feel that streaming children at secondary level is harmful.
2 The main drawback is that if children are not taught in mixed-ability classes, it does not prepare them for the real world they will encounter in the future.
3 … I feel that streaming children at secondary level is harmful.
4 harmful
5 … it does not prepare them for the real world they will encounter in the future.
This could then hold them back …
… and reduce their career opportunities considerably.

**4** Students can do this exercise in groups followed by similar feedback to exercise 3.

**POSSIBLE ANSWERS**

The first sentence contains a topic sentence stating that streaming is a disadvantage with two possible reasons. A consequence (result) of not having mixed-ability classes is stated. This is then followed by other consequences/results in the last sentence.

**5** Students complete this exercise in groups. Emphasise that it is essential for cohesion and coherence to be maintained throughout the essay: from the question through the introduction to the topic sentences and then the conclusion. Stress that if they master this, they can achieve a high score in this area. Refer them to the band descriptors for this on the Student's Resource Centre. Discuss whether for them it is easier to achieve a higher score in organisation of their answer than in accuracy.

> **POSSIBLE ANSWERS**
>
> There is a thread all the way through the answer. The introduction mentions the two specific areas about education in the first sentence. In the second sentence, a statement of opinion is given as required in the question of the Task.
> The topic sentence in the first body paragraph acknowledges the benefits of streaming as per the introduction.
> The two topic sentences of the next two paragraphs state the writer's opinion i.e. that streaming has a negative impact and is a disadvantage.
> The conclusion reflects the order of the presentation of the information in the introduction (advantage followed by disadvantage). The topic sentences (and hence, the
> three body paragraphs) follow the same structure as the introduction and the conclusion. The whole answer is tightly bound together.

**6** Students can do this in pairs or groups preparing as full a justification as possible for their choice. As part of whole-class feedback, ask one or more students to use the answer they have chosen to explain the structure of the model answer. How much detail you elicit will depend on your students.

> **ANSWERS**
> A

**7** Ask students to do the exercise for homework, or in class, time permitting. Apart from focusing on gathering ideas and checking for errors, ask them to focus on organisation. Tell them to use the checklist on page 139 to check their answers. You might want to ask them to review the answers they write at home or in class and write an outline summarising their answer as in exercise 6. You can ask them to submit their summary with their answers. This will obviously depend on the size of the class.

Ask students to number and/or date their writing test answers so they can review and track their development.

At this stage you can start collecting good sample answers to show students as examples of good practice. With the students' permission, you can keep and laminate the samples for use in class analysis where students gauge the score band, the structure, the vocabulary range, etc. Do not allow students to keep the samples or to copy them. Over time, you can build up a large resource bank of Task 1 and Task 2 samples. Point out to students that the tasks in the exam vary so much that they cannot learn answers by heart to regurgitate them in the exam.

---

*Model answer*

Experience and knowledge are both crucial in the modern work environment. However, I personally feel that the focus on the former is much more beneficial in the modern knowledge-based economy.

The importance of knowledge for workers cannot be underestimated. For example, employees need qualifications and knowledge of skills such as numeracy and literacy, as well as knowledge of how systems, such as computer systems, work. In order for professionals such as engineers, teachers or doctors to be successful, for example, in their careers, they need knowledge as well as experience. While certain types of knowledge can be acquired during work experience, it is essential for a body of knowledge such as medical and engineering information to be acquired beforehand.

In today's world, however, where knowledge is effectively controlled by machines, it is essential for workers to focus on developing the skills to manipulate this knowledge, as it is so voluminous that it is now impossible to acquire. Knowledge, in effect, plays a secondary role to skills and experience.

There are, therefore, clear advantages to attaching greater value to experience compared to knowledge in the workplace. The modern world demands that companies and institutions have employees with very sophisticated skills not just in technology, but in dealing with modern systems. As a result, frequently workers' technical expertise often takes precedence over basic knowledge and without workers with the necessary experience, it is impossible for companies and organisations to flourish.

As we have seen, despite knowledge being very important in the modern workplace, it is clear that the advantages of a greater emphasis on experience outweighs any disadvantages.

*Word count: 268 words*

**COMMENTS**

The answer shows and develops the writer's position regarding the fact that the advantages of the focus on experience outweigh the disadvantages. The importance of knowledge is looked at first and this is contrasted with the greater importance of having experience.

## REVIEW 7 ANSWERS pages 102–103

## Vocabulary 1: Work

The <u>occupations</u> that my friends want to go into are varied. Some want to find a permanent <u>job</u> in banking or business, while others want to go into the medical or legal <u>professions</u>. It is possible to find <u>work</u> in the former without specific <u>qualifications</u> and considerable <u>experience</u>, but for medicine and law the first of these is essential in order to find something where it is possible to have a good <u>livelihood</u> and a successful <u>career</u>.

## Vocabulary 2: Collocations

1 Do you think it's possible to achieve success without qualifications?
2 Some people think that technology has made huge improvements in the workplace. To what extent do you agree or disagree?
3 Do you think the advantages of working part-time outweigh the disadvantages?
4 What do you think is your most impressive achievement so far?
5 I think giving up rather than the lack of ability can lead to failure.

## Language focus: Conditionals 1

**1**
1 If, wouldn't have been
2 otherwise, will become
3 If, will limit
4 Unless, will be
5 If, would help
6 If, hadn't worked
7 If, focused
8 If, wouldn't have done

**2**
1 Had I not passed my exams at university, I would not be able to follow the profession I wanted.
2 Unless people in today's world have both qualifications and experience, finding a job will become slightly harder.
3 Unless I learn to drive, it will limit my job opportunities.
4 If more money is not invested in the education system, the workforce will be less well-trained.
5 Were people to do some kind of volunteering, it would help them when they started looking for a job.
6 Had I not worked as hard as I did in the past, I wouldn't be as successful as I am now.
7 Were people to focus on achieving a good work-life balance, their working lives would be less stressful.
8 I had the chance to change my career otherwise I wouldn't have done it.

**1**

| | |
|---|---|
| improvement | dissatisfied |
| excellence | opportunity |
| livelihood | aspirations |
| guaranteeing | |

**2**
An efficient workplace is one where the work **environment** encourages people to be **successful**, to develop their **professional** skills and **achieve** their aspirations. If people are denied the **chance** to develop in this way, then their own and the company's success is limited. Furthermore, if everyone has the same **opportunities** at school and at work, there is a good chance their **career** prospects will be improved dramatically and the economy will benefit from a happier and, subsequently, a more productive workforce.

# 8 Mapping the world

Photocopiable activity: Pairwork – Describing maps page 135
Workbook pages 60–67

## Content overview

This unit focuses on maps, places and migration.

**Listening** SECTION 4

Human migration

Question types: Note completion

**Reading**

Cartography

Question types: Matching sentence endings; Table completion; Multiple-choice

**Writing** TASK 1

Describing changes in maps

**Speaking** PARTS 2 AND 3

Part 2 Describing a neighbourhood

Part 3 Social interaction with neighbours

**Vocabulary:** Nouns relating to places

**Language focus:** Referring in a text

## Digital overview

**Presentation Kit**

Interactive versions of Student's Book exam tasks

Embedded audio and answer key for all activities

**Teacher's Resource Centre**

Communicative activity: Pairwork – Describing maps

Workbook audio, answer key and wordlists

**Student's Resource Centre**

Class audio

Wordlist

Speaking Part 1 videos (3) and video worksheet

Speaking Part 2 video and video worksheet

## Vocabulary: Nouns relating to places

**page 104**

### Lead-in

Elicit predictions about the content of the unit by asking students to look first at the title and then the images in exercise 1. You can then ask them to survey the whole unit, checking if their predictions are correct.

**1** Ask students to do the exercise in pairs, encouraging them to develop their answers to the questions, not just by giving reasons and examples but also using cause/effect chains, etc. If necessary, refer them to IELTS essentials on page 205. Then, as a whole class, discuss the similarities and differences between the maps and discuss some or all of the questions.

**2** Students do the exercise in pairs, followed by whole-class feedback.

> ANSWERS
>
> **1** Urban
> **3** Possible answer: the gardens

**3** Students do this exercise with a partner, checking their answers with another pair before whole-class feedback.

> ANSWERS
>
> **1** place, spot    **2** district, area
> **3** location, region    **4** area, spaces
> **5** vicinity, neighbourhood    **6** places, regions, spots
> **7** setting, region

**4** Ask students to do this in pairs. If you haven't already started doing so, you might want to begin giving students a time limit for exercises from now on. This will help focus their attention and increase their awareness of time management, which is essential for the exam. Start by eliciting how much time they might need or by setting a limit, depending on your students.

> ANSWERS
>
> **1** e, f
> **2** a, b, c, d, g, h, i and possibly j
> **3** b, c, d, g, i and possibly j
> **4** a, b, c, g, h, i, j
> **5** h, j
> **6** e, f
> **7** b, c d, g, i
> **8** a, b, h, j
> **9** a, b, d, g, h, i
> **10** a, b, d, g, i

**5** Ask students to look first at the sentence and establish which words the italicised ones are referring to first (e.g., where there are adjective and noun combinations) and if there's a complete clause. You may want to do a quick review of basic word order.

ANSWERS
1 overlooking a small garden, neighbourhood with old buildings, located near a large park full of flowers and plants
2 stretching for miles along the seashore, with plenty of opportunity for lots of boating and swimming, built two hundred years ago
3 surrounded by beautiful mountains, with its purple flowers
4 surrounded by a forest full of wildlife, covered with trees but with views looking out

**6** Students work in pairs and discuss the questions, followed by whole-class feedback.

### Round up

Review the vocabulary learnt, reminding students to add words to their (electronic) vocabulary lists. Have a brief discussion about time management in preparation for reading in the next section.

## Reading Passage   page 106

### Lead-in

By way of a brief lead-in, elicit what *cartography* is about, asking students to work out the meaning from *cart-* and *-graphy*.

**1** Students do the exercise with a partner, and check their answers in whole-class feedback. You might like to give students a time limit.

ANSWERS
1 sophisticated/complex    2 innate
3 constitutes              4 primary
5 depicting                6 associated
7 network                  8 progress

**2** Students share their ideas in groups, followed by whole-class feedback. Elicit whether the passage is factual or argumentative, and ask for reasons e.g., *look at Questions 6–11*.

### Questions 1–13

Continue the focus on time management. Before students answer the questions, ask them to look at the three sets of questions and decide which are likely to take them longer. For many students, Questions 1–5 require more time and Questions 6–11 less time as they are fairly contained, relating to specific people given in the first column of the table. Questions 12 and 13 are also factual questions. Go through Questions 1–5 with students, along with the *How to go about it* box, analysing the

beginnings of sentences and eliciting and noticing clues in the questions, e.g., the general and specific nature of the first two sentence beginnings and the specific topic sentence-like beginning of question 5.

Elicit what students expect from the sentence beginnings before they read through the endings. Don't expect perfect answers, but try to start them thinking about the process of completion. Then they can look at the stems.

For Questions 6–11, ask students to circle/box the names from the first column of the table in the text to help them focus their information search. Remind them to predict the word type for the gaps.

Give the students 20 minutes to do the test, and to write their answers on a separate grid.

Ask them to check their answers in pairs before whole-class feedback, and to justify their choices and not just matching answers.

ANSWERS
1 C
2 E
3 F
4 G
5 D
6 bark, cave
7 Dream Time
8 aids
9 clay tablets
10 title deeds
11 expeditions
12–13 IN ANY ORDER: B, E

**3** Students discuss the question in small groups.

### Extension

Ask students to work in pairs and select at least one collocation from each paragraph that is worth remembering. Students then form groups and compare their collocations, followed by whole-class feedback. As a whole class, decide whether the phrases are worth remembering (for writing, reading, listening) or not and why. This can all be adapted, depending on time and student level.

### Round up

Review time management and discuss any strategies and/or issues.

## Language focus: Referring in a text
### page 109

**1** Do this exercise as a whole-class activity. Discuss how the words in the second sentence are used to refer back to a previous noun or noun phrase.

ANSWERS
The study and practice of making maps.
The charts are memory aids …
These tablets are title deeds …

**2–4** Go through the explanations carefully so that the students grasp the difference in use between *it* and *this*. Basically, pronouns like *it* and *they* refer to the last nouns before they occur. The pronoun *it* has to have something specific to refer to, while *this* and *that* can focus on the last idea mentioned or a whole sequence of ideas up to a paragraph. Refer the students to the Grammar reference on page 223.

You might want to encourage students to start thinking about their own writing briefly here, by way of *transfer of knowledge and skills* to stop their skills being compartmentalised.

> **ANSWERS**
>
> **2**
> 1 the neighbourhood
> 2 the region
> 3 the cost of farming
>
> **3**
> The nouns would need to be in the latter part of the sentence or the whole sentence. They are too far away from *this* to refer to.
>
> **4**
> It is not really possible to work out what *it* refers to: *cost/farming/period*/the whole sentence/part of the sentence. If you keep the word *rise*, the phrase *This rise* refers to the latter part of the sentence from *increased* onwards. If you use *this* on its own, it can refer to the same part of the sentence or the whole sentence.

**5** Students complete this exercise individually and then compare answers in pairs, before whole-class feedback.

> **ANSWERS**
>
> | | | | |
> |---|---|---|---|
> | 1 | It | 2 | it |
> | 3 | This new development | 4 | it, it |
> | 5 | This | 6 | they, This |
> | 7 | those | 8 | these |

**6** Ask the students to do this exercise with a partner and then discuss their answers in groups. Encourage them to talk about/reflect on *referring* in their own writing and speaking, before whole-class feedback. Elicit reasons for student answers.

> **ANSWERS**
>
> 1 The price of property in this region is increasing, and **this/it** is set to continue.
> 2 The neighbourhood was poor once, but **it** is rich now.
> 3 I like visiting the seaside when nobody is around; **it** is very relaxing.
> 4 If people make an effort to clean up after themselves when **they** visit parks, then **these places** will be much more inviting for the public in general.
> 5 My friend suggested I should go away for a few days for a break. **This** was a good idea, but **it** might be expensive.

> 6 The government should pass laws to protect more areas of great natural beauty. **This** would benefit all of us.
> 7 Change in the local area cannot be stopped. **It** is inevitable, even if **it** is very slow and **it** stops altogether for a while. But **this** is unlikely to happen.

**7** Use this exercise to generate ideas which may be useful in a Writing Task 2 or Speaking Part 3 tasks. You could also do this as a whole-class discussion.

## Round up

Briefly discuss the importance of noticing and using *referring* in all exam skills.

## Listening SECTION 4 page 110

### Lead-in

Elicit whether Section 4 is a monologue or a dialogue. Review the strategies the students usually need to employ when listening to this type of test. Ask them to underline the words in the questions that will warn them that they are about to hear the answers. Make sure they look at the information after the gaps, as the information in the test may be the other way round. Also remind them to look at two questions at a time if they can, in case the answers come close together. Emphasise the need to concentrate throughout and also not to worry about any big gaps, which can sometimes occur between the answers.

**1** Elicit that lectures are usually organised like a written text with an introduction, several points with examples and support, and a conclusion. Discuss with the students the linking devices and sequencers used to signal the stages of the talk. These will help them identify when one topic (main idea) is ending and another beginning: *first of all, next, now,* etc., *Before we look at … I'd like to look at …*

The speaker will usually introduce the main topic at the beginning, '*Well, in today's lecture we are going to explore early human migration out of Africa to colonise the world.*', and often give an outline of what secondary topics are to be covered in the introduction. The headings in the questions relate to the focus of the different sections of the talk.

When students have done the listening test, ask them to look at the Listening script on page 233. Tell them to mark any devices they think will help guide them through future listening tasks.

**2** Elicit the subject, and find out what students already know about the subject generally. Ask them the reasons for early man migrating and the geological influences. Pre-teach *AD* (vs *BC*) if necessary and *steppes*. Elicit that there are three main sections to the talk and ask how they know this.

## ANSWERS

| | |
|---|---|
| **31** number | **32** noun |
| **33** number | **34** noun (phrase) |
| **35** noun (phrase) | **36** number (fraction/percentage) |
| **37** noun | **38** noun (place) |
| **39** noun (phrase) | **40** noun (phrase) |

### Extension

Time permitting, ask students to use the questions to describe the content of the talk, expanding the notes into sentences. Students complete the test and then go through their answers in pairs before whole-class feedback.

### Questions 31–40

#### ANSWERS

**31** 100,000 /one hundred thousand
**32** temperature
**33** 45,000
**34** land mass
**35** simple boats
**36** 30%/per cent
**37** yam
**38** Sudan
**39** work fields
**40** military advantage

**3**  Discuss in pairs followed by whole-class feedback.

---

### Listening script 13

Well, in today's lecture we are going to explore early human migration out of Africa to colonise the world. Throughout history, there've been waves of humans migrating as people have moved from one locality to another, sometimes quickly over very short distances … and sometimes slowly over very great stretches of land, mmm … in search of a new or different or better life. There now appears to be general agreement that the first movement of people of any real significance in any part of our planet originated in East Africa approximately <u>100,000</u> years ago. This first group of modern humans made their way across the Red Sea, which was then a dry bed. Then through Arabia and into what is now the Middle East. But these early pioneers soon died out.

Just like today, the Earth was subject to shifts in <u>temperature</u>. About 70,000 years ago, the planet became warmer and another group of modern humans migrated out of their homeland of Africa, following basically the same route, and then moving on to South Asia. By about 50,000 years ago, modern humans had colonised China, and about <u>45,000</u> years ago they had reached Europe. These early humans settled in the wide open spaces of Siberia about 40,000 years ago, and about 20,000 years ago, modern humans reached Japan, which was

connected to the main <u>land mass</u> at that time.

Now, there was no land connection between Australia and South East Asia, so the first Australians who arrived around 50,000 years ago must have made the journey across the sea in <u>simple boats</u> to settle on the Australian continent.

Modern humans moved from Asia to North America, which was reached across what is now the Bering Strait through Alaska. This migration happened between 15 and 13,000 years ago. There is also some evidence to suggest that modern humans came across pack ice via the North Atlantic, but this theory has been discounted by some. Since that time, the American continent has been the destination of waves of human settlement.

......................................................

Before we look at more modern examples of human movement, like the Anglo-Saxon migrations to Britain in the 5th century AD, the migration of Turks during the Middle Ages and the migration of the Irish to America in the mid-19th century, I'd like to look at a migration within the continent of Africa itself, that I'm personally very interested in.

If we look at the map of Africa, we can see some patterns that are common to other waves of human movement throughout history. The routes here show what is probably the most significant migration in Africa itself: that of the Bantu, who spread out from a small region in West Africa near the present day border of Nigeria and Cameroon, just around here on the map … to occupy roughly <u>30 per cent</u> of the continent by the year 1,000 AD. A trigger for this movement may have been the result of the cultivation of the <u>yam</u>, a starchy root vegetable, which Bantu farmers started to grow as part of their staple diet. This cultivation began around 2,750 BC, resulting in the expansion of the population. The Bantu people then spread out into the neighbouring territories, which were at that time sparsely populated. As the land of the rainforest could not sustain the farmers and their families for longer than a few years, they moved on, felling trees and creating new clearances in the forest to cultivate yams. With the numbers of the Bantu on the increase between 2,500 and 400 BC, the people were constantly on the move, migrating south down through modern day Congo … in central Africa, and reaching Zimbabwe and modern-day South Africa by about 100 AD.

It was contact with <u>Sudan</u> in North Africa that introduced the Bantu to iron production, in which they excelled. Once they had exchanged knowledge of working in iron from Sudan, the quality of their work rivalled that produced by the Mediterranean people of the time. They now had better tools to cut down trees, clear forests and <u>work fields</u>. And there is one other benefit iron gave them, and that was a <u>military advantage</u> over their neighbours.

I'd say that migration has transformed the world from early times, and we all reap the benefits of different peoples coming into contact with each other.

## Round up

Briefly discuss globalisation, generally, and/or a subject like the spread of world languages. You can map where certain languages are spoken using a world map. Students might want to discuss language spread historically as well, time permitting.

## Writing TASK 1 page 111

**1** Ask students to do the exercise in pairs, followed by whole-class feedback. Focus on noun-verb collocations, especially on verbs with trees and buildings and also the use of the passive. Elicit other words or phrases students know that could be used in the context, e.g., *pull down*, *change*, *convert*, etc.

> **ANSWERS**
> **1** b **2** g, c **3** a, d **4** g, c **5** g, c **6** e **7** d, f, b

**2** Students can complete the exercise in pairs followed by whole-class feedback.

> **ANSWERS**
> **a** replaced **b** transformed **c** turned into
> **d** built **e** chopped down **f** converted
> **g** knocked down/demolished.

**3** Students do this exercise individually, followed by checking in pairs and then whole-class feedback.

> **ANSWERS**
> **1** was extended
> **2** expanded
> **3** was constructed
> **4** was completely changed/was changed completely/ changed completely
> **5** became
> **6** took place, altered
> **7** became
> **8** was developed

**4** Elicit the answers from the whole class.

> **ANSWERS**
> extension     expansion     construction
> demolition    alteration    conversion
> development

**5** 🔊 Students can do this in groups as well as pairs, followed by whole-class feedback.

## Extension

In advance of the class, ask students to bring in two photos of a place they know (or don't know) at different points in time. They can play *spot the difference* in groups or as a whole class followed by a description of the changes by the students.

## Lead-in

Elicit the points of the compass and show these on the board. Review adverbs of place with the students and list them on the board. Remember that for some cultures it is natural to use the points of the compass to describe location, but for others, less so, and they might use prepositions of place instead.

Give students a map or use the one provided to make five sentences about buildings or places on the map, but not to state which particular building they are referring to. Ask them to read the description to their partner, who has to guess what each building/place is.

**6** Follow the instructions in the Student's Book. Focus only on the first map and not the whole task. Monitor the pairwork discussion and give feedback.

As an alternative exercise, ask students to ask each other questions: *Is … in the north of …? Where is …? What is north/east of …?*

Go through the whole task and maps with students, checking they understand the task. Point out the generic rubric and stress that they have to cover all the changes in their response in the exam and that an overview is necessary. Elicit the purpose of writing tasks like this – to check an awareness of and use of location descriptions.

**7** Students can complete the exercise in pairs. Monitor and take notes of good practice before whole-class feedback.

**8–9** Once students have done exercise 8 with a partner, ask them to check their answers with another pair and then add the phrases a-g to the model.

> **ANSWERS**
> **8**
> **a** the shops <u>in the east</u> of the area
> **b** the square <u>south of</u> the open-air market
> **c** the woodland with the lake <u>to the east of</u> the farmland
> **d** the disused car factory <u>in the north-east</u>
> **e** the farmland <u>in the north-west</u> of Wetherby
> **f** <u>South of</u> Main Street, the area witnessed even greater change.
> **g** the office block <u>south of</u> the house was extended in 2016
> **9**
> **1** e **2** c **3** d **4** f **5** g **6** a **7** b

**10** Elicit the verbs from the whole class, making sure you discuss the difference between the past simple and past perfect.

> **ANSWERS**
> <u>Present simple:</u> as it is the introduction.
> illustrate
> is
>
> <u>past simple:</u> for events in the past
> underwent
> experienced
> was turned into

remained
was converted into
witnessed
was extended
became

Past perfect: the verbs below are governed by the phrase "by 2016" and actions that had happened before that time.
had given way
had become
had also been added

**11** When students have done this, emphasise that the overview is usually written in the present simple, and ask them to compare overviews from previous units. Allow them to use the past simple in the rewrite but indicate a preference for the present simple.

**ANSWER**

The overview is the second sentence.

Possible answer
Overall, it is clear that the town is/has been completely transformed/changed with the …

**12** 🗣 Designate Student A and Student B in each pair. Do the pairwork as it is set up checking that the students have the right information at each stage because if they have made any errors, it will have an impact on the subsequent step. Ensure students do not just look at each other's maps, but that they use the language as required.

**Extension**

Ask students individually or in pairs to draw their own basic map: a rectangle with roads, rivers buildings, etc. and remind them of the compass. Ask them to describe their map (basically) to a new partner, who then draws the map. As a follow-up, students can ask you to draw a map on the board, but only draw the feature if/when the description is completely correct.

**13** Students can do this exercise in class or for homework. Stress the need for an overview, the correct use of the passive and the use of the past perfect. Encourage students to use the Writing checklist on page 139.

---

*Model answer*

The maps illustrate the developments that occurred in Harton between 2008 and 2016.

Overall, it is clear that the town of Harton undergoes a complete transformation during the period with a significant reduction in residential areas. For example, the residential neighbourhood in the southwest gave way to a shopping centre, while the industrial complex east of the river expanded replacing a substantial part of the wooded area, where the lake was drained and reduced to a pond.

---

Moreover, by 2016 the derelict warehouses in the north of Harton next to the residential area had been converted into a car park and where the old town once stood south of the warehouses, offices and a university have been built. Another significant change was the conversion of the arts centre in the west of the town to a multi-screen cinema. The school next to the arts centre west of the river, meanwhile, remained unchanged.

*Word Count: 153 words*

**COMMENTS**

The answer to the task covers all the developments in the two maps, indicating the location of the features. There is a wide range of structures including complex sentences and a range of vocabulary relating to change and location.

## Speaking PARTS 2–3 page 113

**1** 🗣 Review Speaking Part 2 and then ask students to do the exercise in pairs. Monitor students for accuracy and use of the new vocabulary.

**2** 🗣 Follow the instructions in the Student's Book, emphasising advice given about time in the *Don't forget!* box. Let students work in pairs and take control of this activity. Ask them to time their partners both while taking the notes and as they speak. Tell them to check their partner's notes when they finish to make sure they are as brief as possible. Encourage them to check the rhythm of their partner's description.

**3** 🗣 Ask students to work in pairs. As preparation for taking turns asking and answering the questions, ask students to discuss a few ideas, and possibly the organisation of the answers. Then ask them to ask and answer the questions, followed by pair and whole-class feedback.

---

### REVIEW 8 ANSWERS pages 114–115

## Vocabulary: Nouns relating to places

1 neighbourhood, area, vicinity
2 area, spot, place
3 zone, district, space
4 location, regions, place
5 setting, vicinity, place.

## Language focus: Referring in a text

**1**

1 The ruined castle
2 residential areas in the city
3 holidays

**2**
1  This, it
2  that, it
3  This, it
4  it, that, it
5  it, this
6  they, it
7  this, those

# Verbs relating to changes in places

**1**
construction, conversion, demolition, replacement, transformation, renovation

**2**
1  The old houses **were demolished** to make way for a block of flats.
2  The area was completely **transformed** with new houses and shops.
3  A supermarket was **knocked down** to make way for a wider road.
4  A line of trees was **chopped down** and houses were constructed in their place.
5  The bank was **renovated and converted** into a restaurant.
6  The main street was **turned into** a small pedestrian area.
7  A new bridge **replaced** the tunnel.
8  The offices were **demolished** and rebuilt again.

**3**
1  The demolition of the old houses made way for a block of flats.
2  The area underwent a complete transformation with new houses and shops.

**ACCURACY IN IELTS**
1  The tramline was extended to the suburbs and three new stations were added.
2  As the town expanded, the fields were **used for** housing.
3  A retail complex was constructed on a greenfield site on the **edge of town**.
4  The neighbourhood was completely transformed with the building **of huge** apartment blocks.
5  The area in the northwest of the town **became** more built-up.
6  A number of dramatic developments took place, **which altered** the character of the town considerably.
7  The neighbourhood to the northwest of the town centre became less rural and leafy with the building of new offices.
8  The empty **space west** of the university campus was turned into a technology development centre.

Photocopiable activity: Group game – Description and evaluation board game pages 136 and 142

Workbook pages 68–75

## Content overview

This unit focuses on beauty, architecture and beautiful surroundings.

### Listening SECTION 3

A film project

Question types: Sentence Completion; Matching information

### Reading

The architect, Giles Gilbert Scott

Question types: Sentence Completion; Classification; Matching information to paragraphs

### Writing TASK 2

Describing effects and consequences

### Speaking PARTS 2 AND 3

Part 2 Describing a building or monument

Part 3 Discussing buildings and traditions

**Vocabulary 1:** Beauty

**Word Building:** Prefixes *under-* and *over-*

**Language focus:** Modal verbs for evaluating

## Digital overview

### Presentation Kit

Interactive versions of Student's Book exam tasks

Embedded audio and answer key for all activities

### Teacher's Resource Centre

Progress Test 3

Communicative activity: Group game – Description and evaluation board game

Workbook audio, answer key and wordlists

### Student's Resource Centre

Class audio

Wordlist

Speaking Part 2 video and video worksheet

Speaking Part 3 videos (4) and video worksheet

## Vocabulary: Beauty page 116

### Lead-in

As a lead-in, ask students to look at the photographs and decide if the buildings are beautiful or not and briefly discuss as a whole class who decides what is beautiful and how. You can extend the discussion *briefly* to advertising and fashion and then revisit it at the end of/later in the unit. This can be done to whet students' appetites.

1 Students describe the buildings in groups and answer the questions. Encourage them to give their reactions to the buildings and discuss their feelings about them, giving opinions on beauty. Also ask them to compare them with buildings and monuments they are familiar with and like. In the whole-class feedback, elicit students' evidence for their answers by way of examples, reasons, etc.

> **ANSWERS**
> 1 Dubai Rotating Tower, Dubai
> 2 The Egg, Beijing, China
> 3 Jal Mahal, Jaipur, India
> 4 La Boca, Buenos Aires, Argentina
> 5 The Royal Tombs, Petra, Jordan

2 Ask students to rank the buildings individually. Students should then discuss them in groups, comparing any similarities and differences. Encourage them to justify and to support their justification with examples. As part of the whole-class feedback, to reinforce organisational skills for all parts of the exam, you can briefly tabulate the information on the board, e.g.: *Building, Rank, Similarities, Differences, Justification*. When you have completed the table, you can select a student from each group to summarise the items in the table.

3 Students complete the statements with their own ideas. You can elicit examples from individual students.

4 When students have completed this exercise, ask them to transfer the adjectives to their (electronic) vocabulary lists.

> **ANSWERS**
> A tall, ancient, spacious, stone
> B evocative, melancholic, thoughtful, dazzling, humbling, magnificent, impressive, overwhelmed, emotional, ecstatic, nostalgic, majestic

5 Students complete this activity individually and check their answers in pairs. As part of the whole-class feedback, ask for reasons for answers. Also, elicit other words students might want to add to the list/use. Ask them briefly why it is important to

know and use words in this way, e.g., flexibility in the use of language, improvement in paraphrasing, improvements in spontaneity and fluency and, hence, competence in IELTS. This then leads into exercise 6.

ANSWERS

1 humble  2 emotion  3 nostalgia
4 evoke  5 think/thoughtful

**6** Go though the example with the students, pointing out the greater flexibility in language use needed here. Students can work in groups of three and transform three chosen sentences. They can then share their transformed sentences with the class.

ANSWERS

1 … the Sphinx was very humbling/filled me with humility.
2 The sight of the Himalayas made me feel emotional/moved me.
3 … that I love sometimes makes me melancholic …
4 … my home country, they are evocative of so many memories …
5 … wandering through the ruins made me thoughtful/think about life …

**Extension**

Students work in groups. Ask them to transform two sentences using their own words. As part of the task, the sentences have to keep the same meaning but they must, as far as possible, paraphrase everything except for the names or words that cannot be paraphrased, such as photograph/photo. This increases awareness of paraphrasing, which also involves knowing *what not to paraphrase,* as it can mean changing the subject topic, in speaking and writing questions.

**7** Elicit what is meant by national monuments and give some examples from other countries, e.g., the Parthenon in Athens, the Statue of Liberty in the United States. If you have a monolingual class, you can also select examples from the students' country. Write the following expressions on the board and encourage students to use them:
*What makes/made/has made (the monument) important to people in my country is …*
*I chose this monument because …*
*(The monument) makes people feel …*
Students share their ideas with a partner, and then the whole class.

**Speaking** PART 2 **page 118**

**Lead-in**

Focus briefly on the structure of the Task Card by way of a lead-in. Elicit the relationship between the three prompts after *You should say* and the last

prompt *and explain why …,* i.e. the initial prompts set the scene and are the background for the more detailed evaluation in the last part. Elicit examples of the kind of language used in the evaluation, e.g., adjectives of description, cause and effect developments, and adjectives of evaluation like *important.* Point out that they are going to look at *evaluation/giving an opinion* in another way.

**1** Go through the rubric with students highlighting the linking devices and point out that these can be used effectively in both writing and speaking. Using a variety of these markers will enhance students' cohesion in both these skills. Show how some of the markers can go at the beginning or in the middle of two clauses, but others generally do not go at the beginning.

Check that the students understand the phrases before they write the sentences. Point out that they can use the negative words to emphasise the appeal something has to them by contrasting their positive attitude, feelings, etc. with something negative. Go through the *Useful expressions* box, eliciting the differences in the phrases. Draw students' attention to the structure *What made (the building) important to me is …,* and explain the structure if necessary, i.e. the 'what' clause is the subject of the sentence.

**2** Students do the exercise in pairs. Afterwards, they can read out their sentences to the class. Monitor for correct stress and structural accuracy, and correct as necessary.

**3** Ask students to do the exercise, checking to see which sentences they use.

**4** Tell students they should put their notes to the previous activities away before embarking on the actual test practice and look only at the words relating to the prompts. Ask students to time each other strictly on the note-making and the actual task. Let them check their original notes when they finish and compare them to any new notes made during the task. Ask students to use the Speaking checklists on page 181 to give feedback on each other's work. Point out they do not have to give feedback on everything and that they should be constructive. Suggest extra practice for students who are still not making concise notes and who are not keeping to time or extending their language use.

**Round up**

Summarise the ways of showing opinion in this section and the vocabulary on page 117. Stress how students can now give their opinion, show their position/stance, and evaluate by ways other than just saying *I think, in my opinion.* You might want to elicit in which ways students prefer to express their opinion and gauge this again later in the course.

## Reading Passage  page 118

**1–2** Students suggest and discuss a few things they would expect to read about an architect. They can then skim the text and share the information with the class after discussion in groups. Time permitting, write the Words *General* and *Specific* at the top of the board. Elicit details about the Reading Passage, asking students to tell you under which of the two headings you should write the information, in note form. The order of the information given is not important yet. When you feel you have enough information, elicit the order of the information as it is given in the passage, as far as possible. If you have time, you can also discuss the text from the perspective of general and specific information in the text and texts in general. Refer students to the General and Specific information in IELTS essentials on page 205. Ask students to skim the questions again, thinking about the information collated on the board.

> **POSSIBLE ANSWERS**
>
> a description of (famous) buildings, background history, influences on the architect, dates, etc.

**3** Give students no more than two or three minutes to scan for the antonyms. This can be done in groups with students competing against each other. They can discuss as a whole class how they located the words.

> **ANSWERS**
>
> | | | | | | |
> |---|---|---|---|---|---|
> | **1** | fused | **2** | familiar | **3** | beloved |
> | **4** | romanticised | **5** | obfuscating | **6** | ingenious |
> | **7** | original | | | | |

### Extension

Students can work in groups. Give students a text of 500 to 750 words long. The students take turns choosing important words/phrases, e.g., synonyms/antonyms/collocations/*chunks*, for the other group members to find. Let them decide what is important. Discuss the process afterwards and elicit why they thought the words were important and where they were in the sentence, paragraph/text; whether they are related to general or specific detail, etc. Repeat this several times during the course with students in pairs, groups or as a whole class, reviewing the items chosen afterwards.

### Questions 1–13

Tell students to follow the advice in the *Don't forget!* box. Allow them 20 minutes to answer the questions, giving a time warning after 15 minutes. Tell them to write their answers on a sheet of paper or an answer sheet. Ask students to go over the test in pairs first and then as a whole class, ensuring they all know where the correct answers are in the text.

> **ANSWERS**
>
> | | | | |
> |---|---|---|---|
> | **1** | tradition/modernity | **2** | conservative |
> | **3** | very advanced | **4** | (popular) success |
> | **5** B | **6** C | **7** A | **8** A | **9** B | **10** H | **11** C |
> | **12** E | **13** B | | |

It is worth noting that students may arrive at the correct answers by chance and may not fully understand why they are correct. Elicit detailed justification of even simple correct answers and check the rationale is correct.

**4** Students discuss the question in groups, followed by whole-class feedback.

### Extension

As a variation of reading practice, give students the Reading Passage in the book before they do the test or a new text they have not seen. Ask them to work in groups, select the information in the passage that they think should be tested and justify their choice. If you have chosen the text from the book, they can then answer the questions relating to the test without any further preparation. If you have chosen a new text, you can follow this up with students writing a few IELTS questions, e.g., *sentence completion,* or *True/False/Not Given.* Monitor the students for accuracy as they create the questions. Then ask them to test their questions on another group or the whole class. Throughout, keep strict control of the time, setting clear time limits for each stage depending on your students.

## Word building: Prefixes *under-* and *over-*  page 121

**1** Elicit other examples from the students using *under-* and *over-* as prefixes, if possible. Explain that they sometimes, but not always, have a negative connotation.

> **ANSWERS**
>
> overbearing (paragraph E): too much/more than they should
> understated (paragraph G): below/less than they should

**2** Students can do the exercise with a partner, checking their answers with another pair, followed by whole-class discussion. As the students do the activity, tell them to identify the adjectives that are not negative (6, 9, 10). Ensure they understand the meanings before moving on. Get them to add the vocabulary to their (electronic) vocabulary lists.

> **ANSWERS**
>
> | | | | |
> |---|---|---|---|
> | **1** | underestimated | **2** | overrun |
> | **3** | overrated | **4** | undervalued |
> | **5** | overcome | **6** | overtook |
> | **7** | underfunded | **8** | underrated |
> | **9** | understated | **10** | overawed |

**3** Ask students to do the exercise individually then read and talk about the sentences with a partner.

## Listening SECTION 3 page 122

**1** Ask students to do the exercise in pairs followed by whole-class feedback. Remind students how important prediction is for successful listening.

ANSWERS
The project is about the photographs the student took of India.

**2** Ask the students to work in groups and share their knowledge before using a dictionary. You can clarify any doubts now or wait until after they have heard the words and phrases in context. If the students want to know the definitions, concept check by eliciting examples in sentences as a round-the-class activity.

ANSWERS
1 perception: way of looking at things
2 collage: arrangement/(random) collection of items
3 grandeur: magnificence
4 digital stills: digital images
5 narrow down: limit
6 discipline: control
7 fade: weaken/become pale/disappear
8 access: get into
9 click: select (on a computer)

### Questions 21–30

If necessary, go through the questions before the students do the Listening test. Analyse the questions from the point of view of the purpose of the question type, e.g., *detailed information*. Analyse, as far as you/students can, how to listen for the information, bearing in mind the discussion in exercise 1 above.

Play the recording. Tell students to transfer their answers to an answer sheet and check spelling. Ask them to check their answers with a partner and, if necessary, play the recording again before checking the answers as a whole class.

Point out that if students are aiming for a score band of 7 they should be aiming to get about 7/8 answers correct in this section. Remind students not to leave blanks for any answers, but to predict the answer, either during the Listening test, at the end of the section or at the end of the test during transfer time. Remind them not to linger on answers they can't provide whilst they are listening or they may miss other answers.

ANSWERS
21 too abstract      22 completely overawed
23 dazzling          24 ten/10 (images)
25 pop video         26 G          27 E
28 B                 29 F          30 D

**3** Students discuss the questions in pairs or small groups.

### Listening script 14

**(T = tutor; M = Malcolm)**

**T:** Hi Malcolm. How are you?
**M:** Fine, thanks. And you?
**T:** Yes, I'm OK, thank you. You left a message when you booked this tutorial to say that you wanted to talk about your film project. Am I right?
**M:** Yeah.
**T:** So, how can I help you?
**M:** Well, I'm having difficulty getting my project started. I should've been about halfway through by now, but I haven't done anything at all really. I think I'm feeling a bit overwhelmed by it all.
**T:** Overwhelmed? In what way?
**M:** Mmm … I don't know. I may've chosen something that's <u>too abstract</u>.
**T:** Which is? Remind me what the focus of … ?
**M:** The title's 'Perceptions of Beauty in India'.
**T:** Yeah. That's a good subject; it's probably quite challenging, but very appealing.
**M:** I wanted to put together a moving digital photo collage of my travels around India last summer, showing the beauty of the place. I was <u>completely overawed</u> by the whole experience.
**T:** How many did you take in all?
**M:** At least 600.
**T:** That is a lot. I'm sure it's a wonderful photographic record, but I think your problem lies there. Can you tell me? What did you take photographs of?
**M:** Buildings like palaces and official places like the government buildings in New Delhi by Lutyens – I think they're really underrated. People just think of the Taj Mahal and poverty, but India's not all like that. It's huge: it's got tradition, colour and beauty at every corner. I've also got some <u>dazzling</u> images of places like the Ganges at Varanasi; the grandeur and splendour of the images simply take your breath away.
**T:** OK, I have a suggestion.
**M:** Yeah?
**T:** What about going through your digital stills on the computer and selecting the <u>ten images</u> which appeal to you the most? And …
**M:** I don't know if I could narrow it down to that.
**T:** Well, you'll be surprised. Select the top hundred, and then narrow that down to 25. And then you could …
**M:** I've just thought of an idea.
**T:** Yes?
**M:** I could mmm … Yes that's it! I could select the top ten as you suggest, and then find various people's views on these … and then do a video collage with the pictures swirling around like a <u>pop video</u>. Why didn't I think of that before! That's it!
**T:** Problem solved?
**M:** Yes, but now I have to do all the work!

T: Before you submit the project, there are a few things I'd like to say. The length …

M: Can the film be longer than 15 minutes?

T: I wouldn't advise it. There might have been a few people on the course last year who made 20-minute, or even 25-minute films, but I have to say they were the least successful. I think you'll find that it's good discipline to try to work within a short time limit and <u>overall concentrate on having an end product that is simple</u>.

M: Mmm …

T: And I'd say that ten minutes might be good …

M: Ten minutes! That's almost nothing.

T: You'll be very surprised. One minute per place fading out and in. It could be very effective. Remember the work we did on adverts and <u>the short attention span of people generally</u>, especially these days.

M: Yeah, I suppose you're right. I'm just thinking of all the materials – 600 plus stills down to ten, and then reduced to a ten-minute film. What about the format? How do I need to submit it?

T: Mmm … <u>all the information is on the department website. You can access it as per usual</u>.

M: What's it under?

T: Go to 'Digital Photography'. Then 'Year One', and then click on 'Film Project', and everything is there. And don't forget <u>you have to fill in a submission form detailing the background of the project</u>.

M: Yeah, I … I know all that. But can't I just email it to you when it's done?

T: I'm afraid not, it has to go through the central process. We used to ask for copies burned on DVD, … four copies with the submission form, but we've been overtaken by technology, so you hand it in <u>on a memory stick</u>.

M: OK, I can do that.

## Round up

Review how difficult students find Section 3 compared to Sections 1 and 2.

## Language focus: Modal verbs for evaluating page 123

### Lead-in

Go through the example and explain this use of modals for evaluating situations. Ask students to provide examples in their own lives, saying when they should or shouldn't have done something. Refer them to the Grammar reference on page 224. Remind students of the other ways of evaluating that they have encountered so far, e.g., adjectives like *important* and *evocative*, etc. Point out that modal verbs like *might/could/should/will* and adjectives like *possible/probable/certain* allow them to indicate their evaluation on a scale running from possibility to certainty.

1 🔵 Students do this exercise in pairs. Elicit examples from students asking them to explain why they think they *shouldn't have* or *should have* done something.

### Extension

You can give students local/regional/national/ international situations that are uncontroversial, like sporting events, competitions and films, and elicit the following: *Do you think [...] should have won? Should they have played better? I think they shouldn't have lost …* Or list *should have/shouldn't have* statements on the board, possibly elicited from the students, and invite comments.

2 Students do this exercise on their own, checking their answers in pairs followed by whole-class feedback.

ANSWERS

| 1 should | 2 could have dealt |
|---|---|
| 3 might have | 4 might |
| 5 must | 6 could be |
| 7 should be | 8 ought to |
| 9 must | |

### Extension

During the feedback process, students could be encouraged to create more context for sentences to explain their answers in more detail, e.g., in 1 *There is a building in the neighbourhood, which is not very attractive and people think it should have been pulled down and something more attractive should have been built instead.* Students can also contextualise the expansion in their own locality, *… in my neighbourhood …* or make it abstract in a national context, *… in the city centre … .*

3 This can be done as whole-class exercise.

ANSWERS

1, 2, 4

4 Do the the first item in the list with the whole class and ask them to do the rest of the exercise in pairs or groups. Invite students' comments on the use of the modals in this way: *Have you used them? How often have you used them? Do you think you can try to use them? Do you think they will make your writing and speaking richer? How/Why?*

ANSWERS

a conclusion: 5, 9
a regret: 4
a suggestion: 8
a criticism: 1, 2, 4
an expectation: 7
a possibility/weak suggestion: 6
a possibility: 3

**5** Put the students in groups and ask them to choose someone to take notes and someone to give feedback to the whole class. If you have a multi-national class, group the students according to country or make sure each group is from a different country. If you have a mono-national class, group them according to region. Alternatively, tell the students to discuss the town/city they are studying in, if they have been there long enough to have obtained some local knowledge. Give the students 15 minutes to discuss the task. Monitor and encourage them to use the modals and vocabulary previously studied. As the 'reporters' report back, encourage the other groups to notice where ideas are similar or different from their own so they can comment when it's their turn, using terms like *We agree*/*We differ* …, etc.

## Round up

Ask students how they can express criticisms, expectations, conclusions, etc. using modals, and/or give them a few sentences and ask them to label them functionally.

## Speaking PART 3 page 123

**1** Put the students into groups for this discussion at first, to pool ideas. Go through the *Don't forget!* box with the class. Ask half the class to discuss the questions on *Beautiful buildings* and the other half the questions on *Buildings and traditions*. Then pair them up so there is one student from each half and conduct the interview as in the exam, with one student as the examiner and the other as the candidate. Ask them to switch roles. This way they both obtain ideas for the two topics.

## Extension

Students can work in groups of three with the third student acting as prompter. If the student roleplaying the candidate wanders, overgeneralises or does not provide much context or development, the prompter suggests a word/phrase like *because*, *such as*, *if, for example* and *so*, etc. and the candidate has to continue by using the word/phrase. By the time students have rotated roles around the group, their fluency and confidence will have increased. Monitor and then give and invite feedback and evaluation.

## Writing TASK 2 page 124

### Lead-in

You might like to expand on this topic by using all the vocabulary from the start of the unit and discussing different architectural styles. You could bring in some photos of different styles of architecture, e.g., Russian, Chinese and Japanese, as well as more Western styles like Palladian, Art Deco, Gothic, etc. Remember to accommodate all your students' backgrounds, if possible. Before the class, you could ask each student to bring in a photo of a building to discuss in groups. When students have discussed their photos in their groups, they can swap photos with other groups. You can ask them to vote on the three most popular buildings.

**1** Students do this in pairs, followed by whole-class feedback.

> **ANSWERS**
> A view/opinion of other people which is expressed using a comparison.

**2** Students by now will be able to work more independently. Give them a time limit and ask them to give feedback to the whole class after they have changed partners and shared ideas. Collate/tabulate the ideas on the board.

**3** Students work in groups followed by whole-class feedback.

> **POSSIBLE ANSWER**
> The preservation and upkeep of old buildings is seen by some as essential, while others think they should be demolished and new ones built instead. In my opinion, it depends on the buildings concerned, but I favour the protection of older buildings, where possible.
>
> It is clear that modern buildings do have their attractions compared to older ones.
>
> Yet, I believe that older buildings such as old houses or factories of architectural interest should be preserved, because they are part of people's heritage.
>
> The visual appeal of some old buildings is another factor in the need to preserve them. Another reason is that some old buildings are worth preserving, as they are very appealing visually.
>
> As we have seen, although modern buildings do have their attraction, many older buildings play a vital role in the preservation of people's heritage and are also attractive.

**4–5** Students do this in pairs, followed by checking with other students and then whole-class feedback. By way of reflection, elicit the processing skills used in this exercise: identifying the linking devices where overt, identifying cause and effect, the use, or not, of signalling words, and putting the two sentences in order.

> **ANSWERS**
> **4**
> **1** b, a    **2** b, a or a, b    **3** a, b
> **4** a, b    **5** b, a or a, b    **6** b, a or a, b
>
> **5**
> **a**
> **1** cause b, effect a    **2** cause b, effect a
> **3** cause a, effect b    **4** cause a, effect b
> **5** cause a, effect b    **6** cause b, effect a

**b**
Cause: **2** thanks to
Effect: **1** and so  **3** leading to  **4** and then
**5** with  **6** as a result of

**c**
**2** the prepositional phrase *thanks to* indicates the cause without any linking device.
**3** the gerund is used to show a result.
**5** the effect is contained in the prepositional clause beginning with the preposition *with*.
**6** the prepositional phrase *as a result of* introduces the cause.

**d**
**4** the word *then* could be left out.

**6** Ask students to do this exercise in groups, followed by whole-class feedback. Elicit as much explanation analysis as time permits. Emphasise the importance of cause and effect.

ANSWERS
**1** shouldn't have relaxed, There are, as a result,
**2** should be attractive, thanks to
**3** Thanks to/With, now lighten up
**4** has a positive effect, which in turn
**5** With/Thanks to, are focusing on

## Extension

Give students a list of about 10 short sentences each containing a cause and effect, e.g.:
1 *The safety of the area was improved by the new street lighting.*
2 *New street lighting resulted in improvements in the safety of the area.*
3 *The safety of the area was a result of the new street lighting.*
  Ask students to identify the cause or effect or both. Give a strict time limit. This can gauge students' ability to process information/meaning rather than just words. Cause and effect can be changed to *purpose*, etc. You can increase the number of sentences or the length of the sentences. Information processing exercises like this can be done before reading and writing to help students limber up.

**7** Students do this in pairs first and explain their list to a new partner. This is followed by whole-class discussion.

**8** Ask the students to discuss the topic in pairs. Get them to write the essay in 40 minutes, either in class or for homework. Remind them to use the checklist on page 139. At this stage in the course, they should be seeing an improvement and should have fewer areas for attention than at the beginning.
  Encourage students to look at the model answer only after they have written their own answer. Ask students to go through the model, working out how it complies with the requirements of the task. They can use the Comments as a starting point.

*Model answer*

The skylines of cities around the world are changing rapidly as more modern building are being constructed, replacing older buildings, which require more money to renovate and maintain. Personally I feel that preserving older buildings is often a waste of money for various reasons.

There is no denying that it is worthwhile keeping certain old buildings. Many castles and mansions, for example, around the world are of great historical interest and they deserve to be preserved, but in some cases old buildings are often overrated, while many new buildings are undervalued. Instead of money being spent on improving them, many old buildings should have been demolished, because they are not fit for purpose. Many people like them for nostalgic reasons, and there is no doubt that they are evocative of another era, but they are in many instances not very practical to work or live in.

On the other hand, new buildings are generally cheaper to build and maintain than keeping old buildings. The costs involved in the latter arise because it is difficult sometimes to find the correct materials for renovation. It is also time-consuming to modernise them while at the same time keeping the original features.

Some people dislike modern construction methods because they use a lot of glass and steel rather than old-fashioned materials such as bricks. Personally, I find certain modern skylines in cities like Doha in Qatar, Shanghai and New York, impressive and beautiful. Cities which don't have modern buildings can seem rather melancholic and not as dazzling as some people feel.

As we have seen, the construction of modern buildings is more worthwhile than maintaining older ones.

*Word count: 273 words*

COMMENTS

The answer is well-organised with clear paragraphing. Each paragraph presents and develops an argument that is supported with reasons and examples. The conclusion reflects each paragraph and is linked with the task.

## Round up

Elicit from students what they learnt in the unit and the three most important things they will carry forward.

3 For example, local neighbourhoods could be given funds to improve their surroundings by creating mini-gardens and decorating buildings.
4 a beautiful environment (cause of positive impact) with fewer days off work and increased productivity (part of cause of the economic health of the nation)

**REVIEW 9 ANSWERS** pages 126 AND 127

## Vocabulary: Beauty

**1**
1 Breathtaking  2 Magnificent  3 Spacious
4 Nostalgic  5 Overwhelmed  6 Thoughtful
7 Melancholic  8 Ancient  10 Ecstatic

**2**
Accept all suitable answers.

## Word building: Prefixes *under-* and *over-*

**1**
1 underrated  2 underfunded  3 overstated
4 underpriced  5 overcome  6 undervalued
7 overtaken  8 underestimated

## Language focus: Modal verbs for evaluating

**Possible answers**
1 Conclusion: They <u>must have</u> closed it.
2 Expectation: People <u>should be</u> happy.
3 Conclusion: The transport <u>must have been</u> on time.
4 Mild criticism: The government <u>could have</u> invested money earlier.
5 Criticism: She <u>might at least</u> have phoned me!
6 Suggestion: <u>The town should be made</u> more attractive.
7 Conclusion: It <u>must have cost a lot of</u> money./It <u>must be worth a lot of</u> money.
8 Suggestion: The building <u>could be renovated</u> rather than being knocked down.
9 Expectation: <u>It should help to make</u> the environment more pleasant.

**ACCURACY IN IELTS**
**1**
1 … *a positive impact <u>on</u>* (wrong word)
2 *As <u>a</u> result* (missing word)
3 … *the nation <u>should also improve</u>* (wrong tense)
4 … *neighbourhoods could <u>be</u>* (missing word)
5 *This <u>should</u> definitely* (wrong word)

**2**
1 The main reason is that a beautiful environment has a positive impact on people's mood, …
2 … which in turn should increase the health status of the general population.
As a result, the economic health of the nation should also improve with fewer days off work and increased productivity.
This should definitely have a beneficial effect on people's mood.

## Ready for Writing

## Introduction page 128

Go through the information in the introduction with the students, checking comprehension by asking students to summarise the contents in their own words.

## Task 1 page 128

**1–2** These can be done as whole-class exercises giving the students time to read and think.

ANSWERS

**1**

1 (stacked) bar chart  2 pie chart  3 bar chart
4 graph  5 table

**2**

1 False. Barcharts, tables and a sequence of pie charts can also show trends.
2 True. Pie charts usually show proportions with percentages, but they can show proportions where the values are given in numbers, e.g., hundreds, thousands, etc.
3 True.
4 True. Stacked bar charts are like horizontal or vertical pie charts. They are used because it is easier to compare visually the various proportions.
5 True.

### Graph

**1** Ask students to study the task and the model before completing the exercise individually or in pairs followed by whole-class feedback.

ANSWERS

1 the overview:
*Overall, it is clear that regarding the two main reasons, not needing the internet and a lack of skills, the trend was upwards throughout the period, while that for the other reasons was fairly flat.*

**2** examples of complex sentences:
*By contrast, while there was a rise in the proportion of households without internet access because of lack of skills from about 15% in 2008 to just over 30% in 2014, the trend in the proportion for high equipment costs was slightly downwards, 10% compared to 13% in 2000 and 2014 respectively.*
*As regards high access cost, the trend was flat with a peak of about 15% in 2010 from 11% in 2008 , but privacy and security was less of a concern with the proportion giving this reason falling between 2008 and 2014, approximately 6% and 3%, respectively.*

**3** examples of language of comparison:
*(For example, approximately one third (about 34%) … compared to more than a half (approximately 54%) in 2014.*
*By contrast, while there was a rise in the proportion of households … (the trend in the proportion for high equipment costs was slightly downwards, 10%) compared to 13% in 2000 and 2014 respectively.*
*… but privacy and security was less of a concern …*

**4** sentences where high access and high equipment costs are described:
*… the trend in the proportion for high equipment costs was slightly downwards, 10% compared to 13% in 2000 and 2014 respectively. As regards high access cost, the trend was flat with a peak of about 15% in 2010 from 11% in 2008 …*

Elicit from students an explanation of:
- the structure of the model overall
- the structure of a selection of the sentences in the second paragraph looking at where the data are in the sentence
- the tenses used.

Ask them what they think the word count of the model is. Refer them to the Writing Task 1 checklist on page 139 of the Student's Book.

### Further practice

Ask students to work in groups and select seven chunks of text or phrases that might be useful to remember for recycling in future.

### Bar chart

**1** Ask students to study the task and the model before completing the exercise individually or in pairs followed by whole-class feedback.

ANSWERS

1 d  2 e  3 a  4 c  5 b

### Extension

Time permitting, ask one or more groups to explain the bar chart and/or present the bar chart to the whole class before doing the exercise. After students have done the exercise, ask one or more groups to present the completed model to the whole class, and explain the structure of the model, including the stages, from general to specific. Ask a group to choose seven chunks of text or phrases that might be useful to remember for recycling in future. The class can discuss and revise the choices.

## Pie charts

1 Follow the same procedure for bar charts, including the extension activity.

> **ANSWERS**
>
> 1 almost three quarters of employees putting in at least 30 hours per week and just over half of self-employed people doing so.
> 2 more than 45 hours per week compared with 25.3% for self-employed homeworkers.
> 3 a much larger proportion of employees (42.1%) do so.
> 4 self-employed workers working 30 hours or less per week accounted for 40.2% of the total as opposed to a much smaller proportion of employees, only 26.4%.

## Extension

To increase students' awareness of the concept of proportions, ask them to draw two large circles on an A4 sheet of paper, labelled 2010 and 2016. Then, choose a topic like attendances at a football stadium, art gallery by age group or sales of items by department/in a department store. To the students, describe the proportions for the age groups or the department stores, e.g., *the 15–24 age group accounted for 30% of those attending … in 2010, while in 2016 the attendance for this group had fallen to …/the sales in the furniture department constituted 30% of total sales in the department store in 2010, while … .* Students label the pie charts for both years adding the percentage and the legend.

You can vary this:

- by asking students to do the exercise in pairs
- by giving students already prepared pie charts without labels and percentages
- by asking them to complete just one year
- by asking them to create their own pie charts and dictate to another pair/partner/group, with or without pie charts prepared in advance.

## Table

1 Follow the same procedure for pie and bar charts, including both extension activities.

> **ANSWERS**
>
> Comparison: comparative adjectives, adverbs, *conjunctions*, or *other*.
> The table shows the volume of various types of cereals that were produced in a selection of European countries in 2000. Overall, it is clear that France and Germany produce *the largest amounts* of the cereal crops with Belgium producing *the least*.
> The volume of common wheat and spelt, for example, produced in Germany was 27 711 tons *compared to*

37 501 for France and 5153, 5442, 5319 and 1919 for Denmark, the Czech Republic, Bulgaria and Belgium respectively. By contrast, France produced only 128 tons of rye and maslin as opposed to 3854 tons in Germany, with no data available for Belgium. Likewise, Denmark produced 678 tons *in contrast* to 130 tons in the Czech Republic and only 28 tons in Bulgaria. The largest producer of barley was France with 11 775 tons *followed closely by* Germany with 11 563 tons. By comparison, Denmark produced *more barley than* the Czech Republic, Bulgaria and Belgium together, 3548 tons *against* 1967 tons, 851 tons and 400 tons, respectively.

Other
Prepositions: *compared to-, in contrast to, against*
Zero relative: *followed closely by*

## Extension

As a variation in the dictation described in the Extension for pie charts, give students a table like the one in the Student's Book and remove 5–7 items. Describe the items in the table and ask students to insert the missing data. This can be varied by removing some of the legends relating to the table, e.g., parts of the title and the countries, etc. Students can also do this individually or in pairs. They can also be given two sets of the same table, A and B, with different information missing on each and asked to describe the table to a partner or group who complete the table. You can also give the class a complete table and ask them to describe it so you complete missing data in the same table presented on the white board.

## Plan A

### Lead-in

Go over the possibilities for maps and plans in the IELTS exam: changes to a place such as a town, area, island over a period of time; changes to the layout of a building or complex; proposed changes in a street, etc.

Ask students to study the plans and describe the changes in their own words before looking at the model. Elicit where they should start and/or how they should organise their description – from the entrance and go clockwise; and group/classify the changes according to type.

1–2 Ask students to do the exercises in pairs, and check their answers with other students, followed by whole-class feedback.

> **ANSWERS**
>
> 1
> relocation, addition, replacement
>
> 2
> relocation: *the reception was moved to the right hand side of the entrance*
> addition: *New seating areas were also introduced to the left and right of the entrance with a new electronic turnstile being added just between the reception area and*

*the lift and stairs. Another addition was the electronic databank to the right of the lifts.*
*replacement: the three offices for 10 workers each on the left hand side had been turned into an open plan office for 45 workers. Moreover, the kitchen and staff lounge on the back wall had been replaced with meeting rooms. Similarly, the two offices for 10 workers each on the right had been turned into an office for 30 workers.*

## Extension

Give students two partially completed plans for different years with words missing and describe the plans. Students listen and label the plans, check their answers and then they describe them in their own words and/or write a description.

## Plan B

1 Students do the exercise in pairs, checking their answers together before whole-class feedback.

> **ANSWERS**
>
> | 1 railings | 2 High Road | 3 park |
> | 4 zebra crossing | 5 Staple Road | 6 major junction |
> | 7 roundabout | 8 traffic lights | |

## Extension

Ask students to work in groups of four and paraphrase part or the whole of the completed model answer. Half of the model can be given to each pair in the group and the text then amalgamated. They can write their answers on a sheet of paper. The paraphrase can be displayed and students circulate and choose the best. This can also be done electronically.

## Process

1–2 Ask students to do the exercises in pairs and to check their answers with other students before whole-class feedback.

> **ANSWERS**
>
> 1 *Overall, the production of the energy from tidal power using the artificial circular lagoon involves several stages relating to the opening and closing to the inflow and outflow gates in the lagoon.*
> 2 *First of all, before the high tide comes into the estuary, the inflow gate is opened to allow the water to flow into the lagoon …*
> *… at the same time the outflow gate is closed to prevent the water escaping again.*
> *Then, when the tide is at its highest, the lagoon is full of water.*
> *Subsequently, as soon as the tide turns …*
> *… the inflow gate is closed and the outflow gate, is opened and the water flows out of the lagoon …*
> 3 *Overall,*
> *First of all, before*
> *and at the same time.*

> *Then, when*
> *Subsequently, as soon as*
> *to which*
> 4 *falls and rises*
> *turns*
> 5 *Overall, the production of the energy from tidal power using the artificial circular lagoon involves several stages relating to the opening and closing to the inflow and outflow gates in the lagoon.*
> *First of all, before the high tide comes into the estuary, the inflow gate is opened to allow the water to flow into the lagoon and at the same time the outflow gate is closed to prevent the water escaping again.*
> *Subsequently, as soon as the tide turns and it is at its lowest level, the inflow gate is closed and the outflow gate, to which a turbine is attached, is opened and the water flows out of the lagoon, generating electricity.*

> 2
> Yes, 166 words

## Extension

As a project, students can research in groups a process or lifecycle and prepare a short explanation consisting of no more than two minutes. Students display their process/lifecycle and describe it to the whole class or other groups. This can, of course, be done electronically or on paper.

Keep a record of the processes/lifecycles described.

## Task 2 page 136

### Lead-in

Elicit the difference between Writing Tasks 1 and 2, stressing that: Writing Task 2 carries twice as many marks as Task 1; in Task 1, the description is objective, while in Task 2 the answer often contains opinion, argument and evaluation, which can draw on students' personal experience, but preferably still in the abstract, e.g., … *for example, in France/in China*, etc.

Go though the introduction and elicit further details and/or explaining information.

1 Ask students to work in pairs and to analyse the Writing Task using the items listed. Then elicit the analysis as a whole class, ensuring that the students lead the feedback and intervening for facilitating, correcting and clarifying only.

2 Students can do this exercise on their own first of all, followed by checking in pairs and then in whole-class feedback. To check comprehension, ask students to explain the organisation in their own words.

Students can be encouraged to analyse their own writing in class and at home to make them more aware of the stages in the writing process. This will help them see how the information in paragraphs fits together and make them more aware of discourse in reading and in speaking/listening. Refer to this during feedback.

ANSWERS
1 *The main factor behind the decrease in walking among the general population is the modern lifestyle that is much more sedentary, especially for people working in offices. The main solution is to encourage people through advertising to become more physically active.*
2 *With the advances in technology, people's lifestyles are changing and are becoming much more sedentary.*
3 *The modern lifestyle that is much more sedentary, especially for people working in offices.*
4 *… especially for people working in offices. For example, if people are sitting at a desk in an office for long periods of time rather than doing manual work on the land, this can reduce the time for people to do simple activities like walking.*
5 *… if people are sitting at a desk in an office for long periods of time rather than doing manual work on the land …*
6 *… this can reduce the time for people to do simple activities like walking.*
7 *Moreover, people are more inclined to travel by car or bus …*
8 *… so there is less need for people to walk.*
9 *… to encourage people through advertising to become more physically active.*

## Extension

Elicit different types of hooks, e.g.: *Walking is a less popular activity than it was in the past./Compared to previous generations, people walk less frequently./ Walking is less common than it was for previous generations.*

 Look at the functional nature of possible hooks: a comparison with the past, a cause and effect statement, a statement with a development/ situation/problem.

3 Students can do this in pairs followed by whole-class feedback.

POSSIBLE ANSWERS
educational, entertainment, financial, i.e. cheap leisure activity/attracting visitors, technological, developmental, national/international, e.g. attract people from around the country not just local, regional, national, environmental, e.g. 'visitors don't have to travel'.
You can use other perspectives here and you can use the perspectives to analyse and trigger ideas.

4 Ask students to do this exercise in groups eliciting a comparison from each group. Also ask each group to describe the structure of the model.

POSSIBLE ANSWERS
1 Two statements with two views and a statement asking candidates to write about each of the views and then give their own opinion.
2 One statement giving a development, followed by a question that asks whether the development in

the statement is negative or positive, i.e. students have to give their opinion/an evaluation: positive or negative. The rubric asks for reasons and examples in support of the candidate's ideas.
3 One statement giving a solution, with an evaluation, to a problem, followed by two questions asking whether they agree with the evaluation and what other measures could be effective. Students have to give their opinion/an evaluation of the measures, and suggest other measures. The rubric asks for reasons and examples in support of the candidate's ideas.

5 Students can do this in groups, followed by whole-class feedback. You might want to ask students to write their answers on a large sheet of paper, or write them electronically, for display to the whole class. Each group can present and explain their paraphrases. Point out that in tasks like this the introduction and conclusion change according to the opinion/position/stance of the writer.

POSSIBLE ANSWERS

The curriculum at primary school is in a permanent state of change with the constant educational advances. It is suggested by some that software programming needs to be taught to primary school children, but others argue that play is more important. Personally, I think the latter is more valuable for children at this stage than immersing them in technology. From my point of view, I agree mainly with the second group, but I think the importance of technology in the modern world means that it is a valuable skill for primary school children to acquire.

6 Go though the Writing Task, the topic sentences and conclusion with students, eliciting and stressing the connection at each stage with the task itself. Students can then do this in pairs or groups, followed by whole-class feedback.

POSSIBLE ANSWERS

Many museums and art galleries around the world are making the content of their institutions available to the general public by uploading them onto the internet. While some feel this is a negative step, I personally think that it is primarily positive for various reasons.

7 This exercise can be done individually followed by pair and then whole class checking.

ANSWERS
1 c   2 b   3 d   4 a

8 Ask students to do this exercise in pairs, checking their answers with other students before whole-class feedback.

## Ready for Writing

**9** Students can do this as a test or homework exercise using the Writing Task 2 checklist on page 139. It can be done without any input or the task can be discussed, eliciting the focus of the task, ideas and structure of the response.

### Model answer

In recent years, the lack of such soft skills as communication and working in teams ha grown. This development is the result of various factors, which can have a negative impact on both employees and employers.

A deficiency in soft skills is caused by various factors such as the current emphasis on computer-based work, automation, and as a consequence a lack of socialisation in general. Take the impact of working electronically, for example. This can lead to a decline in the experience of dealing with colleagues face-to-face on a daily basis. As a result, workers are less able to communicate effectively with their fellow workers, their managers, and, if applicable, the public. From the automation perspective, many business processes such as dealing with the public have increased the distance between people generally, and have further led to decline in overall socialisation.

The above factors have a direct impact both on the employees and businesses and the public. From the perspective of the employee, the effect can be both psychological and financial. A bank worker may, for instance, become dissatisfied with their work and their efficiency may decline. This, in turn, can lead to a lack of promotion or bonuses, leading to further dissatisfaction. From employers' perspective, such as situation is not healthy as it can affect profits and ultimately the viability of the organisation. The consequences are also felt by the general public who are then faced with a reduction if the quality of service.

As we have seen, there are various reasons behind the lack of soft skills like communication and team working among modern employees, which can have a huge impact on people in the workplace, companies and the general public.

*Word count: 283 words*

COMMENT

The response satisfies all part of the task. It has two body paragraphs of similar lengths dealing first with causes, and then effects. The paragraphs are well balance with the third paragraph analyzing the impact from three perspectives: the employee, the employer and the general public. Note the use language relating to cause and effect throughout.

## Extension

Students can be encouraged to make a class list of the rubrics for Writing Task 2, e.g., *Discuss both these views and give your own opinion*, which can be used for revision purposes during the course.

# 10  Is it art?

Photocopiable activity: Pairwork – Matching paragraphs and headings page 137
Workbook pages 76–83

## Content overview

This unit focuses on the arts, graffiti, describing a work of art, and involvement in the arts.

### Listening SECTION 2

Radio interview about an art exhibition

Question types: Selecting items from a list; Multiple-choice; Sentence completion

### Reading

Fern Garden – an art installation

Question types: Summary completion; Labelling a diagram

### Writing TASK 2

Discussing an opinion about a statement

### Speaking PARTS 2 AND 3

Part 3 Discussing the arts

Part 2 Describing an art form

**Vocabulary:** Art

**Language focus:** Defining and non-defining relative clauses

## Digital overview

### Presentation Kit

Interactive versions of Student's Book exam tasks

Embedded audio and answer key for all activities

### Teacher's Resource Centre

Communicative activity: Pairwork – Matching paragraphs and headings

Workbook audio, answer key and wordlists

### Student's Resource Centre

Class audio

Wordlist

Speaking Part 3 videos (4) and video worksheet

Speaking Part 2 video and video worksheet

## Vocabulary: Art  page 140

### Lead-in

Ask students what they think the question means. Elicit whether they think it demands just a yes/no answer or whether it questions legitimacy of some art forms. Ask for, or point out, examples. Students by now should be starting to question whatever they encounter. This is an essential strategy - see IELTS strategies page 203.

**1–2** Students can do these exercises together or in smaller groups. Encourage them to give their opinions/position/stance on the art forms. They should evaluate them using the array of strategies they have encountered thus far, e.g., adjectives such as *important*, *beautiful*, and modals. During whole-class feedback, elicit comments and evaluations.

> **ANSWERS**
> **1** Music   **2** Sculpture   **3** Dance
> **4** Theatre   **5** Painting

**3** Working in the same groups, students do the exercise. Go through the example and elicit more examples or encourage students to add more if possible during their discussion. During whole-class feedback, write the types of art forms, vertically as per the exercise or across the top of the board, and elicit words to write associated with each one. Add any you think they have missed. Ask the students about any local or national art forms that are not mentioned here. For example, is the word *symphony* familiar to them? What different forms of dance are there?

> **POSSIBLE ANSWERS**
> **1** play: actor, actress, lead (role), playwright, director, producer, costume designer, set designer
> **2** exhibition: visitor, exhibitor, designer, artist, sculptor, painter
> **3** musical: singer, actor/actress, writer, song-writer, producer, conductor, musician, pianist, violinist, percussionist
> **4** book: novelist, writer, illustrator, author, reader, editor
> **5** sculpture: sculptor, artist
> **6** video game: designer, writer, illustrator, artist, software programmer, producer, engineer
> **7** film: actor/actress, director, star, producer, distributor, scriptwriter, fan

### Extension

You could extend this into a brief discussion about outside influences or local/national influences at an international level.

Students can also take any word from the lists they have generated and make a list of words they associate with it. The association does not have to be restricted to nouns; it can also extend to evaluations, including emotional/personal associations. Elicit from students the importance of this skill in prediction, and in activating schemata in reading, listening and in developing speaking and writing. See the Listening and Reading sections below.

**4–5** Students do these exercises in pairs, checking their answers with another before whole-class feedback. For brief further practice, to show students how much they know, select some of the nouns from exercise 4 and ask students to give other verbs they can link with the nouns. Then do the same for a selection of the verbs. At this point in the course, these may come thick and fast.

ANSWERS
**4**
1 artist/draw (an artist draws pictures/images)
direct/play (a director directs plays)
design/clothes (a fashion/clothes designer designs clothes)
video game/programmer (a software programmer creates video games.)
2 drama/plot,
drama/writer,
novel/plot,
novel/writer (a writer writes novels and dramas. Novels and dramas have plots)
musical/sing (singers sing in musicals) ballet/perform (a dancer performs in a ballet)
3 construct/art installation (an art installation needs to be constructed)
soap opera/act (actors act in a soap opera.)
compose/symphony (a composer composes symphonies)

**5**
1 exhibition   2 sculptures   3 criticism
4 collection   5 critics   6 scenery
7 visual

**6** Students work in pairs. Give them a time limit, depending on the level of your students. This exercise can be expanded into a group discussion, with students combining with another pair after a fixed time. Elicit whole-class feedback with evaluation and justification. Give students a fixed time for this stage. Tell them they can move on when the time is up.

**7** Ask students to do the exercise on their own, followed by pair checking and then whole-class feedback. Set a time limit for the exercise and extend if necessary, but let students know that the time is up and that you are extending the time. Indicate when you think students should have moved on and should be checking their answers in pairs.

ANSWERS
1 drama, scenery, produces, play, highbrow
2 modern, appreciate, critical
3 works, Abstract, exhibitions, classical

**Extension**
You might want to have a discussion about new forms of art, e.g., video games, graphic design, video art, etc. Limit the items to seven words/phrases on the board and write them as students mention them. Then quickly elicit words that they used connected with the words on the board. Ask students if they need to write down all the words here. Elicit and/or point out how the initial seven words/phrases summarise the discussion. Remind students of summarising in IELTS strategies on page 204. Elicit where they do this in IELTS, i.e. in Speaking Part 3 specifically and also mentally before they answer spoken or written questions. Point out that nouns can act as prompts for students to attach their ideas to or hooks to hang them from.

**Round up**
Encourage students to add words from the section to their (electronic) vocabulary lists..

**Speaking** PART 3  page 142

**1** Students do the exercise in groups, followed by whole-class feedback. Elicit the importance of the *Don't forget!* box.

ANSWERS
1 What are the advantages of making some form of the arts compulsory at secondary school?
2 How do you think institutions involved in the arts such as museums and art schools should be funded? Should it be from public funds or private donations?
3 In what ways, do you think an interest in the arts can be used to help to improve the lives of all people in society? Give reasons and examples.

**2** Allocate a question to each group of three students or let them choose their own groups ensuring you have a spread of questions across the class. Avoid giving help with ideas of questions and vocabulary at this stage. After students have shared ideas, briefly summarise as a whole class, eliciting or adding ideas. Encourage the use of items from the vocabulary section and of evaluation. Remind students of the use of cause and effect chains as they develop ideas, adding a few phrases as reminders, e.g., *which, in turn, ... result in/from.*

**3** Either keep students in the same groups or ask them to regroup. Remind students of the checklist and encourage them to choose what they would like feedback on. Monitor students as they discuss and elicit/give feedback on examples of good practice. Also elicit/give some suggestions for improvement.

## Extension

Set one of the questions from exercise 2 as a writing exercise/test in class or for homework at a later date.

## Reading Passage  page 143

1 Ask students to work in groups and discuss the statement. Set a time limit, but allow them to continue for longer if the discussion is going well. Ask groups to volunteer a member to give feedback to the whole class. Make sure you give enough time for each group to have a chance to give feedback.

2 Let students stay in the same groups and decide on the answers. If they do not know an answer, tell them to ask other students.

**ANSWERS**

1 d  2 e  3 i  4 h  5 a  6 g  7 c  8 b
9 f  10 j

3 Students work in the same groups, scanning for the words from exercise 2. When you have checked the answers, ask the students what they can tell you about the text and list the information on the board. They will probably be very surprised by how much they have picked up, even when they have not been focusing on the content. Use this to reassure the students about not having to read every word and as evidence for the effectiveness of skimming and scanning.

## Questions 1–13

Ask students to look at the questions for the Reading Passage and at the picture. Set a strict time limit of 20 minutes. Give the students a five-minute warning after 15 minutes and ask them to note which question they are doing but to continue for a few more minutes. Remind students to write their answers on a sheet of paper or on an answer sheet. Ask them to check their answers in pairs, paying attention to spelling in Questions 10–13. Remind the students that the answers they choose for the summary need to reflect the meaning in the text and not just fit grammatically. Elicit whether they think the summary covers part or the whole of the passage and why.

Watch the students while they are reading and give feedback on technique: reading rather than skimming/scanning; underlining too much; spending too much time on one question; not leaving a question and coming back to it at the end. You may want to focus on one or more of these areas.

To help students navigate the diagram, ask students to read the notes thinking of the types of words that are needed. Ask them to predict the types of words and complete the blank spaces with possible answers. Tell them that you do not expect them to predict the exact answers but something general, a synonym, a paraphrase that they can

then search for. Point out that this is part of the prediction process.

**ANSWERS**

1 O  2 D  3 Q  4 B  5 I  6 P  7 J  8 C  9 H
10 vortex patterns      11 gentle ramp
12 ledge      13 jets

4 Students discuss the questions in small groups followed by whole-class feedback.

## Extension

As a pre-reading exercise, you can give students a selection of words and phrases, 7–10 items, from a text or just the first two or three paragraphs of a reading text. Ask students to think of what picture/schemata the items produce. For example, for the first paragraph of the Reading Passage on page 143 you can give them: *art, commission, work, sculpture, garden, instead, site, public, courtyard.* Students can then read the paragraph, checking their schema and whether it helped them to read the paragraph more efficiently. As a further extension, you can ask students what words they associate with the items or give them words to match to the items: *gallery, consider, garden, building, concrete walls, window wall.* After this they can read the paragraph. After any tasks like this, discuss how they can prepare themselves for reading and how they naturally predict in their own languages when reading, as well as in discussions, e.g., *I knew you were going to say that* … and in other everyday situations.

## Language focus: Defining and non-defining relative clauses  page 145

Go over the grammar points carefully and refer the students to the Grammar reference on page 224 for further explanation. These clauses are essential for students so they add additional information by way of context and development, e.g., *non-defining relative clauses and defining relative clauses.* Students often use longer, simpler grammatical expressions for additional information to avoid using defining and non-defining clauses. Such clauses also have an effect on students' ability to use and recognise complex sentences in all four main skills.

While discussing the sentences in this section, indicate how much more interesting for the reader/speaker/listener they are, because relative clauses can be used to add information and aid fluency. When monitoring students' spoken practice or marking their written work, point out any places where they missed the chance to use them.

## Extension

In a multi-lingual class, it is worth asking students to compare the use of relative pronouns, or the lack of them in English and other languages they know.

This not only highlights why issues may arise, but also develops tolerance and patience in the classroom.

Ask students to explain how relative clauses are translated into their own languages. Write a sentence with a defining clause on the board and then write a literal translation underneath. If you have a multi-lingual class, write several examples. This can lead to a lively discussion and make students aware of the languages of their peers. In addition, it can give you insight into the mistakes the students make and why they make them. This type of activity can also be used for other grammar areas.

**1–2** Go though the explanation in 1 and ask students to find the examples in the text, followed by a brief look at the Grammar reference, if necessary.

> **ANSWERS**
>
> Paragraph 4: *Pebbles of the required size were sorted from a stockpile and laid into a base of dry mortar* <u>*which was watered to make the cement set.*</u>
> Paragraph 7: *The main path is decorated in vortex patterns much like the movement of the eddying stream* <u>*from which the pebbles originated.*</u>

**3** Students do the exercise in groups. If necessary, go through the first pair of sentences with the whole class as an example. Follow this with whole-class feedback eliciting students' justification for their answers.

> **ANSWERS**
>
> **1** a: … *which the playwright wrote when he was young* … Adds additional information about the play related to when it was written.
> b: … *that he wrote at the age of 21* … A defining clause needed to identify which particular play won the award.
> **2** a: … *which is taken from Beethoven's 9th symphony* … Additional information not necessary for identification.
> b: … *that I heard on the car radio yesterday* … A defining clause needed to identify which pop song.
> **3** a: … *that I would like to talk about* … A defining clause is needed to identify the artist.
> b: … *who is still alive* … Additional information about the artist.
> **4** a: … *I go to regularly* … A defining clause is needed to distinguish between museums.
> b: … *which often have interactive displays* … Extra information given about modern museums which is not needed.
> **5** a: … *that need to be taught at school* … A defining clause is needed to point out which arts subjects need to be taught.
> b: … *which include painting and drama* … Additional information which is not necessary for identification purposes.

**4** Go through the rubric with the students highlighting the fact that they are leaving out the relative pronoun where appropriate. It is essential

that students are aware of this, because sometimes they overgeneralise and leave all of the relative pronouns out.

> **ANSWERS**
>
> **1** no pronoun necessary, that/which are possible
> **2** whose
> **3** which
> **4** which
> **5** no pronoun necessary, that/which are possible
> **6** who
> **7** that/which
> **8** no pronoun necessary, that/which are possible

**5** Students do this individually and check in pairs. Ensure the punctuation is correct here when you go over this. An awareness of correct punctuation is essential in writing.

> **ANSWERS**
>
> **1** ,c, **2** ,d, **3** ,b, **4** ,f, **5** g **6** ,c, **7** ,e,

**6** 🗨 Ask students to do this in pairs. Monitor the class carefully for correct usage. Share good examples with the whole class. Tell them you'll be looking for use of relative clauses in their writing and speaking practice. When you set an essay in future, you may want to insist that it contains at least one defining or non-defining relative clause as a way to show they are able to write complex sentences, but also point out that they should not overuse them.

## Round up

Elicit the importance of using relative clauses in writing and speaking and in noticing and recognising them in reading and listening.

## Listening SECTION 2 page 146

**1** 🗨 Elicit vocabulary concerning art exhibitions, especially regarding the types of exhibits. Ask students to discuss in groups. Note that the question concerns the 'kind' of opinions people in general might have, not just the opinions of the students themselves. Point out that they are looking at the opinions in the abstract.

**2** Ask students to scan the questions and underline words that will help them identify the answer as they listen.

> **ANSWERS**
>
> proposals: suggestions, recommendations
> aims: objectives, purposes

**3** Students can do this in the same groups and then check their answers with the whole class. For Questions 18–20, point out that, as a general rule for completion, they should also look at the information after the gaps.

ANSWERS

15 public
16 website survey
17 Jenny Driver, art world, concerned
18 radio show
19 outside broadcasts
20 second reporter

## Questions 11–20

**4** Play the listening test. By this stage you should be playing the recording once only. Ask students to check their answers in pairs, and then check the answers with the whole class. Ask the students to listen to the test again in their own time. Only play parts of the test now for clarification. Answer any questions that come up about vocabulary.

ANSWERS

**11–12** IN EITHER ORDER: B, D
**13–14** IN EITHER ORDER: A, E
**15** A
**16** A
**17** B
**18** the street
**19** public reaction
**20** department store

**5**  Ask students to discuss the questions in pairs/groups, followed by whole-class feedback. You might want, for a change, to have whole-class discussion instead of the pair/groupwork.

---

### 🎧 Listening script 15

**(P = Presenter; D = Director)**

**P:** Welcome on this lazy Saturday morning to Radio Hope. This is Charlie Carter, your host on your favourite show, *Your Chance* … and we have a lot for you this week.
I've got Jenny Driver the Director of the Horn Art Gallery in George Street and we'll be talking about developments on the art scene this week.

**D:** Thank you Charlie. Well, first, there's the new Public Art Project throughout the city, which opened last weekend in conjunction with the Horn Gallery and which has caused a sensation judging by the response on Twitter. And then we have a debate about charging for entrance to museums and art galleries. But first to the Public Art Project.
There has been some criticism that the public art on display is a waste of public money, but also many people have suggested the sculptures on display could be made permanent, which could encourage more people to visit the city and its museums and art galleries. Gallery attendance has definitely been on the increase since the public art sculptures were installed. The idea of a

permanent public display is a very good one. But some people have also emailed in suggesting that instead of having only international artists, the gallery could use the exhibition as an opportunity to support local sculptors who get no help from the public funds, which is a valid suggestion.

**P:** Do you think the Project will achieve its objectives?

**D:** Well, I think so. The Public Art Project had two broad objectives, which were to raise public awareness about art, especially sculpture, which I think has been achieved with the increase in museum attendances. And, secondly, through tourism in the area, we wanted to make people more aware of the city nationally and internationally. Both are difficult to gauge in the long term, but for the moment the number of people visiting the city seems to point to success.

**P:** What do you think about the idea of making all museums and art galleries free of charge?

**D:** There has been a fierce debate about this over the past year or so, because people are deterred from visiting places of a cultural nature, like the Horn Gallery, because of the cost. And while children are able to get in free, they rarely come with their parents, which is a bad thing. So, basically, I am for the change. From the survey we've had on our website, I think about 75 per cent said they were for entrance being free, only ten per cent were very definitely against and 20 per cent said they didn't know.

**P:** Have you any concerns about the removal of charges?

**D:** There is one thing I and other people working in the gallery world are worried about, and that is the level of government funding. We've always had subsidies from the government to run the galleries, but this has always been topped up by entrance fees. We're waiting to see if this will be reflected in the government's arts funding for next year.

· · · · · · · · · · · · · · · · · · · · · · · · · · · · · · · · · · · · · · · · · · · ·

**P:** Now, as you all know, we've been wanting to do some outside broadcasting on the show for a long time, and this week for the first time we will have two reporters on the street … because we think this is an important issue, … mmm and we want to gauge mmm … public reaction to the museum charge debate. We have one reporter, Angie Hunter, standing by outside the Horn Gallery. And we'll see what people really think about their art galleries being free or not. To make sure we get as wide a spectrum of people as possible, we have another reporter, Alex Grey, who's standing in front of the department store in the pedestrian shopping precinct. So, if you're listening and want to make your views known, pop down to the precinct or the gallery. We'll be starting the outside broadcast in 15 minutes at 12.45, after we have got through the other items today, so …

## Speaking PART 2 page 147

**1** Ask students to do the exercise in pairs and check as a whole class. Ask for a volunteer to read the extract.

> **ANSWERS**
>
> Defining clause: *The art form I'm going to describe is …* (to identify which art form)
> Non-defining clause: *… part of the performing arts, … dancing, which to me is exciting and inspiring …* (to give additional information)
> Non-defining clause: *… a dance show, which was very noisy and energetic …* (to give additional information)

**2** Students can do this in pairs or groups, adding their own ideas if necessary. During feedback, elicit justification for their choices.

**3–4** Go through the examples with students and, after the discussion in pairs, discuss their answers.

> **ANSWERS**
>
> *which, in turn, can improve your chances of finding a good job*: effect of what went before and cause of what comes next *and hence of earning a living*: effect

**5** Students repeat the procedure in exercises 3 and 4. Discuss their answers.

**6** 👥 Students follow the procedure as before for Part 2, using the checklist for feedback. Remind them to use relative clauses where possible.

## Writing TASK 2 page 148

**1** Students do the exercise in groups. Give them a time limit and make them responsible for their own time management. Monitor the discussion to help them focus. After discussing students' answers, briefly discuss time management again.

Remind students, as they discuss, to recycle some of the vocabulary they used in the previous unit on the feelings architecture induces and in other units, e.g., cause and effect, *-ing* and *-ed* adjectives. Write some of their ideas on the board under 'positive' and 'negative' headings.

> **ANSWER**
>
> The statement describes a trend and compares a situation in the past with a present situation. In the present, the focus in education at all levels is more on science and business studies compared to the arts, i.e. the former is becoming more important.
> The question asks students to give their opinion as to whether this is a positive or negative development. Students can say it is positive or negative or a mixture of both.

**2** This exercise can be done as a whole-class exercise, as a revision or as a focusing exercise.

> **ANSWERS**
>
> No, because the statement in the task is a development not an evaluation or view/position/ stance/opinion. If the statement said *'Some people think that nowadays there is too much focus at all levels in education on science and business studies rather than the arts'*, then it would be possible to replace the question with *'To what extent do you agree or disagree?'*

**3** Students can do this in pairs or in groups, followed by whole-class feedback.

> **ANSWERS**
>
> negative

**4–5** Students do both exercises in pairs. Give them sufficient time to complete the exercises and take time to go over their responses.

> **ANSWERS**
>
> **4**
> 1 an introduction saying that it is a positive development; a second paragraph discussing why it is a negative development and supporting an (equal/greater) emphasis on sciences and business studies; two paragraphs showing the positive side of the sciences and business studies; a conclusion.
> 2 an introduction saying that the development has positive and negative aspects; a second paragraph discussing why it is a development, (with positive perhaps being stronger than negative or vice versa); a third paragraph discussing why it is a negative development; a fourth paragraph saying it is both positive and negative and why; a conclusion.
> **5** The introduction contains a hook in the first sentence, which states the importance of the two main areas (science and business studies and the arts) for society, i.e. both are positive for society. The second sentence then states that the current focus on science and business studies is a negative development. In the first topic sentence, the writer acknowledges the value of science and business studies. In the second topic sentence, the writer contrasts this with the importance of the arts for society. In the third topic sentence, the writer gives another reason why the arts are important.

**6** Ask students to do this in groups, and check their answers with another group before whole-class feedback.

> **POSSIBLE ANSWER**
>
> Introduction: Science and business studies and the arts are all important for progress in society in general. However, I think the current emphasis in education on science and business studies is a positive trend.
> First topic sentence: There is no doubt that the arts are invaluable in today's world.

Second topic sentence: Science and business studies, however, play a key role in the development of society.
Third topic sentence: Another reason is that training in science and business studies can open up many career opportunities for young people.
Conclusion: As we have seen, the present focus in education on science and business studies is a positive development.

**7** Ask students to complete the gaps individually and then check their answers in pairs. Go over the answers with the whole class.

ANSWERS

**1** arts **2** field **3** trend **4** participation **5** Take **6** physical **7** coordination (concentration may also be possible) **8** Likewise **9** exhibition **10** gallery

**8** This exercise can be done as a whole class quick-fire exercise. Elicit explanations for each item 1–5.

ANSWERS

**1** *However, I think the current emphasis in the field of education on science and business studies is a positive trend.*
**2** *Drama, which requires lots of activity, is obviously good for physical and mental health …*
*…coordination, which is a skill that is missing in education today.*
**3** No examples
**4** *… the purpose of involvement in the arts is to help them relax …*
**5** *Take drama, for example.*

**9** Ask students to write their responses in class or for homework. Encourage them to (or insist that they) write at least one relative clause. Tell them to use the checklist on page 139. Advise students to look at the model answer *only after* they have written their own answer. Ask students to go through the model working out how it complies with the requirements of the task. They can use the Comments as a starting point.

*Model answer*

The advances in technology are being keenly felt in modern art in fields like design, painting and film. Such a trend I think is beneficial for those studying and working in these areas, as well as the public.

The main criticism levelled at the use of technology in the areas above is that it is de-skilling workers. With computer painting and design, including on tablets, students in the above areas are losing basics skills in producing objects by hand. Likewise, children are losing the ability even to hold implements like pens and brushes, to coordinate their actions, to plan and to think through the basic processes for producing something. The same applies to workers in these areas.

This is a valid criticism, but the benefits derived from the increasing use of technology in the areas above are huge. Computer software, such as 3D printing, supplements the skills of the students and workers in design, paint and films. The technology does not replace people, but is an additional tool like any other.

Another reason why the effect technology is having on the fields above should be seen in a positive light is that these areas have through the ages adapted to the available technology to improve their work for the benefit of society. The latest technology now allows efficient car design and mechanics, as in hybrid cars. Artists and film makers can use computers to create more entertaining interactive art works and films with computer-generated imagery for the public's benefit.

As we have seen, while there may be some downsides to the increasing role of technology in modern art such as design, painting and film, its increasing influence is a positive development.

*Word count: 281 words*

COMMENT

The answer is clearly presented in five paragraphs with an introduction setting out the writer's position. The first body paragraph looks at the negative impact of technology' in the modern art fields mentioned, while the other two support the writer's position on the value of its use. The conclusion brings everything together and reflects the introduction and task.

**Round up**

Review or ask students to review/reflect on the Writing Task 2 type covered here and compare it with other Writing Task 2 rubrics, especially the rubric featured in exercise 2.

## REVIEW 10 ANSWERS pages 150–151

## Vocabulary: Art

**1**

1 Actors and actresses act in plays or films. Sometimes some of them become famous because they star in soap **operas**.
2 He **wrote** the symphony and conducted the orchestra at the performance.
3 She has written many fantasy novels but people still do not think that she is a great **author**, but there are many children and adults who would disagree.
4 As a playwright, he wrote many **plays** and even directed some of his works in well-known theatres, appearing from time to time on the stage himself.
5 Is a newspaper journalist an **artist**? Many would like to think they have artistic qualities.
6 He was a great **sculptor** and painter, having carved many famous statues and painted many of the world's greatest paintings.
7 The producer got on well with the actors and **actresses** in the film, but he didn't always like the way the director directed it.
8 The choreographer arranged the ballet very carefully, but some of the **dancers** found it very difficult to perform.

**2**

1 drama, stages, scenery, Drama, produce, plays, highbrow
2 abstract, classical, illusions, art
3 appreciate, favourable

## Language focus: Defining and non-defining relative clauses

**1**

1 that has influenced me the most
2 (that) I want to talk about
3 that is free for all schoolchildren.
4 I admire the most is Frida Kahlo
5 that is close to my flat.
6 the café you usually go to
7 that was announced last night on TV.
8 that you know very well

**2**

2, 3

### ACCURACY IN IELTS

| | | | | | |
|---|---|---|---|---|---|
| 1 | children | 2 | art | 3 | art |
| 4 | Correct | 5 | people | 6 | art |
| 7 | schoolchildren | | | | |

# 11 The family and society

Photocopiable activity: Whole class – Commonly confused letters/numbers bingo page 138
Workbook pages 84–91

## Content overview

This unit focuses on family and society.

**Listening** SECTION 1

Registering to be a host family

Question types: Note completion

**Reading**

Growing up in an African village

Question types: Sentence completion; Matching information to paragraphs; Selecting items from a list

**Writing** TASK 2

Agreeing or disagreeing with a statement; Discussing views, causes, solutions

**Speaking** PART 2

Describing a friendship, relationship, period of your life, membership

**Vocabulary:** The family

**Word building:** Suffixes -*hood* and -*ship*

**Language focus:** Conditionals 2

## Digital overview

**Presentation Kit**

Interactive versions of Student's Book exam tasks

Embedded audio and answer key for all activities

**Teacher's Resource Centre**

Communicative activity: Whole class – Commonly confused letters/numbers bingo

Workbook audio, answer key and wordlists

**Student's Resource Centre**

Class audio

Wordlist

Speaking Part 2 video and video worksheet

## Vocabulary: The family  page 152

### Lead-in

Ask students what they think the title of the unit relates to. Elicit information about family relationships in their countries, and what (if anything) has changed in recent years. Ask them about family sizes, and the concept of nuclear and extended families.

**1** 🗣 Ask students to describe the photographs in groups, and to relate them to their own local or national background, if possible.

> ANSWERS
> 1 village community
> 2 nuclear family
> 3 large extended family
> 4 grandparent and grandchild

**2** Ask students to do this in pairs or in the same groups as in exercise 1. Elicit any words relating to family relationships that students might know, e.g., *son*, *daughter*, *aunt*, *uncle*, etc. You might also like to explain first the difference between *home*, relating to place, and *household*, relating to the people in that place.

> ANSWERS
> 1 parents                2 grandparents
> 3 siblings               4 family tree
> 5 widow: someone whose husband has died;
>    widower: someone whose wife has died
> 6 relatives              7 ancestor
> 8 niece/nephew           9 family
> 10 household

**3** Ask the students to do the exercise in pairs, and to check their answers with another pair before whole-class feedback. If you think your students need consolidation, ask them to write out the complete sentences.

> ANSWERS
> 1 b  2 e  3 f  4 a  5 c  6 d  7 g

**4** 🗣 This exercise is an extension of exercise 3 and the lead-in discussion incorporating the new vocabulary. Monitor the pairwork discussion. Give examples of good practice during feedback as well as examples of common errors. Elicit a selection of examples of sentences and/or questions and answers from selected students.

## Reading Passage  page 153

**1** Students do the prediction activity in pairs and discuss their ideas.

**2** Ask them to underline the key words in each paragraph individually and follow up with whole-class feedback. You may have time to do only two or three paragraphs. The aim is to get students to engage with the text without looking just at answering questions

POSSIBLE ANSWERS

Paragraph A: African village, bring up, socialise, child, community, relatives, kinship, familial and kinship relations, network of relatives, upbringing

Paragraph B: adolescence, society, initiation ceremonies, mark the transition from childhood, adulthood, conduct and behaviour, duties and responsibilities, interests of the entire community.

Paragraph C: Kinship and family, individual interests, Young people, process, initiation from childhood to adulthood, the society, good and bad times, bond, members, same age-grade, taught the historical information, cultural group, rituals, marry

Paragraph D: Seniority, age, respected and admired, wisdom, respect, counsel, crisis, certain responsibilities, elder, unemotional, arbiter, above partisan differences, synonymous with honour (etc) manifest these qualities in old age, elevated status in society.

Paragraph E: good care of senior citizens, good example, respect, good treatment in old age, procreation, somebody, old age, Children brought up well, asset, children see that their grandparents are treated well, learn by example

Paragraph F: elder is the pillar, nuclear, extended family, link between the living and ancestors, unite the family, reinforces kinship ideology, helps to socialise, provide guidance, pass the baton, all members of the society take socialisation seriously

## Questions 1–14

Briefly review the strategies for sentence completion, matching information/phrases to paragraphs, and selecting ideas. Give students 20 minutes to complete the questions. Make sure they write their answers on a piece of paper or an answer sheet. Remind them to be careful about spelling and to put the answers against the correct number.

Students discuss their answers in groups. Ask them to justify all their answers. Elicit the answers and feedback from the whole class.

ANSWERS

1 Western society
2 interests
3 societal values
4 responsibilities
5 candid, sincere
6 C
7 E
8 A
9 E
10–14 IN ANY ORDER: A, C, E, F, G

**3** Put students into groups and ask them to choose someone to write down ideas and someone to report back. Discuss as a whole class. As a follow-up, you might like to ask students to write an answer to the second set of questions in this exercise.

### Extension

Select a text that is on a similar theme to the Reading Passage in the unit and add letters (e.g., A, B, etc.) to the paragraphs. Set a time limit for the task. Ask students to work in groups and on a sheet of paper write between three and five phrases, not sentences, paraphrasing specific, or chunks of, information from the paragraphs. Leave it up to the students as to what information they select to paraphrase. Monitor the phrases for accuracy. Students write a *key* on the back of the sheet. Students then give their phrases to another group who have to find the information.

Elicit from students what type of information they chose and why, and whether groups chose the same or different information to paraphrase. Keep a copy of the students' phrases with the text for future reference. This task applies to all question types. Limit the number of items you want students to write to the time available.

## Word building: Suffixes -*hood* and -*ship* page 155

### Lead-in

Remind students that in IELTS they need to be able to understand, write and talk about abstract concepts or ideas. Elicit examples of such concepts from the Reading Passage. Ask them to look again at exercise 2 in the pre-reading, if necessary.

Go through the examples of the suffixes, explaining that they are used to make abstract nouns to express a concept, a state of being or a quality rather than an object.

Write the five categories on the board, and ask students to add words of their own.

**1** Ask the students to do the exercise in pairs, checking with another pair, before whole-class feedback.

ANSWERS

State: kinship
Period of time: childhood, adulthood

**2** Students do this in the same pairs. You can write the nouns on the board as per the categories in the lead-in. Remind students to record the words in their (electronic) vocabulary lists.

ANSWERS

1 relationship
2 childhood
3 neighbourhood
4 Parenthood

| 5 | membership | 6 | adulthood |
| 7 | partnership | 8 | apprenticeship |
| 9 | sponsorship | 10 | Leadership |

**3** Students do the exercise in pairs, followed by whole-class feedback.

**ANSWERS**

| 1 | hardship | 2 | nationhood |
| 3 | leadership qualities | 4 | childhood |
| 5 | Parenthood | 6 | sponsorship scheme |
| 7 | relationships | | |

**4** Elicit what *collocate* means. Students do the exercise in pairs, followed by whole-class feedback.

**ANSWERS**

1 cultivated, relationship
2 withdrew, sponsorship
3 facing, hardship
4 spent, childhood
5 nationhood, reached
6 showed, leadership
7 prepare, parenthood

### Extension

Time permitting, you can ask students to work in groups and choose one or two of the nouns with the suffix *–hood* or *–ship*. Ask them to research examples of words that collocate with the words and find or create example sentences. If permissible, allow students to use their mobiles to search the internet or use dictionaries, the Macmillan Dictionary or the Macmillan Collocations Dictionary. Students can present their words to the class electronically or on large sheets of paper. The task can also be done at home with students collaborating outside the class and the presentation delivered the following day. Allow time for each group to present and set a time limit for the presentation.

**5** This exercise is done in pairs, but you could also let students work in groups. During feedback, elicit examples of good practice from students, if possible, as well as giving your own.

## Speaking PART 2 page 157

**1** Ask students to read the topics on the Task Cards on their own and choose the one that relates to the text, followed by whole-class feedback.

**ANSWERS**

Task Card C

**2–3** Ask students to do the exercises in pairs. They then check with other pairs, followed by whole-class feedback after each exercise or when both have been completed.

**ANSWERS**

**2**
Describe a friendship that is/was important to you:
*I'm going to talk about a friendship that I had when I was in my early years of secondary school.*

who the friendship is/was with:
*It was with my best friend at the time, Jane, …*

when you first met your friend:
*… whom I met when I first went to secondary school.*

what you and your friend do/did together:
*We were in the same class throughout our secondary school years, and we would sit next to each other in most classes, play the same games together – we were just like sisters …*

and explain why this friendship is/was important to you:
*The friendship was very important to both of us … firstly, because we gave each other support at a time when we were both nervous about being in a new place. And secondly, where we grew up we both had a happy childhood, but neither of us had any siblings, so it was nice to have the companionship of someone at school … And I suppose I felt that I was leaving childhood behind, and it was, in fact, the first friendship of my adolescence.*

**3**
Possible answers
friendship, secondary, same class/games, support, companionship, first friendship, adolescence, still friends

**4** Students do the exercise with a partner and then form a group with another pair for a full discussion. Ask them also to consider the amount of time devoted to each prompt and discuss.

### Further practice

As an awareness exercise, ask students to work in pairs/groups and gauge how long they think the response in the extract is in exercise 1. Ask them to time each other reading part of the extract, say 20/30 words and then work out how long the whole extract might take. Ask them to discuss the different speed calculations as they speak at different speeds, with hesitations. Remind them that reading and speaking will lead to different calculations but this gives them a rough guide.

**5–6** Students do these process exercises in pairs. Point out the *Don't forget!* box. Remind them of the Vocabulary on families and Word building on *-hood/-ship*. Encourage them to manage their own time. Give feedback on the final prompt, eliciting and giving examples of good reasons. As a further step, you might want to write one or two examples on the board and elicit paraphrases.

### Further practice

You might want to ask one or two volunteers to talk about their selected topic in front of the class.

## Listening SECTION 1  page 158

### Lead-in

Elicit what students think is involved in being a host family for language students. Give hints by asking questions, if necessary.

**1** Ask students to do the exercise in pairs and compare their predictions to Questions 1–10.

**ANSWERS**

Registering to be a host family for international students

Go over the *Don't forget!* advice. This should be automatic for them by this stage in the course. Monitor those who may still not be doing this effectively.

### Questions 1–10

Play the listening through once. Give students a chance to transfer their answers to an answer sheet or a piece of paper. Rather than playing the test again, except for illustrating particular questions, encourage students to listen to the test in the library or at home if necessary.

Students can check their answers in pairs, paying particular attention to their spelling.

**ANSWERS**

| | |
|---|---|
| **1** informal/preliminary chat | **2** two references |
| **3** weeks | **4** September. |
| **5** 2/two | **6** neighbourhood |
| **7** Friday afternoon | **8** 53 |
| **9** 08977 392251 | **10** MAW973 |

**2**  Ask students to discuss the questions in pairs, groups or as a whole class.

### Listening script 16

**(A= administrator; P = parent)**

**A:** Accommodation Office, Tom speaking. How may I help you?

**P:** Yes, hi. My name's Margaret Williams.

**A:** Oh, hi.

**P:** Mmm … I understand that you're looking for host families for international students.

**A:** Yes, we're always looking for suitable families, as we have a lot of demand at the moment. How did you hear about us?

**P:** Mmm … from a friend, Mrs Dalton, who's already with your agency. We live in the same street as her in Maltby.

**A:** Ah yes … I know who you mean. You're quite close to several of our schools.

**P:** … and I just wanted to ask some questions about registering with you.

**A:** No problem.

**P:** OK. Can you tell me how we go about becoming a host family with you?

**A:** Well, once a family first approaches us, we like to make a preliminary visit to the home, have an <u>informal chat</u> and discuss all the registration details first.

**P:** That sounds great. Do we need to make an application at this stage?

**A:** No, we like to come and visit you first and provided we're then both happy after the <u>preliminary chat</u>, we usually begin the registration process there and then, and you can complete it and send it in by email.

**P:** What about references and things like that?

**A:** Mmm, if the application for registration is submitted and accepted, we need to do some background checks first of all, and we like to have at least <u>two references</u> from families or professional people. We'd only do these if you made a definite commitment to proceed.

**P:** OK.

**A:** We think it's better to check that a family's clear about what is involved in the whole process … then we can begin the application process.

**P:** How long does the process take?

**A:** It depends, but it's usually a few <u>weeks</u>, unless there are any delays. Once everything is agreed, we match students with suitable families at the beginning of a term and usually at the beginning of the academic year in <u>September</u>.

**P:** That all sounds reasonable.

**A:** Can I ask how many students you were thinking of hosting?

**P:** We thought that we would like to take <u>two</u> to start with. We have two daughters aged 14 and 15, so we'd like two students around a similar age … that would be ideal … it's easier then for them to strike up a friendship.

**A:** That shouldn't be a problem.

⋯⋯⋯⋯⋯⋯⋯⋯⋯⋯⋯⋯⋯⋯⋯⋯⋯

**A:** Obviously, we have to look at things like how far the host family home is from schools we cover, access to libraries, whether you have wi-fi, access to public transport and the <u>neighbourhood</u> in general.

**P:** OK. That sounds very reasonable. I think we'd like to proceed.

**A:** OK, that's good. We could actually do a preliminary visit at the end of this week, Thursday morning or Friday afternoon, or any time on Saturday, and have a more detailed chat and start the application process, if appropriate.

**P:** OK, we're both free on <u>Friday afternoon</u>.

**A:** That'd be fine. Can I have the number of your house?

**P:** It's <u>53</u>.

**A:** 53 and two more things … could I take a mobile number?

**P:** Yes, it's <u>08977 392251</u>.

**A:** … 392251.

**P:** Yes, that's right.
**A:** … and your email address is?
**P:** It's MAW973@maltby.co.uk.
**A:** OK, I'll email you the confirmation of the meeting, and shall we say 2 pm?
**P:** Yes, that'd be …

# Language focus: Conditionals 2

**page 159**

**1** Ask students to look at the examples and answer the questions. Refer them to the Grammar reference on page 225. You may also want to go through examples of the Conditionals 1 on page 223.

> **ANSWERS**
>
> Example 1: Second conditional: *We'd only do these …* (present); *… made …* (past).
> Example 2: Zero conditional: *… we're then both happy …* (present); *we usually begin* (present)
> In the second example, the following is also possible with no change of meaning: *… we will usually begin …*

**2** Students can do this in pairs or groups. Encourage them to underline the conditional marker in each case. During feedback, elicit explanations for both the correct paraphrases and those which do not work.

> **ANSWERS**
>
> **1** Paraphrase
> **2** I won't do the psychology option on the course if there aren't any free places.
> **3** There's a possibility there will be a change in society if the government addresses social issues like crime and poverty.
> **4** If future generations are even more highly trained than they are now, will their lives be better?
> **5** Unless/(If) people are (not) psychologically well adapted to …
> **6** Paraphrase
> **7** Paraphrase

## Extension

Ask students to work in groups. Give them 5–7 sentences similar to those in exercise 2, ensuring you have a range of sentences with and without conditionals. Make sure those without can be paraphrased using conditional sentences. Students then compare their paraphrases with other students/groups/the rest of the class, eliciting comments/feedback. Alternatively, you can ask students to write their own sentences, adapting those in exercise 2 for other students to paraphrase, or you can give them phrases to build into sentences for other groups to paraphrase, again with peer feedback as above. Keep examples of student output for future reference.

**3–4** Follow the instructions in the Student's Book and check as a whole class at the end of the exercises

> **ANSWERS**
>
> **3**
> **1** Unless
> **2** If only
> **3** Even if
> **4** Provided
> **5** If
> **6** Supposing
> **4**
> 2, 5

**5** Go through the example. Ask students to do the exercise in pairs and check as a whole class.

> **ANSWERS**
>
> **1** Families can play a part in making society a better place, provided the government gives them support.
> **2** If the government funded more community centres, this would provide a place for people to meet.
> **3** If globalisation hadn't occurred, there would now be fewer social and cultural problems around the world.
> **4** If it were not for volunteer workers helping people deal with the psychological aspect of change, the situation would have been worse.
> **5** Even though today trade between different countries is increasing, there are sometimes big differences between various business cultures.
> **6** Supposing social intelligence were taught in schools, would it be beneficial?

**6** 🔊 Write the following expressions on the board and encourage students to use them in their discussions:
*If I hadn't … , I'd …*
*If only I'd … , I'd …*
*If it weren't for … , I'd …*
*Provided I … , I'll …*
*Unless I … , I'll …*
Monitor the discussion for correct structure and usage, and give feedback.

## Round up

Elicit the function of the conditional in speaking and writing, e.g., explaining, developing ideas generally, arguing, persuading, hedging, etc. Remind students to think of the purpose of the conditional sentences rather than thinking of them just as grammatical constructs. Recap the different ways to paraphrase from/to conditional sentences, referring specifically to exercise 2. Elicit how frequently students use the conditional sentences in their speaking and writing, and encourage them to increase their use.

## Writing TASK 2 page 160

You can use this section as a review of Writing Task 2 for revision purposes.

**1** Ask students to do the exercise in groups, ensuring that all the tasks are covered. The groups then compare their lists with another group. During feedback, elicit explanations of the tasks as well as ideas, summarising the main points in a table on the board.

  The ideas could also be put onto A3-sized sheets, one for each group. When the groups have finished, they circulate the sheets, look at the other groups' ideas and add any of their own to the list.

> **POSSIBLE ANSWERS**
>
> **1** Agree: world smaller, some countries richer than others, have responsibility, unethical not to help
> Disagree: charity begins at home, responsibilities to local communities
> **2** Agree: gives people confidence/opportunity to interact with others
> Disagree: not the only way, social help, financial help, basic necessities, depends on situation and individual
> Other measures: government help with better housing, local facilities, better environment, better education/more interesting jobs, developing friendships
> **3** View 1: parents' responsibility, their children, early years with parents
> View 2: children spend time at school, parents at work need help, financial/social support needed, parenting skills, share the responsibility – 'three parties'

**2–3** Students do both exercises in groups, followed by whole-class feedback. Ask students to justify their answers.

> **ANSWERS**
>
> **a** 2
> Structure: introduction, a paragraph saying it is a good way, a paragraph saying why it is a good way, two paragraphs giving two or three other measures, a conclusion.
> **b** 3
> Structure: introduction, view 1, view 2, opinion, conclusion.
> **c** 1
> Structure: introduction, paragraph about concentrating resources on own citizens, two paragraphs about helping other people, conclusion.

### Further practice

Time permitting, elicit paraphrases/improvements of the conclusions, as well as comments, and write them on the board. Or dictate them to the whole class as the students construct them, asking

students to read what they have so far as you go along. Alternatively, just do one conclusion. Paraphrasing of all three is also a suitable homework activity for small classes.

**4** Ask students to do the exercise in pairs, comparing their answers with other students before whole-class feedback. Focus on the reason for matching, looking at clear links between the extracts and the tasks, not just the themes.

> **ANSWERS**
>
> Extract 1: The paragraph relates to helping other people.
> Extract 2: The paragraph relates to other ways for people to improve their social and psychological well-being.

**5–6** Students do the exercises in pairs.

> **ANSWERS**
>
> *For instance, people could volunteer just one day a week to help others …*
> *[So] this characteristic should be harnessed as it leads to the betterment of people's lives.*

**7** Students can do the task for homework, or in class. In both cases, stress the need for them to be strict about the 40-minute time limit. Tell them that as you mark their work, you will be looking for examples of the vocabulary and conditional sentences practised in the unit. Alternatively, you could do this writing task as a class test.

  Encourage students to look at the model answer *only after* they have written their own answer. Ask students to go through the model, working out how it complies with the requirements of the task. They can use the Comments as a starting point.

> *Model answer*
>
> A good community spirit can certainly be promoted by various means, including investment in local amenities such as leisure complexes. While I agree that this approach is worthwhile, it is not necessarily the best, as there are other equally important strategies.
>
> Local amenities like leisure complexes are important for bringing people of all ages together and for providing them with opportunities to mingle with friends and meet new people. As well as facilities, such centres can provide a wide range of activities like swimming clubs and yoga classes as well as art classes, which give people the chance to meet old and new friends and strengthen the local community spirit.
>
> Other amenities such as libraries that are open to the public can also play a role in developing a community. Other measures that are also useful are holding local festivals and fun days, not just in parks but in streets that are closed off to traffic for the day or weekend. In fact, any activity that involves local people coming

together, such as volunteering in the clean-up of local neighbourhoods or tidying up local spaces, is worthwhile.

Another important strategy is the design of local neighbourhoods. Unfortunately, the enormous pressure to increase accommodation for growing populations means that there is less space for houses with gardens. However, it is possible to provide well-maintained open spaces that attract local people along with venues to give them a chance to interact with each other, like local shops instead of large supermarkets, all of which can nurture a local identity and spirit.

In conclusion, investing in local amenities is one among many approaches that can contribute to the fostering of a good spirit within communities.

*Word count: 282*

**COMMENTS**

The response fulfils the task requirements. The introduction gives an evaluation of the opinion in the task. The second paragraph comments on the value of investment in leisure centres and the two other body paragraphs provide alternative approaches that are equally important.

**REVIEW 11 ANSWERS** pages 161–162

## Vocabulary: The family

1  tree
2  grandparents
3  grandfather
4  widower
5  ancestors
6  family
7  relative
8  household
9  siblings
10 relatives

## Word building: Suffixes *-hood* and *-ship*

1  He started his apprenticeship in electrical engineering last year.
2  He received sponsorship (money) to pursue his dreams of being an athlete.
3  When I had club membership, I met many new friends.
4  I remember my childhood with fondness.
5  Before adulthood (begins), people are generally much more carefree.
6  My father and my uncle had a business partnership when they were very young.
7  My neighbourhood is generally very quiet.

## Language focus: Conditionals 2

**1**
1 d  2 c  3 a  4 g  5 b  6 e  7 f

**2**
1  Even if the psychology course is expensive, I'll pay for it.
2  I will do the technology component of the course, unless it's in the morning.
3  People can contribute to society, provided the government gives them support.
4  If the government funded more crèches, it would enable more people to go to work.
5  Unless parents and schools both play a role in teaching good behaviour to children, they will not know right from wrong.
6  If it were not for private sponsorship of some university places, it would be harder for people to develop their careers.
7  If we want to ensure a healthy society, it is essential that socialisation of children takes place at home and school.
8  If there had not been heavy investment in social and technological development programmes, the world would not be in its present advanced state.

**ACCURACY IN IELTS**

Some people think that the sole responsibility for bringing up children lies with parents, while others **argue** that schools also have an important role to play in this respect. Personally, I feel that both parents and schools should share the responsibility for a child's upbringing.

If **we look** at the situation from the perspective of social skills, for example, it is clear that both parties should share the responsibility. Obviously, parents can teach children to form deep and meaningful relationships with friends and family at home. Schools could also **show** how to develop such relationships outside the home with their **peers**, while **at** the same time picking up knowledge and information. If we as adults had not been introduced to the social norms of society we would not know how to behave **ourselves** nor **would** we know how to pass on the skills essential to our children.

## Content overview

This unit focuses on travelling around the world, journeys and places of interest.

### Listening SECTION 2

Talk on St Petersburg as a holiday destination

Question types: Multiple-choice; Sentence completion

### Reading

The Great Barrier Reef

Question types: Summary completion; Identification of information in the text – *True/False/Not Given*; Short-answer questions

### Writing TASK 2

Developing ideas

### Speaking PARTS 1 AND 2

**Part 1** Discussing travel

**Part 2** Describing a journey

**Vocabulary:** Adjectives with multiple meanings

**Word building:** Words related to memory

**Language focus:** Articles

## Digital overview

**Presentation Kit**

Interactive versions of Student's Book exam tasks

Embedded audio and answer key for all activities

**Teacher's Resource Centre**

Progress Test 4

Communicative activity: Group game (groups of 3) – Visualisation

Workbook audio, answer key and wordlists

**Student's Resource Centre**

Speaking Part 1 videos (3) and video worksheet

Speaking Part 2 video and video worksheet

## Vocabulary: Adjectives with multiple meanings page 164

### Lead-in

Elicit from students predictions about the contents of the unit, using questions to give them hints if necessary: *Do you think it might …?* Then ask them to survey the whole unit to check their predictions.

**1** 👥 Students do this exercise in pairs, forming groups with other pairs to compare their answers, especially to the questions.

> **POSSIBLE ANSWERS**
>
> 1 pristine, unspoilt, beautiful
> 2 unique, alien, impressive
> 3 ancient, strange

**2** This exercise can be done as a whole-class activity, relating the concept of multiple meaning, or polysemy, to languages they know.

> **ANSWERS**
>
> It means 'original', 'new', or 'different'. It can also mean 'a work of fiction'.

**3** After going through the example, ask students to do this exercise in pairs, followed by whole class checking. Explain that because of the breadth of the English language many words have similar meanings, and compare this with other languages.

> **ANSWERS**
>
> | 1 apathetic | 2 native | 3 treasured |
> |---|---|---|
> | 4 local | 5 similar | 6 uncomfortable |
> | 7 odd | 8 extra | 9 treasured |

**4–5** Students work in pairs followed by checking with other students and then whole-class feedback. Allow students to check with more than one partner or in groups.

> **ANSWERS**
>
> **4**
>
> | 1 different | 2 strange | 3 unique |
> |---|---|---|
> | 4 curious | 5 foreign | 6 odd |
> | 7 new | 8 fresh | 9 alien |
>
> **5**
>
> | 1 difference | 2 strangeness |
> |---|---|
> | 3 uniqueness | 4 curiosity |
> | 5 foreignness | 6 oddity/oddness |
> | 7 newness | 8 freshness |
> | 9 alienation | |

**6** 👥 Students can do this exercise in pairs, but it also works as a group activity with other group members eliciting further information by asking questions. You can write the following expressions on the board and encourage students to use them:

*A _____ thing happened to me when I was …*
*What happened was …*
*It was really …*
*It changed my life.*
*I have never seen/experienced anything like it.*

## Round up

Give students words from the section and elicit their different meanings either in or out of context.

# Listening SECTION 2 page 166

## Lead-in

Ask students what places they would most like to visit in the world and why.

**1** Tell students to do the exercise in groups, followed by whole-class feedback.

## Questions 11–20

Ask students to look at all the Listening questions and underline key words, as advised in the *Don't forget!* box. At this stage of the course, you might want to omit the previous task and start with the test. Before they do the test, analyse the structure of the multiple-choice Questions 11–15 with students. Look especially at the stems and how they prepare students for the answer; predict a possible answer and suggest why the other two options may not be not possible. Remind students to predict the word type for Questions 16–20, and also possible answers where they can.

Play the recording. After the test, ask students to transfer their answers to a grid or answer sheet and check their answers in pairs, before whole class checking.

**ANSWERS**

**11** C  **12** A  **13** B  **14** C  **15** A
**16** summer cruise       **17** palaces, gardens
**18** explore             **19** popular
**20** novel experience

**2**  Students can discuss the questions in pairs.

>  **Listening script 17**
>
> Good evening. I'm really pleased to be asked to be part of your winter series on cities around the world and I can see from your programme that you have had speakers talking about a wide range of places from Asia to Africa and South America. This helped me narrow my choice down to three different places, and I finally decided on a city that made a huge impression on me, namely St Petersburg in Russia. Before we start, … <u>if you'd like more information</u>

<u>about the places mentioned in the talk you can find it on my website and in my blog</u>, details of which I'll give you at the end.

All of the places I've visited over the years have made a profound impression on me. But my trip to St Petersburg will always stay in my memory. … <u>And I have to say that the city is definitely in the top ten places that I have ever visited for a holiday.</u>

The first time I went there was in winter … it was memorable, partly because I visited various cultural places like the Hermitage, the famous museum on the bank of the River Neva, a place that I had always wanted to visit. <u>But I remember my visit particularly well because it was very cold … the river was frozen solid and I saw moisture freezing in mid-air as the wind came off the frozen river.</u> The place was so magical. It's moments like this that make travelling so worthwhile. It was such a different experience from anything I'd ever had before.

The city is famous, like Venice, for its canals, but there is just so much to see, as it is a city full of beauty. The people are so welcoming, … <u>and what strikes you as a visitor is the richness of the heritage.</u> Near to the Hermitage Museum, that I have already mentioned, is a very striking statue, the Bronze Horseman, which is a memorial to Peter the Great. Other places that are worth seeing are the Mariinsky Theatre and the metro of St Petersburg which, although is not as famous perhaps as that of Moscow, is still worth seeing, especially the Avtovo metro station, which is without doubt one of the most beautifully decorated metro stations you're ever likely to see. <u>But for me, if I had visited nothing else in St Petersburg and had only gone round the Hermitage Museum, it would've been well worth the visit.</u>

• • • • • • • • • • • • • • • • • • • • • • • • • • • • • • • • • • • • • • • • • • •

For breaks to a city like St Petersburg, you have different ways of travelling and different types of holidays. You can fly direct to St Petersburg from London or you can visit the city as part of a <u>summer cruise</u> of the Baltic Sea that also takes in the Gulf of Finland. Visits don't have to be restricted to the city itself. In the city suburbs there're fabulous <u>palaces</u> and <u>gardens</u> to entice visitors. Apart from the famous Peterhof Palace, there's also the Catherine Palace with its famous Amber room and extensive park. So, if you are thinking of visiting the city, leave yourself some time to <u>explore</u> further than the centre of the city.

But of course, any holiday destination is a personal choice. For many people the word 'holiday' conjures up different things. For example, adventure holidays to places that are generally inaccessible are now increasingly <u>popular</u>, as are those to pristine beaches untouched by humans, but for me, even as a seasoned traveller, my trip to St Petersburg in the heart of winter among the ice and snow was a <u>novel experience</u> and a true adventure.

Now let's look at …

## Word building: Words related to memory page 167

**1** Elicit the word *memento* from the students, using dictionaries if necessary. Ask them to talk about any mementoes they may have brought back from a holiday. Compare the word with *souvenir* and *keepsake*.

**ANSWERS**

souvenir or memento
Words with the root *mem-*: memento, memo/
memorandum, memoir, memoirs, memorable,
memorial, memorabilia, memorise, memory,

**2** Ask students to do the exercise in pairs, checking their answers with other students/pairs and then the whole class. Students can record words in their (electronic) vocabulary lists. Remind them of the benefit of word building for common words they encounter.

**ANSWERS**

| | | |
|---|---|---|
| **1** memories | **2** remember | **3** memoirs |
| **4** memorabilia | **5** memorise | **6** memorable |
| **7** memorial | **8** memento | |

### Further practice

Time permitting, write a root like *cycl-* in the centre of the board and ask students to suggest words that they can make from it. Students do this in groups as quickly as possible. Instead of a root you might want to have a prefix like *con-* or even a word like *success*. You can go a step further and ask students to give collocations and positions related to the words they create. Keep a record of the board work allowing students to photograph the board.

**3** Students can do this on their own, checking their answers in pairs before whole-class feedback.

**ANSWERS**

| | | |
|---|---|---|
| **1** memories | **2** memorabilia | **3** mementos |
| **4** memoirs | **5** memorial | **6** memorable |
| **7** remember | **8** memorise | |

**4** 🗣 Students do this exercise in pairs. Monitor the questions before the pairwork begins. Elicit a few examples from the class and allow them to ask you questions.

## Speaking PART 1 page 168

**1–2** Elicit the appropriate answer beginnings and explain why the structure of the others are inaccurate, if necessary. Monitor the answers students give for form and variety of response and ask two or three to give their own examples. You might like to put up some of their ideas on the board for reference.

**ANSWERS**

**1**
**a** 2  **b** 1  **c** 4  **d** 3

**3** 🗣 Ask students to ask each other the questions in turns, and monitor the roleplay. Remind them they do not need to develop their answers beyond one or two sentences.

Also, remind them that, as they practise for the exam, preparing how to begin their answers gives them valuable time to think in the exam. Remind them to try to avoid repeating the question in the answers and using empty phrases that play for time, e.g., *This is an interesting question, …* as such beginnings sound unnatural.

## Speaking PART 2 page 168

**1–2** Ask students to do both these exercises in groups and check the answers as whole class.

**ANSWERS**

**1**
Possible answers
tour, excursion, expedition, outing, trip, voyage,
travel luggage, suitcase, plane, train, car, tickets,
hotel, boat

**2**
1 pleasant, exciting, long, tiring, excruciating,
   memorable, fantastic, comfortable, uncomfortable
2 travel, fly, stay, stop, stop over, journey, sail
3 hotel, seaside, mountains, beaches, city centre,
   ski resort
4 for a holiday, for/to work, to visit friends, to study

**3** Ask students to compare their lists of words with at least two other students and allow them to change their words or refine their lists.

**4** 🗣 Remind students of the contents of the *Don't forget!* box. Give the students a moment to choose two of the criteria to give their partner. Ask them to take turns talking about the prompts on the card in exercise 2. Monitor for examples of good practice, especially the use of vocabulary and organisation of the description. Give individual feedback if necessary before whole-class feedback.

## Reading Passage page 169

**1** 🗣 Students do the exercise in pairs, check their answers with other students, and then check and discuss as a whole class. Discuss the statements relating to the photographs and elicit whether the students would like to visit the places in the photos/statements and why.

**ANSWERS**

| | |
|---|---|
| **1** True | **2** True |
| **3** False – Australia | **4** True |

| 5 False – Athens in Greece | 6 False – East Africa |
|---|---|
| 7 True | 8 True |
| 9 False – St Petersburg | 10 False – Iran |

**2** Ask students to do the exercise in the same pairs. As a whole class, elicit and discuss at least three facts about the Great Barrier Reef, e.g., *it's off Queensland, Australia, it's a coral reef, it's a conservation area,* etc.

**3–4** Ask students to predict the possible meanings used in the passage, and then underline the words as they scan the passage to check which meaning is actually used. As a whole class, check the answers. By now students will have a good idea of the contents of the passage.

ANSWERS
1 ledge (of rock or land)
2 the state of being fully developed
3 organism
4 variety
5 catalogue
6 in danger
7 reproduce
8 group
9 ancient
10 place of safety

## Questions 1–13

Elicit what type of text the Reading Passage is, factual or descriptive. Review briefly both the Summary completion and *True/False/Not Given* statements, eliciting the skills needed from students. For Questions 11–13, elicit what word type is needed in the answers. Set a 20-minute time limit, encouraging students to be responsible for their own time management. Ask them to write their answers on a sheet of paper or an answer sheet. Remind them to be careful with the spelling.

Tell students to check their answers in groups, before whole class checking. Ensure students can justify correct answers as well as incorrect answers. You might want to analyse one of the three sets of questions closely, looking, for example, at the words and phrases in each sentence, e.g., 7 *… for turtles;* 8 *No (other) … ;* 9 *…plans to …;* 10 *All ….* Explore the relative importance of the words/ phrases in the sentences compared to, for example, *food, World Heritage, ruins, industrial activity.*

ANSWERS
| 1 continental shelf | 2 diversity |
|---|---|
| 3 ecosystem | 4 coral reef |
| 5 biological | 6 marine life |
| 7 TRUE | 8 NOT GIVEN |
| 9 NOT GIVEN | 10 FALSE |
| 11 impacts and conflicts | |
| 12 (the) regulatory framework | |
| 13 overall management | |

**5** In the same groups, students discuss the questions using any new vocabulary they have come across in the unit so far.

### Round up

Review the question types in the Reading test and any issues involved in dealing with them.

## Language focus: Articles  page 172

Students often have a problem with articles as they do not occur in all languages, or are used differently. In all parts of the exam, especially the Reading and Listening tests, they are often not noticed by learners, and in writing and speaking their their (over-/under-)use can be a problem. Articles give signals to what is being said, and so this failure to notice or use them can cause miscommunication. If your students have persistent problems with them, advise extra practice from the various grammar books that are available.

**1** Elicit the three kinds of articles and give students a few minutes to find them in the extract. Refer them to the Grammar reference on page 225. Students will be very familiar with this area of grammar, but it is important to focus students' attention on articles and their use.

ANSWERS
1 the Great Barrier Reef, the mainland
2 popular belief, 2,900 individual reefs, fringing reefs, islands
3 a continuous barrier, a broken maze

**2** Students do the exercise in pairs, checking their answers with other students. During the feedback, elicit as much explanation of the use of the articles as time allows.

ANSWERS
1 The sun
2 Stars, the moon, the Milky Way
3 A star
4 We can call it a star when we look at it in the galaxy or when we look at it as an astronomical object.
5 Yes
6 Mount Everest
7 The Himalayas
8 Tokyo
9 Yes. The Atlantic Ocean, the Pacific Ocean, the Indian Ocean, the Arctic Ocean, the Southern Ocean.

**3–4** Ask students to do the exercises as per the instructions in the Student's Book. Monitor and assist the students as they complete the exercises and elicit justification for each answer. For exercise 4, use the photograph to introduce the activity, eliciting information and a description from students. Monitor correct usage as they speak.

**3**

1  b  The. ... *I visited were old*. makes the monuments specific, not just any or all 'old monuments'.
2  b  the. The Himalayas are a particular group of mountains, not just mountains in general.
3  a  the. The sun in the sky/our solar system.
4  b  the. The Nile is a specific river.
5  a  The. The phrase ... *of Mexico* ... makes the word capital-specific. *Mexico City* does not need an article as there is only one Mexico City.
6  a  The. 'The United Kingdom' is used to distinguish the kingdom from other kingdoms.
7  a  The. The definite article can be used if it refers to a particular country. Sentence b is about prime ministers in general.
8  a  The. There is only one heart in the body, not various hearts.

**4**

the Brazil, the sisters, the Rio de Janeiro, the beaches, the fun, a sightseeing, the living, the holidays

## Extension

Ask students to work in groups. Give them a text on travel, or any subject of about a page long, and tell each group to focus on a particular paragraph. Select 2 or 3 paragraphs overall, depending on the size of the class. Ask each group to identify and explain the use of the articles, including zero articles, in their paragraph. They then check their answers with another group who focused on the same paragraph. You can vary this by having all the groups focusing on only one paragraph in the text. You can also restrict the focus in each group with, for example, one group looking only at the use of the definite article and another at the zero article. Allow a group to lead the feedback, and monitor and correct use.

## Round up

Encourage students to focus on noticing the use of articles as they read, listen, etc. and to try and think about their usage. They can focus for part of the time as they read, listen, etc. rather than over-focusing.

## Writing TASK 2 page 172

1  Ask students to work in groups and do the exercise. Collate/tabulate information on the board as part of the whole-class discussion. Highlight the generic parts of the rubric regarding time and word limit and especially the prompt to give reasons and examples, which is often overlooked.

ANSWERS

Respond to the opinion in the second sentence in relation to the first opinion; talk about other effective measures.

Write an introduction.

Write a paragraph stating that the effect travelling has is/isn't significant and explain why it is a good/bad measure, but there are others. Give reasons and examples to help explain.

Write two paragraphs stating and explaining two or three other measures. Give reasons and examples to help explain.

Write a conclusion.

2  Students can do the exercise in the same groups. Discuss students' answers and give suggestions.

ANSWERS

2, 3, 4, 7

3  Ask students to do the exercise on their own, within the same groups, and then check their answers with other group members, before whole-class discussion.

ANSWERS

1  Relevant
2  At the moment, for example, more people are travelling by train than by plane.
3  Relevant
4  Relevant
5  This is surely because of the cheapness and availability of fast means of transport.
6  Relevant

4  This can continue to be done as a group activity, with responses and justification elicited during whole-class feedback.

5  You can start the exercise as a whole-class activity, going through the main parts of the question. Students can then list and discuss their ideas in groups, followed by whole-class feedback.

ANSWERS

Positive:
gives people new ideas and experiences, languages
helps develop international relations
provides education
removes prejudice
helps people appreciate other cultures

Negative:
may lead to people emigrating and brain drain
makes people more insular
bad for the environment

6  Students can do the task for homework, or in class. In both cases, stress the need for them to be strict about the 40-minute time limit. Tell them that as you mark their work, you will be looking for examples of the vocabulary and the use of the articles practised in the unit. Alternatively, you could set this as a class test.

Encourage students to look at the model answer *only after* they have written their own answer. Ask students to go through the model working out how it complies with the requirements of the task. They can use the Comments as a starting point.

---

*Model answer*

The volume of international travel is increasing with globalisation and cheaper travel. As a result, it is argued that the environment is suffering and that restrictions should be imposed on such travel. I think that international travel does pose some risks for the environment, but the effects can be mitigated.

There is no doubt that as the number of international travellers increases there is increased danger of the environment being harmed. This risk comes not only from the growing volume of flights, but also from the impact of huge numbers of people visiting vital ecosystems, especially fragile areas around the world like Antarctica and the Great Barrier Reef. Another worrying development is the increase in cruise ships ferrying thousands of passengers around the world. Therefore, some are calling for international travel to be restricted.

People have always travelled around the world and it would be very difficult to restrict international travel, especially for tourism and business as it is economically beneficial for local communities. If people are concerned about the impact of international travel, rather than trying to impose restrictions, taxes can be introduced to help protect local conservation areas. Such projects can also provide local jobs and help develop local communities.

Moreover, people nowadays are much more conscious of the impact of international travelling and seek to offset the impact by paying for the planting of trees for example. People are also travelling more by railway than in the past as railways become faster, more convenient and integrated, which reduces any threats to the environment.

As we have seen, there are risks to the environment from increased international travel, but such travel is important and any risks can be offset by different measures.

*Word count: 284 words*

**COMMENTS**

The response is divided into clear paragraphs with a stance/position given in the introduction, maintained and developed throughout.

---

## Round up

Review the main areas in each main skill, along with the grammar and vocabulary. Elicit the information, including important strategies, from students in the first instance, giving hints if necessary.

---

**REVIEW 12 ANSWERS** pages 174–175

## Vocabulary: Adjectives with multiple meanings

1 a and b: curious
2 a and b: different
3 a and b: fresh
4 a and b: novel
5 a and b: alien
6 a and b: new

## Word building: Words related to memory

Is your memory good?
Yes, but sometimes I leave memos for myself on the fridge to remind me to do things.
What was your most memorable experience in South America?
Mmm, I have so many vivid memories of my time there.
Where did this memento come from?
Don't you recognise it? It's from the famous memorial I visited in India.
Do you collect historical memorabilia?
No they don't interest me, but I love reading the memoirs of famous historical figures.

## Language focus: Articles

1 zero article, a, the
2 zero article, a, the
3 zero article, the, a
4 The, zero article, a
5 an, zero article, the
6 zero article, a, the
7 zero article, the, a
8 A, the, zero article
9 the, a, the
10 the, zero article, a
11 The, zero article, a

**ACCURACY IN IELTS**

1 An irrelevant piece of information: *And it will also help the environment.*
Two extra articles: *the Stonehenge, the people*
Two words in the wrong form: *visit* (visiting), *memory* (memories)

2 An irrelevant piece of information: *It has also resulted in an expansion of the leisure industry, which is important.*
Two extra articles: *the distant places, the larger disposable incomes*
Two words in the wrong form: *memory* (memorable), *wealth* (wealthy)

# Ready for Speaking

## IELTS Speaking test

PART 1
Introduction and interview

PART 2
Individual long turn

PART 3
Two-way discussion

## Introduction   page 176

### Lead-in

Elicit what students know about the Speaking test, including the duration of each part and the differences between the different parts, i.e. the progression from talking about personal information to abstract concepts/ideas. Or ask students to read through the introduction and elicit an explanation from students in their own words.

You can also give students a few statements and they check if they are correct or not, e.g., *In Part 2 of the Speaking test, you have a discussion with the examiner./The Speaking test lasts 20 minutes./If you make mistakes in the Speaking test, you will not achieve a good score.*

Elicit the criteria for assessment in the Speaking test and refer them to the Speaking band descriptors on the Student's Resource Centre. Remind students that the exam is recorded.

## Part 1   page 176

1 Ask students to do this exercise in pairs, followed by whole-class feedback.

### Extension

Give students a topic that might come up in the exam and ask them to make sets of questions, e.g., pets: *Do you like pets? What kinds of pets do you like? Have you ever had any pets?* Students can share the questions with the whole class and practise interviewing each other in the class or outside the class. They can also create banks of such questions for revision purposes. Keep copies of any questions for your own reference.

2 Students can do this exercise in pairs, followed by whole-class feedback. Elicit why it is important to begin well, by matching the answer to the question, not just copying the question and waffling, e.g. *this is a very good question ...*

**ANSWERS**

1 is not suitable. The question asks the candidate to state a preference about doing something, e.g., *I prefer going out with a large/small group of people/friends/people I know.*

### Further practice

Each time there is Part 1 and Part 3 preparation for the exam in the class, elicit at least one way of beginning the answer. This encourages spontaneity and, over time, increases flexibility.

3 Go over this carefully pointing out how important it is in the exam. Once students have done this in pairs go over it as a whole class. Focus on this throughout the course, where possible.

**ANSWERS**

many reasons, perhaps, most important

**4–6** Follow the instructions in the book, making sure the students understand. Monitor the roleplay for pronunciation.

**ANSWERS**

**4**
Stressed words in set A:
prefer, go out, one friend, group, friends, Why?
What, do you do, go out
think, important, keep, contact, friends, make, work, courses, Why/Why not?
Stressed words in set B:
like, making, things, cooking, pottery, painting, Why/Why not?
think, crafts, important, our lives, Why/Why not?
Tell, traditional craft, your country
think craft, popular, future, Why/Why not?

**5**
Possible beginnings for set B:
Yes I like/love making things, particularly cooking because …
Yes, I think it's crucial/essential/very important, because …
A traditional craft where I come from is …
Oh yes. I think it will be much more central to our lives than now, because …

## Part 2   page 177

By way of lead-in, elicit what students know about Speaking Part 2, especially as regards the organisation, preparation time and glancing at the notes as they speak. Go through the information in the Student's Book.

**1–2** Students can do these exercises in pairs, followed by checking their answers with other students and then whole-class feedback. As you discuss student answers, elicit the connection between the prompts and the notes. You might want to discuss whether it is easier for students to use the exact works in the prompt as they speak or whether it is useful/difficult/wise to paraphrase as they glance at the notes while speaking in preparation for the next exercise. It obviously depends on the individual students, but it is worth discussing and encouraging them to paraphrase.

ANSWERS
**1**
**1** d **2** f **3** e **4** c **5** b **6** a

**2**
Task Card 1:
Describe a place where you enjoy studying: café
where this place is: near river
when you first visited this place: month ago
what this place is like: cheerful
and explain why you enjoy studying there: relaxing, friendly, great view

Task Card 2:
Describe a skill that you would like to learn/what the skill is: musical instrument
when you would like to learn this skill: soon
where you would like to learn this skill: class – irritating/privately
and explain why you would like to learn this skill: relaxing, healthy, helps concentration

**3** Ask students to do this in pairs, followed by whole-class discussion.

ANSWERS
guitar: musical instrument
last August: at the end of the summer
on holiday: when I had a few days off and was visiting my friend in another town
little time: I haven't really had any spare time
annoying: irritating and challenging
not relaxing: not good at helping me unwind

**Extension**

Read the response to the Task Card yourself or ask a student to do so. Time the response and elicit from the students at the end how long they think the response took. Remind them that this involves reading, not speaking, but it's a useful gauge. Then elicit how long they think the response is in words, 220 words with contractions. You might want to point out that part of the purpose of Part 2 is to check if candidates can organise a response, while maintaining control of what they say over an extended period of time using the prompts.

**4** 🎧 Ask students to listen and then compare their answers in pairs/groups. Play the recording again and then discuss the answers as a whole class.

ANSWERS
musical instrument: same
soon: in the near future.
class - irritating: annoying
privately: to acquire by paying for individual tuition
relaxing: very soothing
helps concentration: same
healthy: same

---

🎧 **Listening script 18**

(**E** = examiner; **C** = candidate)

**E:** Now, I'm going to give you a card with a topic to look at. You have one minute to make notes and then I'm going to ask you to talk about the topic.

**E:** Can you talk about the topic?
**C:** The skill that I'd like to talk about is playing a musical instrument, mmm … like the piano, and I'd like to learn it in the near future. I know it's possible to go to a class to learn to play the piano, but mmm … I know I'd find that very annoying. I think learning to play the piano's one of those skills that'd be better to learn … to acquire by paying for individual tuition. I realise it might be expensive, but it'd be mmm … very rewarding in other ways.
Why I'd like to be able to take up the piano is because … it's mmm … very soothing to play and to listen to. It's a wonderful feeling to lose yourself in the music as you're playing. I've got several friends who are mad about music, and I've listened to them many times. They've played both classical and pop music to me, and they've found it thrilling to play for someone. And to me it is a very peaceful experience just sitting there and listening. As well as helping to calm people down, playing an instrument like the piano's mmm … very good for the brain as it keeps it active. One of my friends, who plays the guitar and the piano, says that he plays for about … half an hour before he does any homework, and it helps him to focus on his work and concentrate more. And it's healthy, because it helps take away part of the stress of modern life. Friends have also told me that it improves their ability to focus, and so they play before they study or do any work, which I think would mm … benefit me too.
**E:** OK. Thank you. Which type of music would you like to learn to play?
**C:** Mmm … I'd like to start with classical, but I'd like to learn jazz music later on and maybe some pop music.

**5** This exercise can be done with exercise 4, in the same pairs/groups separately. Elicit justification for any student evaluation/observation and discuss the benefit of developing the prompts from the point of view of spontaneity and flexibility.

**6** Students do this exercise in pairs. Make sure that the partners choose the Task Cards for each other. Monitor the responses, and give feedback about good practice and anything students need to be careful about. If students are happy to be videoed, they can do so in groups, but be careful about school/college policies and privacy. If you video students, play back the recording for analysis purposes.

## Part 3 page 179

Ensure students are aware of the difference between Part 3 and the two earlier parts of the Speaking test. Elicit the information where possible from students themselves.

**1** Ask students to do this in pairs followed by whole-class discussion.

**2**  Students do this in groups as per the instructions. They listen and then check their answers with a partner before whole-class feedback.

**ANSWERS**
2, 1, 6, 3, 4, 5

### Listening script 19

**(E = examiner; C = candidate)**

**E:** Let's talk about learning new skills generally. Do you do think it's important to keep acquiring new skills throughout one's life?

**C:** Yes, I think it is.

**E:** Why do you think so?

**C:** Well, mmm, at the moment life is changing so fast with the advances that have been made in technology, and also through mmm … globalisation in the past few decades, so it's important for people of all ages to keep up-to-date with skills of all kinds.

**E:** How essential do you think it'll be for workforces in the future to be proficient technologically?

**C:** Mmm, I'd say it'll be vital, because more and more of the work that is done nowadays requires a lot of input using one form of technology or another, so that in the near future it will be almost impossible to find work, even basic work, without practical computing skills. Take car design, for example. It seems that technical drawing done by hand is less important now than knowing how to create new products on the screen. Soon designers'll be creating holograms of cars, not just three-dimensional computer images. And the same applies to architecture and teaching too.

**E:** In what way do you think learning only computing skills can be a disadvantage in life?

**C:** Mmm … first of all, people are already becoming over-reliant on computers for virtually everything. In the current knowledge-based society, where information is available literally at people's fingertips, there's a danger that people's knowledge'll decrease and accessing information'll become just like switching on the light without necessarily understanding what's happening. And people're in danger of losing their ability to do basic things.

**E:** Mmm, should the preparation of children and young people for work focus on computing skills at the expense of practical skills?

**C:** Mmm … I think it's a matter of balance, because we need the people to build computers and so on, and the people to learn to be able to use them for their work. Also, if any machines break down, we need people to be able to fix them. And so if education concentrates on training people to use machines to access knowledge at the expense of training technicians, etc, then there'll be a major problem.

**E:** Do you think people will have to work longer in the future?

**C:** At one time, it was thought that people would have more leisure time in the future, but it seems that the opposite is true. As people are living longer worldwide, they're also being asked to work longer with the result that the age at which people will be drawing a pension, if they have one, will be later than it is now. And in fact it's already starting to happen in many countries like the UK and France.

**E:** How can people ensure that work does not control their lives?

**C:** It's not easy, but not impossible either. One way is to ensure that one has interests outside work, and that these interests are not connected with work in any way. For example, if people are involved in working in computers all day, they could find something that requires manual skills, like pottery.

**3** Students can do this in groups followed by group analysis and then whole-class discussion.

# 13 The importance of infrastructure

Photocopiable activity: Group game (groups of 4–6) – Who's telling the truth? page 140
Workbook pages 100–107

## Content overview

This unit focuses on systems and infrastructure.

**Listening** SECTION 3

A research project

Question types: Multiple-choice; Multiple-choice; Multiple-choice

**Reading**

Cycling for transportation and health: The role of infrastructure

Question types: Matching headings; Identification of writer's views/claims – *Yes/No/Not Given*; Multiple-choice

**Writing** TASK 1

Describing tables

**Speaking** PARTS 2 AND 3

**Part 2** Describing a street/square

**Part 3** Discussing transport systems

**Vocabulary**: Nouns related to systems

**Word building**: Modal verbs to adjectives

**Language focus**: Concession and developing ideas

## Digital overview

**Presentation Kit**

Interactive versions of Student's Book exam tasks

Embedded audio and answer key for all activities

**Teacher's Resource Centre**

Communicative activity: Group game (groups of 4–6) – Who's telling the truth?

Workbook audio, answer key and wordlists

**Student's Resource Centre**

Class audio

Wordlist

Speaking Part 2 video and video worksheet

Speaking Part 3 videos (4) and video worksheet

## Vocabulary: Nouns related to systems

page 182

### Lead-in

Elicit from students what *infrastructure* means. Then elicit examples of different types of infrastructure, e.g., electricity, the internet, roads, transport, water and so on, reminding students of countable and uncountable nouns, and classification. You can ask students to work in pairs and tell their partner the type of infrastructure they access most/least on a daily basis, effectively mapping many of the actions they take during their daily routines. You can begin by stating the part of infrastructure you use most/least yourself. Briefly discuss the importance of infrastructure in students' and other people's lives.

**1** 👥 Students do the exercise in groups. Elicit different ways to evaluate and give opinions, e.g., using not just adjectives, but agreeing and then adding an evaluation, *I think … is important, but …*, using cause/effect structures and modal verbs. Encourage the students to develop their answers to the questions as fully as they can. Discuss which elements of infrastructure they have in cities they know, and the advantages and disadvantages of the various types.

> **POSSIBLE ANSWERS**
> **1** Canal  **2** Wifi network  **3** Bridge

**2** Ask students to look at the questionnaire on page 182 and check they understand the items mentioned, e.g., that *GPS* stands for *Global Positioning System*. Elicit an example of each type and the question they'll need to ask, e.g., *Have you used … today?* Tell students to tick their own answers and then ask two other students in the class (not just their neighbours!) the questions.

**3** 👥 Students collate their answers in groups before whole-class discussion. Time permitting, put their findings on the board as a class survey.

**4** Go through the rubric and the example and ask students to do the exercise in pairs. They then work with another pair to develop the connections more fully. Answer any questions about vocabulary, e.g., *slick*, *viaduct*, *host*, *access*, *appliance* and encourage them to add words to their (electronic) vocabulary lists under the heading *infrastructure*. During whole-class feedback, elicit explanations from students, e.g., for the oil industry: *Field* is where the oil is found and a *well* is the apparatus that brings the oil to the surface, etc.

> **ANSWERS**
> **1** railway  **2** telephone  **3** satellite
> **4** internet  **5** water  **6** electricity
> **7** gas  **8** oil

**5** Students do the exercise in pairs, and then check their answers with other students. Encourage them to discuss any discrepancies before you give whole-class feedback.

**ANSWERS**

1 Electricity, grid
2 Gas, pipelines, fields
3 water supply, purification
4 oil, wells, refineries
5 satellite, weather
6 infrastructure, lines
7 access, web, connection

**6** In pairs, students discuss a recent example from their lives when a system has malfunctioned or been faulty, e.g., a failed internet/mobile connection, a power cut, and their reactions to it. You can give an example from your own life.

### Round up

Elicit people's attitude in general to malfunctions in infrastructure and whether: we are over-reliant on some aspects, such as communication systems/the internet/electricity; whether we take various aspects for granted; and whether, perhaps, we use any malfunctioning as just a good excuse to complain.

## Listening SECTION 3   page 184

**1** Students do the exercise in pairs, and then check their answers as a whole class. Ask them to put them in the correct order.

**ANSWERS**

1, 3, 4, 5 and 7 are directly related. 2 and 6 may be indirectly related.
1 what the research intends to do/show, etc.
3 the question the researcher is seeking to answer
4 the results/conclusions of the research
5 the examination of the data/information collected
7 a review or analysis of the books, journals or articles related to the research

**2** After the pairwork, discuss the question as a whole class.

### Questions 21–30

Play the Listening test without any further preparation. Follow the usual procedure for transferring and checking answers. In this particular test, all of the answers are letters of the alphabet, so students must be careful about transferring the answers correctly. Ask them to check their answers in pairs. Analyse the questions and any issues as you check the answers with the whole class.

**ANSWERS**

**21** B   **22** A   **23** A   **24** A   **25** G   **26** F   **27** B
**28** E   **29–30** IN EITHER ORDER:  A, E

### Listening script 20

**(T = Tracey; A = Andrei)**

**T:** Hi Andrei. How're you getting on with your research project?

**A:** I've just started, and it's giving me a headache. I really thought it'd be nothing like this, but then … I suppose it'll probably get easier, … I hope.

**T:** Getting started is always the worst part for me. I always hate getting down to it.

**A:** Well, yeah, it can be a real problem, but it doesn't have to be.

**T:** So … you're doing something … on the relationship between the public and systems such as roads and other transport in cities?

**A:** Yes, that's it. And you're looking at … ?

**T:** Cityscapes and their impact on people's moods.

**A:** Ah, yes.

**T:** It's given me lots of headaches too. What's your problem?

**A:** Oh, everything basically. I'm just trying to get my head around everything and don't know where to start.

**T:** Mmm … I'm in the middle of looking at data analysis, and I'm having a bit of a struggle myself at the moment.

**A:** You're at the data stage. Oh right. You're quite far on then.

**T:** Yeah. I am …

**A:** Could you tell me what your experiences have been as you're further along than me? It might make me feel a bit better.

**T:** Yeah sure. Looking back I don't know how I got to this stage, but mm … I found it fairly straightforward getting started. I was expecting it to be much harder, but it all came together rather quickly.

**A:** That's good to hear. So that's promising. But can you tell me about your experience say of mmm … coming up with the research question?

**T:** I thought I'd have difficulty turning my ideas into a research question, but it wasn't as bad as I thought. In fact, I found it relatively painless.

**A:** OK … I might ask for your help on that then. What about the literature review?

**T:** The literature review? That I found really took up a lot of time. But I have to admit, I actually like digging into things and getting to the bottom of problems, so part of that was me.

**A:** Yes, I agree it can be fun. I'm reading a lot to try and get myself to frame my research question, and I'm really getting into the literature.

**T:** Well, the thing I was very glad to get out of the way was writing the research proposal. I was exhausted after that, because it's important to make sure the research proposal's really clear on the focus of your research. It's not easy summarising everything and bringing it together.

**A:** And what about designing the methods?

**T:** That was really easy to do – I enjoy analysing systems and putting them together, so I think I sorted the methods design out really quickly. But what I found really agonising was writing the aims and objectives. <u>That was probably particularly hard to deal with.</u>

**A:** Yeah … they aren't easy.

........................................................

**T:** Is all of this any help Andrei?

**A:** Oh yes. One of the problems is that it's OK to see things written on paper but it's the thinking behind it.

**T:** Yes, of course. It is.

**A:** Yeah. I appreciate it. My spoken English is not a problem, I think, but I've not done much writing and I'm going to find that bit difficult.

**T:** Well, you can get help you know.

**A:** Yeah? Mm, do you think I need a private tutor?

**T:** Oh no, that's not necessary, I'm sure. I know there's language support in the university if you are not a full-time student; you just need to contact <u>the Language Centre.</u>

**A:** OK, but there's likely to be a fee involved.

**T:** Mmm well you can get help through <u>the main library.</u> It's not just for lending books you know.

**A:** Really? I never thought of that.

**T:** It's so easy to get isolated and not know everything that's available.

## Round up

Elicit from students whether they expect other discussions on research to follow a similar structure. Stress the similarity of academic processes across disciplines/subjects and how important this is for prediction. Stress how common generic processes and patterns are and how knowledge of them can make the exam simple – after all, the IELTS is a system, which tests a system.

## Word building: Modal verbs to adjectives  page 185

### Lead-in

Review the concepts of possibility, probability and obligation, and elicit the modals and adjectives commonly used, e.g.:
Possible: prospective, at some time in the future, possible in the near future
Probable: expected, eventually, likely, in the course of time, it is probable that, expected
Definite: imminent, inevitable, approaching, impending, certain
Clarify for students the difference between *possible* and *probable*. Look at the example and ask the students to explain the comment to you.

**1** Ask students to do this exercise in pairs, and then check their answers with other students. Go over the exercise with the whole class, clearing up any difficulties.

**ANSWERS**

| | | |
|---|---|---|
| **1** possible | **2** unwilling | **3** unnecessary |
| **4** expected | **5** probable | **6** able |
| **7** compulsory | **8** certain | **9** essential |

**2** Ask students to do this exercise in groups, eliciting examples from the whole class during feedback.

**ANSWERS**

Examiner: Is it possible for communications systems like broadband to have an impact on people's lives?
Candidate: I think <u>it is possible for the development of faster communication systems than we have now to have an impact on</u> local as well as national economies, as <u>the expected outcome</u> is that <u>it will enable</u> people to do business faster. Obviously, it is <u>not possible for them/they aren't</u> able to solve every problem, but <u>it is at least possible for them to help.</u> For a while, governments <u>were unwilling to</u> invest in fibre optics, but now the cables are being installed everywhere. For example, in my home country they provide jobs for local people …

**3** 🎧 Students discuss the questions in small groups. Encourage them to use other language they have learnt in previous units, such as the conditionals, as well as language they have just been working with. Give them a few minutes to think of their answers, helping with language where necessary. They can then discuss their ideas with the whole class.

## Round up

Summarise how competent and rich the students' language is now, especially as regards commenting on and developing ideas/concepts. Point out that they are now ready for IELTS.

## Reading Passage  page 186

**1–2** These exercises can be done in groups, followed by whole-class feedback.

**ANSWERS**

**2**

lanes, paths, boulevards, roads, networks, streets, rail transit lines

### Questions 1–13

Give students 20 minutes to do the test without any further help. Ask them to write their answers on a sheet of paper or an answer sheet.

They should check and discuss answers in groups and follow this with whole-class discussion. They can also discuss one or more sets of questions from the point of view of the testing process and the exam as a whole, e.g., the global aspect of headings; the connection between the headings and writing overviews in Writing Task 1, and the subheadings in the Listening test, especially in Section 4. Compare the nature of the testing involved in questions 7–10, testing discrete elements of the text, and highlight how one set of questions relates to/fits inside the other.

ANSWERS
1 iii
2 ix
3 viii
4 i
5 iv
6 vi
7 NO. Paragraph B: *This is in contrast to cycling in countries such as the Netherlands, Denmark, and Germany.*
8 YES. Paragraph C: *The results can lead to policy recommendations for infrastructure investments and planning and zoning policies to encourage more cycling for everyday travel.*
9 NOT GIVEN
10 NO. Paragraph E: *Most of the participants were everyday bicyclists.*
11 B
12 D
13 B

**3** Students discuss the questions in groups, followed by whole-class feedback.

### Further practice

Students work in groups and describe the structure of the Reading Passage using the headings in Questions 1–6. Ask them to discuss why they should be able to predict the structure and location of headings in similar texts in the future. Elicit similarities between the structure of the elements of the Listening test on page 184 and the structure of the Reading Passage, and emphasise the generic nature of many/most/if not all processes in IELTS, and the predictability of organisation and content.

### Extension

Give students a similar research-type passage reporting/dealing with research methods, results and future recommendations, etc. Ask students to predict the organisation, or map the organisation and/or explain the logical/generic organisation of the text. Students can do this with texts relating to history, processes, classification and so on. Now they are ready for a wide range of IELTS texts.

## Language focus: Concession and developing ideas page 188

**1** Elicit what is meant by *concession* and look at the example. The use of concession in this way is a very common 'softening' device when giving opinions or disagreeing with another's opinions. Explain this is necessary in English to avoid sounding too

forceful, which can happen with some students, and thus cause misunderstanding. You might also like to mention that intonation plays a large part in moderating disagreement. Refer students to the Grammar reference on page 225.

ANSWERS
Both are correct.

Although most of the focus on "active living" may have been on walking, cycling has a greater potential to substitute for motorised vehicle trips ...

Most of the focus on "active living" may have been on walking, but cycling has a greater potential to substitute for motorised vehicle trips ...

**2** Ask students to do the exercise in pairs, followed by whole-class feedback.

ANSWERS
1 Although increasing the capacity of the network may be a good solution to the problem, it is not the only one.
2 This may be a sound argument, but I think I'd want to see more funds made available for new carriages as well.
3 While inner city conditions may be cramped, the facilities available are endless.
4 I don't like the idea of computers controlling systems like transport. Nevertheless, they perform a vital function.
5 Much as I agree with the creation of high-speed communication systems, I can't help thinking that they will lead to more demands on workers and hence more stress.
6 Extensive metro systems may exist in many major cities, but they are expensive to maintain and upgrade.
7 I partly agree with the opinion expressed here, but I think it is naive to suggest that increasing the fares will in the end lead to a better transport service.
8 It's clear the quality of public services is improving. Nonetheless, more needs to be done.

**3** Students can do this exercise in the same pairs, explaining why the connections work, and why they don't work. They can check their answers with another pair before whole-class feedback.

ANSWERS
a 7 b 2 c 4 d 1 e 5

**4** Ask the students to work in pairs and think of further ideas to develop the other three sentences, and report them to the class as a whole.

**5–6** Students should be regularly following current events by now to build up their background knowledge and so should have little problem finding issues to discuss here. Give them time to make some notes first and then let them discuss the points in pairs. Monitor here for the use of the language of concession. Ask each pair to work with another pair to expand the discussion. Give feedback on their performance and usage of the target language.

## Extension

Choose a controversial subject and divide the class into two groups to prepare arguments 'for' and 'against'. Work with both groups and help the students decide on three or four main points which support their arguments. Let them come up with supporting ideas. Ask them to nominate a 'speaker' to represent the group on each point. You can then set up the discussion for the whole class. Some possible topics are: *international money loans, censorship,* etc. However, be mindful of the reaction to more sensitive issues and let the students choose the topic.

## Speaking PART 2 page 189

### Lead-in

Elicit from students information about the photograph and the connection between the photograph and the unit title.

1 Students do the exercise in groups. Additionally, you can ask them to review the structure of the Task Cards saying how the initial prompts introduce/act as a background to the more specific reasoning in the final prompt. Discuss as a whole class.

> **ANSWERS**
>
> Similarities:
> They are both about streets and squares. They both ask about locations; what the street/square is like; and what the reasons for choosing the locations are.
>
> Differences:
> Task Card A is about a street or square that is already a favourite and Task Card B is about a hypothetical situation.
> The tenses used in the last part of each card are different.
> Task Card A also asks about how often you go there and Task Card B when you first came to know about the street or square.
> The order of the middle three prompts is different.

2–3 Tell students to do the exercises in the same groups. They can do this either on large sheets of paper or electronically, for display. Set a time limit and extend if necessary.

Ask them to compare their answers with another group. Elicit students' comments on examples of paraphrases during whole-class discussion.

> **ANSWERS**
>
> 1 What I would like to
> 2 There are many
> 3 While the street has a wide range of cafés and places to eat and a couple of art galleries, it's …
> 4 I find the street very attractive and so
> 5 It appeals to me, as

> 6 but still it's just like
> 7 Another reason I like having a walk along the street is that
> 8 No matter what time of day it is, there are always

4–5 Students write their notes and within their groups take turns to talk about the topic. Group members should give constructive criticism about each other's responses, using the checklist on page 181. Give feedback on examples of good practice and suggest improvements. Allow extra time as they are doing this activity in groups.

## Speaking PART 3 page 190

1 Ask students to work in groups and follow the rubric. Before they do exercise 2, check students' responses for exercise 1.

> **ANSWERS**
>
> I think the government or private companies need …
> More trains and buses can be provided which would …
> Yes, if the predictions are correct, they should be in use in the very near future.

2 Students do this exercise in pairs. Monitor the discussion and select examples of good practice for feedback, eliciting any problems/errors that students notice.

### Round up

Review the skills that are involved in Speaking Parts 2 and 3 and how they differ. Encourage students to take the lead in the review, hinting at, rather than imposing, information/skills/ideas.

## Writing TASK 1 page 190

1 Students do the exercise in groups, followed by whole-class discussion. Encourage them to annotate the table, marking and circling important data.

2 Ask them to do the exercise in the same groups, and check their answers with other students before whole-class feedback.

> **ANSWERS**
>
> 1 Read from left to right, looking at the headings for the columns.
> 2 Visits, not visitors
> 3 Generally it is upward, except for visits from Italy and Sweden by tunnel, and from Portugal by air.
> 4 It is the general trend, while the countries and years show specific trends and data.
> 5 Yes, along with the information in the answer to question 3.
> 6 Overall, it is clear that the number of visits from the selected countries is upward by air and tunnel with the exception of visits from Italy and Sweden by tunnel and from Portugal by air.

**3** This can be done as whole-class activity with a discussion about the options.

ANSWERS

2 and 3.
In 1 the introduction would have to read "visits to the UK" not "visitors to the UK" to be suitable.

**4** It is important for students to engage with the information presented here. Elicit an explanation from the students, encouraging them not just to repeat the words, but to describe the sequence of the information as it is presented.

**5** Go through the example and ask students either to do the exercise on their own or in pairs. They can then check their answers with other students before whole-class feedback.

ANSWERS

**1** There was a gradual increase in visits by air from Belgium between 2011 and 2013, from 167,000 to 183,000.
**2** The general trend for the number of overseas visits by air and by tunnel from Bulgaria was clearly upward, climbing from 57,000 for the former in 2011 to 71,000 in 2013, and by tunnel from 6,000 to 12,000, respectively.
**3** Visits from France by air and tunnel also went up with a rise from 1.339 million to 1.441 million, and 1.514 million to 1.761 million, in 2011 and 2013 respectively.
**4** Trips from Germany by air and by tunnel saw an increase; 2.070 million and 2.129 million for the former and 141,000 and 218,000 for the latter, respectively.
**5** As regards Italy, there were 1.445 million trips to the UK by air and 24,000 trips by tunnel in 2011 with 1.562 million trips by air and 23,000 trips by tunnel in 2013.
**6** Trips from Portugal by air fell and by tunnel they rose with the number of trips falling/decreasing from 260,000 to 251,000 and rising/increasing from 4,000 to 7,000.
**7** The overall visit numbers by air and tunnel went up between 2011 and 2013 from 22.631 million to 23.754 million and from 3.67 million to 4.479 million, respectively.

**6** Students can do the task for homework, or in class. In both cases, stress the need for them to be strict about the 20-minute time limit. Tell them that, as you mark their work, you will be looking for examples of the vocabulary and the use of the structures in exercise 4. Alternatively, you could do the writing test as a class test.

Encourage students to look at the model answer *only after* they have written their own answer. Ask students to go through the model working out how it complies with the requirements of the task. They can use the Comments as a starting point.

*Model answer*

The table provides a breakdown of the number of visits made to various countries through four UK airports.

Overall, it is clear that there is considerable variation in the popularity of the airports for each destination. Whereas 91,000 visits were made from Gatwick to Canada, compared to 187,000 from Heathrow and 50,000 from Manchester, more visits were made from Gatwick and Manchester to Spain, 1.896 million and 1.715 million respectively with 814,000 from Stansted and only 273,000 from Heathrow.

This is in contrast to visits made to Austria via Heathrow, Gatwick, Manchester and Stansted, 86,000, 148,000, 66,000 and 44,000 respectively. Regarding the Irish Republic, a different pattern is seen with 278,000 visits made from Heathrow, 158,000 from Gatwick, 111,000 from Manchester and 187,000 from Stansted.

In comparison, there was a smaller number of visits made to Finland with Heathrow and Manchester being more popular than Gatwick and Stansted, 58,000 visits, 53,000, 25,000, and 8,000 respectively. By contrast, the most frequently used airport for visits to Lithuania was Stansted with 33,000, followed by Gatwick with 15,000, only 1,000 visits from Heathrow and none from Manchester.

*Word count: 183 words*

COMMENTS

The response, summarising the data, is clearly divided into paragraphs with an overview at the start of the second paragraph. A wide range of comparative structures is used. The general information throughout is supported by relevant data.

**Extension**

Students work in groups. Ask them to select a table, graph, etc, and prepare a three-minute presentation explaining the data to another group, or to the whole class. Encourage them to invite questions from their peers. You can give students the sets of data to choose from or they can find their own for homework. Mini-student presentations like this can be done for the revision of skills for this part of the exam. It will give you an insight into misunderstandings and depth of knowledge.

**Round up**

Review the main areas in each skill along with the grammar and vocabulary. Elicit the information, including important strategies, from students in the first instance, giving hints if necessary.

## REVIEW 13 ANSWERS  pages 192–193

## Vocabulary: Nouns related to systems

**1**
1  bridges, lines, tunnels
2  water, treatment, tap
3  pylons, generators, grid
4  wells, fields, exploration
5  access, hosts, connection

**2**
Accept all suitable answers.

## Word building: Modal verbs to adjectives

1  likely
2  should
3  necessary
4  expected
5  probable
6  compulsory
7  essential
8  unwilling
9  needs

## Language focus: Concession and developing ideas

1  The running and maintenance costs may be high, but metro systems are efficient at carrying millions of passengers around major cities worldwide. / Metro systems may be efficient at carrying millions of passengers around major cities worldwide, but the running and maintenance costs are high.
2  Although increasing people's access to the transport system by reducing fares is a good approach to reducing unemployment, it may not be the only one.
3  Electric cars help the environment. Nevertheless, I think the infrastructure is still not extensive enough yet for them to have an impact.
4  I partly agree with this opinion, but I think it is foolish to suggest that increasing the fares at peak hours will improve the train service.
5  Though, personally, I am wary of automation in transport systems such as aviation, computers make them much safer.
6  It is clear the integration of transport systems such as trains, trams and ferries has been transformed in recent years. Nonetheless, more improvement is necessary.
7  It may be worthwhile having more cycle lanes, but the volume of traffic won't be reduced.
8  Much as I agree that communication systems such as broadband should be more advanced, it will lead to a more stressful working and home life.

ACCURACY IN IELTS

1  **Passenger** numbers on the ferry soared between 2012 and 2016, from 135,000 to 567,000.
2  Passenger journeys on the metro system rose in 2016 compared to 2015 with numbers **increasing** to over 4 million a day compared to 3.5 million respectively.
3  The proportion of visitors to the UK by air **fell overall** from 2011 to 2013, decreasing from **8.9%** to **7.5%** respectively.
4  The number of people using the station went **up** substantially between January and June 2016 with a jump from **349,000 to 410,000**.
5  The number of visits made to the UK from Sweden was noticeably lower in 2015 **compared** to 2012 (155,000 and 210,000 respectively).

Money and well-being

Photocopiable activity: Group game (groups of
3–4) – Money and values group interviews page 141
Workbook pages 108–115

## Content overview

This unit focuses on money, happiness, and
satisfaction.

### Listening SECTION 4
Money
Question types: Multiple-choice; Note
completion

### Reading
Subjective well-being
Question types: Matching information;
Matching names; Multiple-choice

### Writing TASK 1
Describing charts

### Speaking PART 3
Discussing well-being and money

**Vocabulary**: Money matters
**Word building**: Values and beliefs
**Language focus**: Substitution and ellipsis

## Digital overview

### Presentation Kit
Interactive versions of Student's Book exam
tasks
Embedded audio and answer key for all activities

### Teacher's Resource Centre
Progress Test 5
Final Test
Communicative activity: Group game (groups
of 3–4) – Money and values group interviews
Workbook audio, answer key and wordlists

### Student's Resource Centre
Class audio
Wordlist
Speaking Part 3 videos (4) and video worksheet

## Vocabulary 1: Money matters   page 194

### Optional lead-in

Put two or three of the following proverbs on the
board and ask students to decide what they mean:
*A fool and his money are soon parted.*
*All that glistens is not gold.*
*Money is the root of all evil.*
*When poverty comes in at the door, love flies out of
the window.*
*One law for the rich and another for the poor.*
*A full cup must be carried steadily.*
*If you don't speculate, you can't accumulate.*
*It's better to be born lucky than rich.*
*Money talks.*
*The best things in life are free.*

Elicit some proverbs from students – you may find
that some are the same in different languages. Add
the other proverbs to the list on the board or dictate
them. Ask the students to discuss the proverbs in
groups, identifying any that are similar in their
own languages.

Elicit the double meaning of the title of the
Vocabulary section, *Money matters*, i.e. topics to do
with money and money is important.

1    Ask students to describe the photos and
answer the questions in groups, followed by whole-
class feedback.

> **ANSWERS**
> 1   Stone money used as currency on the Yap Island
> 2   A credit card payment
> 3   Livestock as currency
> 4   A smartphone used for contactless payment

2   Students can do the exercise individually and
then share their information in the same groups
as in exercise 1. Elicit words from each group and
write them on the board. You might like to elicit
the difference between the words *money* and *cash*,
uncountable nouns, and *coins*, *notes* and *monies*,
countable nouns.

> **POSSIBLE ANSWERS**
> coins, bitcoins, cards, (pre-paid/debit/credit), banks,
> currency, spend, notes, dollars, dinars, pesos

3   Go through the rubric with students, looking at
the collocations and eliciting why word order is
important in compound nouns: the first noun acts
as a modifying noun where there are two nouns,
e.g., money bag – a bag for money. Compound
nouns made up of two nouns can be hyphenated,
two words or sometimes just one word. This can
be confusing for students, but point out that the
alternatives are often acceptable in the reading and
listening test keys. Remind the students that they

must always follow what is in each individual text. Students do the exercise in pairs followed by whole class checking.

**ANSWERS**

1 money management
2 money market
3 pocket money
4 money laundering
5 paper money
6 sponsorship money
7 counterfeit money
8 money box

**4** Ask students to do the exercise in pairs, check their answers with other students and then with the whole class.

**ANSWERS**

1 **cash** reserves/flow/payment/settlement/limit/ crisis/crop
2 **currency** conversion/markets/speculation/ fluctuation/reserves/crisis
3 **credit** agreement/arrangement/facilities/terms/ limit/transfer
4 **debt** collection/burden/mountain
5 **savings** account/plan/bank
6 consumer/government/public **spending**
7 consumer/government/public/welfare/education **expenditure**
8 capital/investment/household/family **income**
9 company/government/state/family/household **finances**

**5** Students can do this activity individually and then check their answers in pairs.

**ANSWERS**

1 cash crop ~~cash~~, cash flow ~~cash~~, cash crisis ~~cash~~
2 ~~Money~~ paper money
3 Education expenditure ~~education~~, expenditure level ~~expenditure~~
4 Family finances ~~family~~, finance minister ~~finance~~
5 ~~Management~~ money management
6 currency reserves ~~currency~~, currency crisis ~~currency~~
7 ~~burden~~ debt burden
8 savings account ~~savings~~

## Extension

Put students in pairs and give each pair two words related to money, such as *cash payment,* or ask them to choose two words. They prepare a short talk of up to one minute on the words without mentioning the words or parts of the words, e.g., *pay/payment.* Students then give their talk jointly to another pair who try to work out the noun phrase as quickly as possible. Select a few volunteers to give their talk impromptu to the whole class, and/or give a talk yourself with the students suggesting the answer.

**6** Give the students two minutes to list three ways that their lives have been affected by money in the past week. Then ask them to describe their experiences in groups. Encourage other members of the group to ask pertinent questions. Point out the link to Speaking Part 3 and elicit examples.

## Round up

Stress the need to think of words that go/collocate/ are associated with other words. Point out that the more common words are the more words they collocate with. Emphasise how important this is for fluency and prediction in IELTS. Refer students to the article on IELTS by Sam McCarter at the beginning of the *Macmillan Collocations Dictionary.*

## Listening SECTION 4 page 196

**1** Students do the exercise in groups followed by whole-class feedback.

**2** Ask students to skim the questions and discuss the topic in as much detail as they can, and then discuss their information as a whole class.

Reinforce the importance of underlining key words and phrases (the students should know all of this and should have practised it many times by now). Check they have underlined the relevant key words.

**POSSIBLE ANSWER**

The talk is about the history of money. Money is more than an economic tool. The talk includes information on bartering goods, commodity money, representative money and the materials used for money.

### Questions 31–40

Play the recording once only. Ask the students to transfer their answers onto an answer sheet or a sheet of paper. Remind them to be careful about spelling. Ask them to discuss their answers in pairs and check differences with other students. Analyse the questions and answers as a whole class.

**ANSWERS**

31 B
32 A
33 B
34 C
35 valuable
36 axes, spades
37 visually attractive
38 standard measure
39 significant evolution
40 abstract

**Listening script 21**

As we continue our series on customs and traditions that influence the values and principles of all societies in the world, today we're going to talk about money. It is easy to think of money as just an economic tool in the world of finance, but it also has a <u>social and psychological dimension</u>. It is woven into the fabric of our society and thinking, and as such has, through history, despite people's criticism of its pursuit, helped lay down the standards and the ethics that govern modern society.

First of all, to look at the history of money we need to ask ourselves what money is. Money is, in fact, an invention of the human mind, … which is made possible because <u>we as human beings are able to give value to symbols</u>. And money is one of the most important symbols in all societies because it represents the value of goods and services. <u>If we accept any object as money – say a gold coin or a digital bank account balance – both the user and the wider community have to agree to this.</u> So, all the money that we use today has … mmm … not just an economic dimension, but a psychological and a social one as well.

Before we look at so-called 'commodity money' … with the introduction of coins and representative money, let's go back to the time of bartering. Before money was invented, bartering was the main way to exchange goods. An individual who had something of value, such as some grain, could directly exchange the grain for another item, which was seen to have an equivalent value, like a small animal, or a tool. <u>The seller of the grain, of course, had to find someone who wanted to buy it</u> and who could offer in return something the seller wanted to buy. There was no common medium of exchange such as money into which both seller and buyer could convert the commodities they wanted to trade.

So, the first stage in the evolution of money was commodity money. This involved accepting objects or commodities, such as grain or metals or animals, as being inherently <u>valuable</u> so they could be used as a common standard of measure and unit of exchange. People could accept any of these objects as money because they had inherent use value for every individual. … And, therefore, they would be widely accepted by other people.

All metals were accepted because they could be easily converted into precious tools, for instance, <u>axes and spades</u>. Metals such as gold and silver also had secondary advantages. They were also easy to identify and <u>visually attractive</u>. Gold, silver, copper as well as other usable objects such as salt and peppercorns are categorised as commodity money, since they combine the attributes both of a usable commodity and a symbol.

So people accepted foods and metals as money because they were sure of their value to themselves and to other people.

Then came metal coins, which were another step in the evolution from usable commodities such as grains to … symbolic forms of money. Metal had a use value of its own, but coins became accepted in trade for their symbolic value. They acted as a <u>standard measure</u> for exchanging other goods and services of value rather than for the use of the metal they contained.

The next stage in the evolution of money is that of representative money. Representative money is symbolic money that is based on useful commodities, such as the warehouse receipts issued by the ancient Egyptian grain banks, or, and more recent, forms of paper currency that were backed by gold or silver. The adoption of representative money was a <u>significant evolution</u> in human consciousness. Psychologically, the individual had to transfer the sense of value from a usable material object to an <u>abstract</u> symbol. Socially, groups of people had to agree on the common usage of the same symbol.

The invention of representative money then had a profound effect on the evolution of both money and society and …

# Word building: Values and beliefs

**page 197**

**1** Elicit what students think the meaning is. Put their ideas on the board.

**2** Before the lesson starts, write sets of words and meanings on card and cut them up. Divide the class into pairs and for this exercise ask them to match the words and their meanings. This should generate some discussion as the distinctions are fine for some items. When the students have finished, they can check their definitions of values and principles in exercise 1.

**ANSWERS**

**1** b **2** e **3** h **4** c **5** a **6** f **7** d **8** g

**3** Encourage students to think of as many words as they can themselves before resorting to the dictionary. Any new words need to be added to their (electronic) vocabulary lists.

**ANSWERS**

standards, standardise, standardisation, non-standard, substandard

**4–6** Ask students to do these activities individually followed by checking in pairs after each exercise. Sort out any difficulties as you monitor, and focus on any that the whole class are finding problematic. Then check the answers as whole class.

**ANSWERS**

**4**

**1** Values

**2** value

3 Valuables
4 invaluable/valuable
5 valueless

**5**
1 principles
2 principled
3 unprincipled
4 principles

**6**
1 idealistic
2 ideals
3 morals
4 ethical

**7** Ask students to work in groups and discuss the question. Make sure students look at both the advantages and the disadvantages so that when you divide them into groups, both sides have something to work on. Religion may play a part for some students in the question of values, so make them aware that their arguments should be objective not subjective and steer clear of the topic as far as possible. Point out that discussions of religion and politics should be avoided in the exam. Monitor the discussion and give feedback, tabulating students' ideas on the board.

# Reading Passage page 198

**1** Ask students to find the synonyms in pairs. They can divide the words between them and then check their answers before checking with another pair. Give the students a time limit to do the scanning.

ANSWERS
1 indicators
2 evaluate
3 emphasis
4 phenomena
5 factors
6 crucial
7 advantage
8 predominantly

## Further practice

In pairs, students can choose about six or seven words or phrases and write synonyms and then ask another pair to find them. This can be extended to finding words, antonyms, paraphrases of clauses/sentences and the location of function, e.g., *examples, effects, reservations*, etc.

**2** Students do the exercise in pairs. If you think students are choosing the same paragraph, allot each pair of students a paragraph to make sure they are all covered by the class. Ask them to skim the paragraph and make brief notes about the main content. They then compare their ideas with another pair. Discuss as a whole class, checking a selection of paragraphs.

## Questions 1–13

Ask students to answer the questions as a Reading test within a strict 20-minute time limit without any further preparation. Allow extra time, only if necessary, asking students to mark which question they were up to at the 20-minute limit.

When the time is up, put them into groups to discuss their answers and then go over the answers as a whole class.

ANSWERS
1 B
2 F
3 G
4 D
5 A
6 D
7 A
8 F
9 B
10 (valid) construct
11 self-reported
12 policy areas
13 A

**3** Students discuss the follow-up question in small groups.

## Extension

Students can work in groups, and then collate as a whole class a strategy list for question types that they can record and share electronically.

Time permitting, students can create their own reading infogram which they can design as a poster, web page or pdf for the class Facebook page/blog, etc. Check any language input for accuracy, etc. and revise periodically.

## Round up

Review/elicit from students the strategies they used for each set of questions and any time issues they had.

# Language focus: Substitution and ellipsis page 200

**1** Discuss the example and emphasise how useful substitution and ellipsis are in developing fluency and cohesion in the writing and speaking tests. Highlight the dangers of overuse, as students need to be clear about the words they are substituting. For example, students need to be aware of what their readers are already aware of so that any reference to it is clear. Students may have a tendency to provide too much information, thus having the opposite effect to that intended, affecting cohesion and comprehension.

Go through the Grammar reference, eliciting how aware students are of this area of grammar. Show students how to write less without losing any of the message. You can do this by highlighting in texts where ellipsis and substitution successfully occur (use some of the reading texts from their books). You can draw their attention to substitution and ellipsis by asking what information is missing and what certain words or phrases refer to. This way students will gradually recognise substitution devices and have more confidence in using them in their own writing and speaking.

ANSWERS

1 person
2 Repeating the words breaks the flow between the clauses.
   This can make clauses and sentences more difficult to follow.
3 *I think so.*

**2–3** Students do the exercises in pairs. Ask them to check their answers with other students before whole-class feedback.

ANSWERS

**2**
1 h  2 a  3 g  4 f  5 e  6 b  7 c  8 d

**3**
1 … by putting back some of the profits they have made from the local people./Such philanthropic behaviour
2 … told us how to behave …/… to do so …
3 … the traditions and ways of the society they belong to … /… such customs …
4 … introduce philosophy into the school curriculum./… Doing so …
5 I left home when I was 18 to go to university./I did so …
6 Detailed analysis … on what makes people happy,/… such research …
7 … adhered to the traditions of the community we came from …/… do so …
8 moral standards on television … should be therefore raised/In doing so …

**4** Students can do this activity individually and then check their answers in pairs before checking as a whole class. Discuss any difficulties with the whole class.

ANSWERS

1 Although the government wanted to stop funding the railway venture, they weren't able to stop funding it.
2 The banks didn't want the policy on extending loans to small businesses to change, but the government did want the policy to change.
3 Some people don't believe that there is a clear link between happiness and money, while others do think there is.
4 The college was praised for student behaviour and success as it hoped it would be praised.
5 The university didn't invest as much in delivering subjects like philosophy as it could have invested.
6 My father laid down the law with us when we were children, but my mother didn't lay down the law.

## Round up
Ask students whether they like using substitution and/or ellipsis. The same can be done with all language and skills.

## Speaking PART 3 page 201

**1** Ask students to do the exercise in pairs, and then form a group with another pair to share and check their answers. As a whole class, list the responses under the two headings, and number the questions 1–3, 4–6 for reference. Against each number, write the focus of each question. Ask students to read the focus for each question and see if they can discern how the focus of the questions develops as the discussion progresses. The structure will then become apparent. They can then link this to the development of arguments in Writing Task 2, and in the Reading and Listening parts of the IELTS exam.

ANSWERS

factors contributing to well-being
whether free time is a key factor (evaluation )
opinion about the evaluation that modern life is too stressful
different ways that money impacts on well-being/the impact of money
evaluation of the pursuit of money
the role of money in our future lives

**2** Students work in the same groups, matching the ideas with the questions. Point out that some may be used for more than one question, and that they can add their own ideas. Monitor the discussion and then go over students' answers as a whole class, highlighting good ideas.

ANSWERS

Well-being:
What factors contribute to people's general sense of well-being? a
Do you think having free time is the key factor in people's well-being? Why/Why not? e, g, j
Some people think modern life is too stressful for people to be generally happy. To what extent do you agree or disagree? b

Money and its effects:
How does money impact on people's well-being in activities such as work and leisure? c, d
In terms of social development, do you think the pursuit of money has a negative or positive effect? Why/Why not? h, i
In the future, do you think money will have a greater or lesser role to play in our lives? Give reasons. f

## Extension
Students can create *idea banks* that they can use across all questions. These can be organised under perspectives such as educational/education ideas, etc.

**3** Students work in pairs and then compare their answers with other students.

ANSWERS
1 Substitution
2 Substitution
3 Ellipsis
4 Substitution
5 Substitution
6 Ellipsis

**4** Students choose two or three of the questions and discuss them, noting down any ideas they come up with for future reference for Speaking or for Writing Task 2.

For exam practice, put them into pairs to practise a timed Part 3 speaking. They can use the checklist on page 181, and note anything specific they want their partner to focus on.

### Round up

Review the Speaking test of the IELTS exam, especially regarding skills, and ask students to evaluate/reflect on how they have developed during the course.

## Writing TASK 1 page 202

**1** Students look at the task and the charts in groups. Check comprehension of the words in the box, and ask them to highlight significant points on the charts. Elicit the tenses they will use and the kinds of trend/descriptive phrases they can use. Check the answers with the students leading the discussion/analysis.

**2–3** Students do this in groups, followed by whole class checking with words listed on the board. Students can photograph the list for their (electronic) vocabulary lists, but encourage them to type/write them and not just to rely on the photograph.

ANSWERS
**2**
proportion: share, percentage
constitute: account for, form, make up, comprise, total
reflect: mirror
vast majority: overwhelming majority
only: just
pattern: trend, development
similarity: is similar to
difference: is different from/differs from
quarter: 25%
age group: those who are … years of age, … year-olds
year-olds: years of age, those in the … age group, the … age group

**4** Students can do this individually and then check their answers with other students before whole-class feedback.

ANSWERS
a (a greater proportion of) part-time workers
b there was a marked difference in the proportions of those aged 25–34
c compared to
d reflect
e the vast majority cited
f illustrate
g a correlation

**5** Students again do this in groups, checking their answers with the whole class. The matching is an essential generic process for evaluation of essays, like the checklist.

ANSWERS
1 cited/stated
2 Overall, there seems to be a correlation between age and the frequency of being happy.
3 reflect
4 some or all/most of the time
5 stated that they were less so
6 Whereas most 35–49 year-olds were happy some or all/most of the time (87.8%), a greater proportion of this age group stated that they were less so (12.2%). The full-time and part-time workers' responses reflect those of the three age groups with identical proportions (91.8%) among both groups being happy at least some of the time, but a greater proportion of part-time workers being slightly happier all or most of the time (66.5%).
7 identical
8 a correlation, the vast majority, difference, two thirds, a quarter, a greater proportion, identical proportions, a greater proportion

### Extension

In groups, students select about seven (generic) phrases from the model that they think would be useful in the future. Discuss the selected phrases and their suitability as generic/recyclable phrases.

**6** Students do this in groups and discuss with the class.

**7** Students can do the task for homework, or in class. In both cases, stress the need for them to be strict about the 20-minute time limit. Tell them that as you mark their work, you will be looking for examples of the vocabulary and the use of the structures in exercise 5. Alternatively, you could do this as a class test.

Encourage students to look at the model answer *only after* they have written their own answer. Ask students to go through the model working out how it complies with the requirements of the task. They can use the *Comments* as a starting point.

*Model answer*

The charts report how happy people in selected groups said they were in the last four weeks.

It is clear that most people in the various groups are generally happy. Among those aged 50–64, the majority stated that they were happy some of the time and all/most of the time, 29.4% and 55.1% respectively, with 15.6% being happy a little or none of the time. The pattern was fairly similar among those in the 65–74 age group, with 58.3% happy all or most of the time and a smaller proportion (27.4%) some of the time compared to 14.2% being less happy.

The happiness responses of the three labour groups generally mirror those of the two age groups. The happiest people are those in education or training with the overwhelming majority (93.7%) being happy at least some of the time. As regards people who were self- employed and retired, the former were generally happier than the latter. Whilst most of those who were selfemployed stated they were happy at least some of the time (87.7%), a slightly smaller proportion (84.8%) of those retired did so.

*Word count: 183*

**COMMENTS**

The response summarises all the information giving all the relevant data. The introduction paraphrases the rubric and there is an overview at the beginning of the second paragraph. Complex sentences are used as well as comparative structures and different noun phrases are employed to avoid repetition, e.g., *among those aged 50-64/in the 65–74 age group/people who were self-employed and retired.*

## Round up

Review the main types of data found in IELTS Writing Task 1, first eliciting from students the grammar and vocabulary areas along with important strategies. Give hints, if necessary.

---

**REVIEW 14 ANSWERS**  pages 204–205

## Vocabulary: Money matters

**1**

| | |
|---|---|
| 1 paper money | 2 Correct |
| 3 Correct | 4 cash payment |
| 5 Correct | 6 Correct |
| 7 currency crisis | |

**2**

1 Countries try to build up currency reserves to buy foreign products.
2 Sponsorship money helps many artists and young people achieve their ambitions in life.
3 When I was a child I kept my savings in a money box shaped like a red telephone box.
4 Many countries are not restricted to just one cash

crop such as rice or wheat.
5 To develop the financial literacy of the general public, children at school should be given lessons on money management.
6 Do you have much spending money left after paying for all your outgoings?
7 Family finances are as much a concern for finance ministers as health, housing and welfare.
8 The cancellation of a debt burden can be an enormous relief.

## Word building: Values and beliefs

1 idealistic
2 values
3 principles
4 value, invaluable, valuable
5 customs

## Language focus: Substitution and ellipsis

**1**
Possible answers
1 It is essential for people to aim for physical as well as mental well-being. If they do so, it will make them feel better.
2 Thinking classes should be introduced in secondary schools. Doing so would improve pupils' performance enormously.
3 Education on money management is crucial to help people control their finances. Such education helps them to cope with their daily lives.
4 Children can attend extracurricular classes relating to their hobbies. By doing so, pupils will progress even more during normal school hours.
5 I will start university next term. I know I'll do so with great excitement.

**2**

1 *did*/didn't/*had*
2 *wasn't able to*/couldn't/*mightn't*
3 *do*/think they are/*think*
4 *would*/will do/*would have*
5 *could have*/did/*should have*
6 will/*won't*/*might not*
7 *could have*/*might have*/would have
8 *is*/*must be*/will be

**ACCURACY IN IELTS**

1 a greater proportion, accommodation
2 education expenditure, projects
3 accounted for, largest age group
4 the 24–35 age group, opening
5 seems, in the first five years
6 information, volunteer
7 the percentage/proportion of volunteers, the 15–19 age group fell from …
8 twice as many, convenient
9 fluctuations, sponsorship

Photocopiable materials

# Photocopiable activities

## Unit 1  We are all friends now
# Describing people

**Student A**

**1** Take it in turns to describe the words. When your partner gives a right answer, they can write it into the crossword.

---

**Student B**

**1** Take it in turns to describe the words. When your partner gives a right answer, they can write it into the crossword.

## Unit 2 Technology – now and then
# Don't say it

| convenient | practical | important |
|---|---|---|
| easy | suitable | useful |
| little effort | effective | valuable |
| needs | possible | significant |
| appropriate | hands-on | necessary |

| necessary | significant | harmful |
|---|---|---|
| important | important | damage |
| needed | special | hurt |
| essential | large | injury |
| basis | serious | effect |

| valuable | useful | effective |
|---|---|---|
| money | effective | successful |
| worth | helpful | efficient |
| important | achieve | achieve |
| worthless | good | good |

| appealing | worthwhile | inspiring |
|---|---|---|
| attractive | useful | encourage |
| interesting | important | want to do something |
| want | good enough | feeling |
| beautiful | suitable | reaction |

| improve | destroy | produce |
|---|---|---|
| make things better | damage | make |
| worse | end | use |
| good | defeat | thing |
| excellent | spoil | object |

| affect | enhance | promote |
|---|---|---|
| result | better | sell |
| effect | quality | advertise |
| consequence | amount | improve |
| outcome | strength | encourage |

| damage | deteriorate | advance |
|---|---|---|
| hurt | get worse | progress |
| destroy | bad | get better |
| harm | become worse | improve |
| injury | situation | develop |

## Unit 3  Thrill seekers
# Grammar grab

| Team name | Correct ✓ Incorrect ✗ | Points bet | +/- Points |
|---|---|---|---|
| 1  I'm really keen about learning foreign languages. | | | |
| 2  She's addicted by exercise. She trains three times a day. | | | |
| 3  I'm mad about running. I get stressed when I don't run. | | | |
| 4  Why do you think so many people are interesting in football? | | | |
| 5  I find climbing mountains really invigorating. | | | |
| 6  What makes extreme sports excited? | | | |
| 7  I get bored in watching sport but I love playing different games. | | | |
| 8  Can you tell me about someone you find inspired? | | | |
| 9  I'm not capable to swimming very far. | | | |
| 10  What sports do you think are the most challenged? | | | |
| 11  I'm passionate about watching the Olympics. | | | |
| 12  I'm fond to eating Italian food. I love cooking it as well. | | | |
| 13  I find people who watch sport all the time really annoying. | | | |
| 14  I'm indifferent with reality TV shows. I watch them occasionally but I'm not a huge fan. | | | |
| 15  What's the most challenged sport you've ever played? | | | |
| | | | .......... points |

## Unit 4  Global issues and opportunities
# World problems

---

### Collocations

| | |
|---|---|
| main/likely/major *cause* | adverse/unfavourable/trying *circumstances* |
| significant/political/special *event* | favourable/false/good *impression* |
| burning/controversial/major *issue* | memorable/festive/state *occasion* |
| golden/excellent/perfect *opportunity* | growing/serious/insurmountable *problem* |
| ideal/dangerous/difficult *situation* | imaginative/effective/perfect *solution* |

---

### Question cards

| | | |
|---|---|---|
| What can individuals do to solve world problems such as climate change? | What do you think are the main problems facing the world today? | What can be done to solve issues such as world hunger? |
| Should governments be responsible for dealing with environmental issues? | What are the main causes of unemployment in your country? | What can be done to solve the growing problem of crime? |
| What serious problems have you solved in your life? | Can you tell me about a difficult situation you have dealt with? | What golden opportunities have you had in your life? |
| What solutions are there to the amount of waste people cause? | Should businesses be made responsible for solving environmental issues? | How can we solve the problem of people being over reliant on their cars? |
| Who is responsible for dealing with problems such as homelessness? | What can be done to encourage people to recycle more? | Should governments be responsible for providing new graduates with jobs? |
| What are the main causes of rising temperatures? | What are the main causes of animal extinction? | Why are cities becoming so overcrowded? |
| Why is water becoming scarcer in the world? | Are you optimistic or pessimistic about the world's problems? Why? | Who faces more significant problems: urban or rural dwellers? |

## Unit 5  The future

# Find someone who …

| **Student A:** Find someone who thinks that, in the future, … | **Name** | **Reason** |
| --- | --- | --- |
| people will work from home more. | | |
| jobs will be very different. | | |
| people will have a better work-life balance. | | |
| people will be healthier. | | |
| people will live longer. | | |
| **Student B:** Find someone who thinks that, in the future, … | **Name** | **Reason** |
| life will be better in rural areas than in urban areas. | | |
| cities will be even larger. | | |
| people will live, work, shop and go to school in the same building. | | |
| modern civilisation won't have changed much in 50 years' time. | | |
| lifestyles will become simpler and more traditional. | | |
| **Student C:** Find someone who thinks that, in the future, … | **Name** | **Reason** |
| cars won't need drivers. | | |
| people will travel less because of fuel shortages. | | |
| people won't have cars as fuel will be too expensive. | | |
| the roles of men and women will become more similar. | | |
| men will become the primary carers for children. | | |
| **Student D:** Find someone who thinks that, in the future, … | **Name** | **Reason** |
| children will learn online and not in a traditional classroom. | | |
| the subjects taught at school will change. | | |
| fewer people will go to university. | | |
| unhealthy foods will be banned by most governments. | | |
| people will only eat convenience food and forget how to cook meals. | | |

PHOTOCOPIABLE

## Unit 6  The fruits of nature
# Processes
### Set 1: Brick making

Initially, raw materials are delivered to the factory.

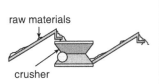

raw materials

crusher

The raw materials are then crushed.

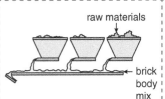

raw materials

brick body mix

Next, the raw materials are batched and mixed to create the mixture for the bricks.

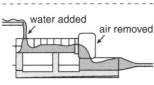

water added

air removed

Following that the material is taken to the brick-making machine where water is added and sludge and air are removed.

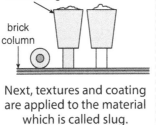

texturing and coating

brick column

Next, textures and coating are applied to the material which is called slug.

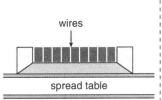

wires

spread table

Wires now cut the slug into individual bricks.

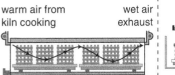 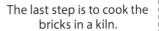

warm air from kiln cooking

wet air exhaust

The last step is to cook the bricks in a kiln.

unloading & packaging

Finally, bricks are held in a holding room before being packed and unloaded.

### Set 2: Cheese making

raw milk

The process of traditional cheese making starts with the use of raw milk.

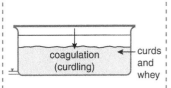

coagulation (curdling)

curds and whey

The raw milk is curdled and produces curds and whey.

cutting

After this, the curds and whey are cut with a rake.

stirring and cooking

Next, the mixture is cooked and stirred.

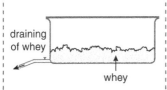

draining of whey

whey

The whey is drained off and the curds are left in the container.

milling

The curds are then milled and made into a finer product.

salting

Afterwards, this finer product has salt added to it.

Next, the salted mixture is poured into moulds to create the shape necessary.

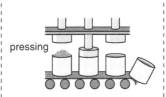

pressing

Then these moulds are pressed to create a firmer cheese.

ripening

Finally, the cheese is ripened over time on shelves.

## Unit 7  The world of work and education
# Collocations dominoes

| throw away | benefit |
|---|---|
| considerable | advantage |
| take | opportunity |
| once-in-a-lifetime | success |
| guarantee | prospects |
| career | disadvantage |
| distinct | failure |
| total | achievement |

| a lack of | improvement |
|---|---|
| room | chance |
| boost | opportunity |
| seize | prospects |
| result in | chance |
| deserve | failure |
| career | prospects |

**Possible collocations**

a lack of – opportunity/success/prospects/achievement/improvement/chance

boost – chances

career – opportunity/success/prospects

considerable – this collocates with all the nouns

deserve – chance

distinct – disadvantage/advantage/opportunity/chance

guarantee – success/failure/improvement

once-in-a-lifetime – opportunity

result in – opportunity/success/failure/improvement

room – improvement

seize – opportunity/chance

take – advantage/opportunity/chance

throw away – opportunity/chance

total – failure

## Unit 8  Mapping the world
# Describing maps

### Student A

Barrow 2005

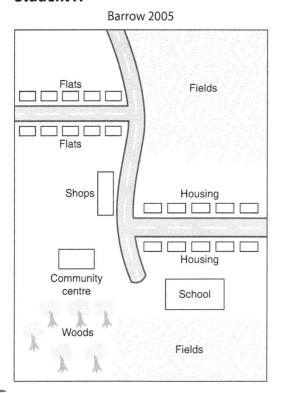

Barrow 2016

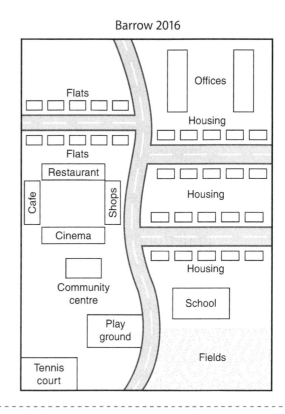

### Student B

Barrow 2005

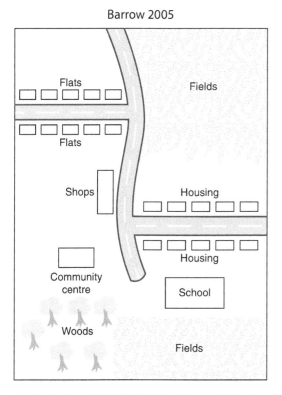

Barrow 2016

Notes

PHOTOCOPIABLE

## Unit 9  What is beauty?
# Description and evaluation

| | |
|---|---|
| evoke<br>tall<br>undervalued<br>overvalued | ancient<br>spacious<br>dazzling<br>humbling |
| magnificent<br>impressive<br>overstate<br>understated | ecstatic<br>stone<br>overcome<br>underestimate |
| underfunded<br>melancholic<br>thoughtful<br>understate | nostalgic<br>awe<br>overestimate<br>overrated |
| overwhelmed<br>emotional<br>underrated<br>overtake | separated<br>hated<br>revealing<br>unoriginal |
| alien<br>attacked<br>talentless<br>fused | familiar<br>admired<br>succumbing<br>disguised |
| ingenious<br>perception<br>collage<br>take in | grandeur<br>digital stills<br>narrow down<br>access |
| discipline<br>fade<br>click<br>conclusion | regret<br>suggestion<br>criticism<br>expectation |
| possibility<br>impression<br>old-fashioned<br>majesty | |

**Unit 10  Is it art?**
## Matching paragraphs and headings

**A** Perfecting the plan

**B** How nature influences the design

**C** An initial proposal

**D** First steps in creating the garden

**E** The use and impact of colour

**F** Sourcing and using ancient plants

**G** The project is given approval

## Unit 11  The family and society

# Bingo

| | | | |
|---|---|---|---|
| **Card 1** | Call 08453906211 | June 21st 1984 | www.soul-rose.com |
| | £688.21 | 12 Elliott Close | Flight PZ 921 |
| | Card 7879 4530 3205 6912 | MN19 6VY | Reference AP19S03 |
| **Card 2** | Call 08543906211 | June 24th 1984 | www.soul-rose.com |
| | £688.12 | 12 Eliot Close | Flight PZ 921 |
| | Card 7879 4530 3205 6912 | MN90 6VY | Reference AP19S03 |
| **Card 3** | Call 08453906211 | June 24th 1984 | www.saul-roze.com |
| | £671.21 | 12 Eliot Close | Flight FS 291 |
| | Card 7879 4530 3205 6912 | MN19 6VY | Reference AB19S03 |
| **Card 4** | Call 08453906221 | June 12th 1984 | www.saul-roze.com |
| | £681.21 | 12 Elliott Close | Flight FS 291 |
| | Card 7879 4530 3502 6912 | NM90 6YV | Reference AP91S03 |
| **Card 5** | Call 08453906221 | June 21st 1984 | www.saul-roze.com |
| | £681.21 | 12 Eliot Close | Flight SS 912 |
| | Card 7879 4530 3502 6912 | NM91 6VY | Reference AB91Z03 |
| **Card 6** | Call 08453960211 | June 12th 1984 | www.soul-roze.com |
| | £618.12 | 12 Eliot Close | Flight SS 912 |
| | Card 7897 4530 3205 6912 | NM91 6VY | Reference AB91Z03 |
| **Card 7** | Call 08453906211 | June 12th 1984 | www.sole-rose.com |
| | £618.12 | 12 Eliot's Close | Flight PS 921 |
| | Card 7897 4530 3205 6912 | NM19 6YV | Reference AB19S03 |
| **Card 8** | Call 08453960211 | June 1st 1948 | www.sole-rose.com |
| | £861.21 | 12 Eliott Close | Flight BZ 912 |
| | Card 7879 4350 3205 6912 | NM19 6YV | Reference AB19S03 |
| **Card 9** | Call 08453960211 | June 1st 1984 | www.soul-roze.com |
| | £861.21 | 12 Eliott Close | Flight PS 921 |
| | Card 7879 4350 3205 6912 | NM91 6VY | Reference PA91S03 |
| **Card 10** | Call 08543906211 | June 1st 1984 | www.soul-roze.com |
| | £671.21 | 12 Eliot's Close | Flight BZ 912 |
| | Card 7879 4350 3205 6912 | NM91 6VY | Reference PA91S03 |

**Unit 12  Travelling around the world**
# Visualisation

**Set A**

| First holiday | Worst holiday | Favourite holiday activities | Worst food eaten on holiday |
|---|---|---|---|
| Favourite holiday | Favourite country to visit | Least favourite holiday activities | A good souvenir you brought back |
| Favourite city to visit | Favourite type of accommodation | A difficult journey you made | A place you would love to go to again |

**Set B**

| Foreign | Curious | Unique | Pristine |
|---|---|---|---|
| Odd | Fresh | New | Different |
| Strange | Unfamiliar | Local | Inquisitive |
| Treasured | Untouched | Irregular | Diverse |
| Dissimilar | Unexpected | Unfamiliar | Uncomfortable |

## Unit 13  The importance of infrastructure
# Who's telling the truth?

**Card 1**

Cars should be banned and bikes given to people for free.

**Card 2**

International flights should be limited to one per person per year.

**Card 3**

Internet access that is not for work or trade should be limited to one hour per person per day.

**Card 4**

People should only be allowed one luxury electric appliance. Luxury appliances include tablets, phones, TVs and stereos.

**Card 5**

1 billion people in the world do not have access to a clean water supply. Everyone should pay a 10% annual tax until they do.

**Card 6**

The oil industry should be closed by 2030 and the world become reliant solely on renewable energy.

## Unit 14  Money and well-being
# Group interviews

| | |
|---|---|
| Money for me is … | One thing I'd like to achieve is … |
| Money and happiness are … | Money affects my behaviour … |
| I prefer spending money on … | I'm satisfied with my life because … |
| People's moods are most affected by … | Work affects people's moods by … |
| Having more money makes people … | Rich people should … |
| Money is more important than anything else because … | The pursuit of money has damaged … |

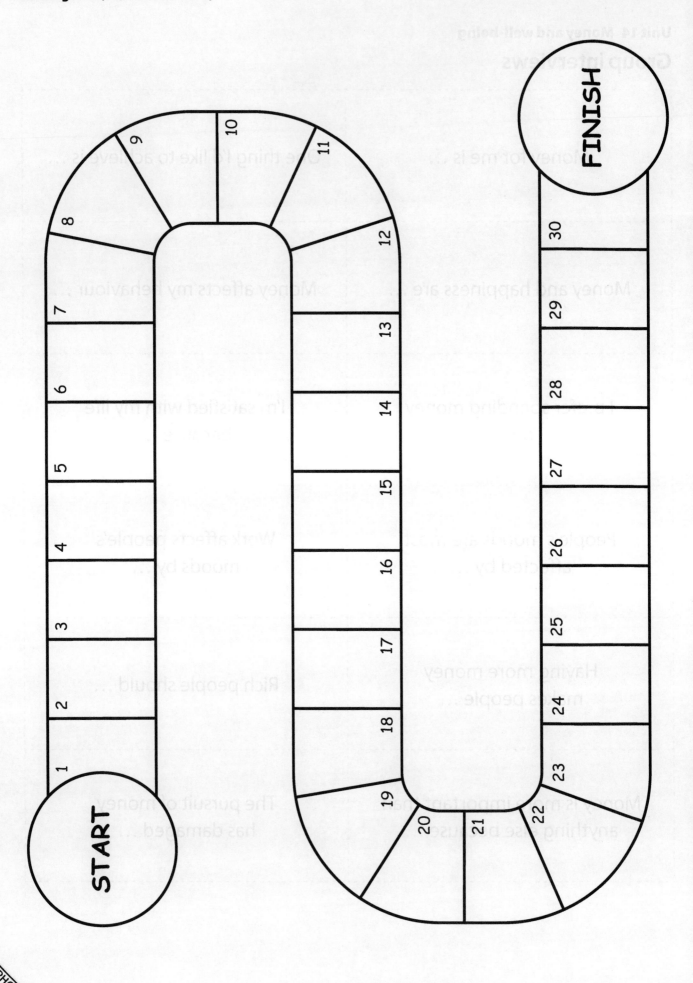

## Unit 1

### Activity
Pairwork: two halves of a crossword

### Aim
To revise Unit 1 target vocabulary. To practise the skill assessed in the Speaking section (especially part 2).

### Grammar and lexis
Adjectives to describe personality

### Preparation
Make one copy of the worksheet for each pair of students, and cut it up into two sections as indicated.

### Time
15–20 minutes

### Student's Book link
Unit 1, page 7.

### Procedure
- Organise students into pairs and distribute the crosswords.
- Explain that students have two halves of the same crossword. They should take it in turns to explain a word without saying that word or showing each other's crosswords.
- Demonstrate how the activity works using the words *sporty* and *confident*. Tell student As that you are going to explain 2 across. Ask student Bs NOT to answer (as they have the words on their crossword). Explain and describe the word until someone guesses it. Then explain to student Bs that you will describe 5 across. Ask student As not to answer. Explain and describe it until someone guesses the word.
- Give students around 15 minutes to complete the crossword. Monitor and help with definitions.
- As an extension, you could write the following Part 2 topic card on the board:

> Describe a person you admire.
>
> You should say:
>   what they do
>   what their characteristics are
>   what positive things they have done in their life
> and explain why you admire them.

## Unit 2

### Activity
Group game (groups of four)

### Aim
To revise the target language of Unit 2. To practise thinking of synonyms useful for Speaking Part 2.

### Grammar and lexis
Evaluating adjectives and verbs of cause and effect

### Preparation
Make one copy of the cut-up card for each group.

### Time
15 minutes

### Student's Book link
Unit 2. Set this task at the end of page 21.

### Exam link
Speaking Part 2 – causes and effects/evaluating adjectives to give opinions

### Procedure
- Organise students into groups of four. Give each group a set of cut up cards. Divide each group into A and B pairs.
- Write one of the cards on the board. Ask students to think about how they can explain the word at the top without using the words below. Also explain that they cannot use other forms of the target word e.g. say *the opposite of inconvenient*. After thirty seconds, ask one student to explain the word without using the other words.
- Tell students that they have to describe words to their partner. While one pair is describing the words the other pair should time one minute and monitor that the student speaking does not use the taboo words. Students should describe as many words as possible in one minute.
- The pairs should then swap roles so that B are timing and monitoring while pair A are describing and guessing.
- Students should rotate roles until all of the cards have been used. For words students describe and guess, they should keep that card. The winning pair is the one with the most cards at the end.
- As an extension, you could ask students to produce their own taboo cards using the target words not used so far, e.g., *harm*, *ruin* and *result*.

# Notes for photocopiable activities

## Unit 3

### Activity
Group game (groups of four)

### Aim
To revise the target language of Unit 3. To practise questions and answers for Speaking Part 1.

### Grammar and lexis
Adjectives with prepositions and adjectives ending in -ing/-ed

### Preparation
Make one copy of the sheet per group (cut up).

### Time
25–30 minutes

### Student's Book link
Unit 3, and end of page 33.

### Procedure
- Organise students into groups of four. Give each group a sheet. Ask them to choose a team name or letter. Write the names/letters on the board.
- Tell students they are going to identify if the sentences are grammatically correct or not. Give each group 10–15 minutes to put either a tick or a cross in the Correct/Incorrect column. They should correct the sentences they think are wrong.
- Explain that each group now has 100 points they can allocate across their answers. The amount of points they put against a sentence should reflect how confident they are it is correct or incorrect. Give each group five minutes to write the amount in the 'Points bet' column.
- Groups swap worksheets. Check answers in whole-class feedback. Students win the points for correct answers and lose them for incorrect answers.
- Ask groups to give the sheets back to the original group. Groups then confirm the amount of points they have and which group is the winner.

#### ANSWERS
1 I'm really keen **on** learning foreign languages.
2 She's addicted **to** exercise. She trains three times a day.
3 Correct.
4 Why do you think so many people are **interested** in football?
5 Correct.
6 What makes extreme sports **exciting**?
7 I get bored **with** watching sport but I love playing different games.
   [Note: no preposition should also be accepted: I get bored watching sport ...]
8 Can you tell me about someone you find **inspiring**?
9 I'm not capable **of** swimming very far.
10 What sports do you think are the most **challenging**?

11 Correct.
12 I'm fond **of** eating Italian food. I love cooking it as well.
13 Correct.
14 I'm indifferent **to** reality TV shows. I watch them occasionally but I'm not a huge fan.
15 What's the most **challenging** sport you've ever played?

## Unit 4

### Activity
Group board game (groups of four)

### Aim
To revise the target vocabulary of Unit 4. To practise giving full answers to Speaking Part 3 questions.

### Grammar and lexis
Collocations of problems, solutions and opportunities

### Preparation
Make one copy of the board game on page 142, one collocations sheet, and one set of accompanying question cards (cut up) for each group of four students.

### Time
20 minutes

### Student's Book link
Unit 4, pages 49 and 55.

### Procedure
- Organise students into groups of four. Give each group a board game, a collocations sheet, and a set of cut up question cards. Each group will also need a coin, four items to use as counters and a watch/phone to time their responses.
- Explain that students have to take it in turns to flip a coin and move around the board. *Heads* means students move two squares. *Tails* means they move one square.
- As an example, write one set of the collocations onto the board. Read one of the questions aloud. Ask a student to time you. Then answer the question using a collocation and speaking for twenty seconds.
- Explain that students can move further round the board by: a. speaking for close to twenty seconds (one additional square) b. using a collocation in their response (one additional square).
- The other students who are not speaking should listen for any of the collocations being used, and also time the speaker. Make it clear to the students that they can use any of the collocations to answer any of the questions, as long as they make sense. Some collocations may be more appropriate than others.

- If a student cannot answer the question appropriately, they move back one space. If they take more than twenty seconds to respond then they also move back one space. If they speak for only fifteen seconds, they cannot move forward one space and if they speak for more than thirty seconds they cannot move forward one space.
- After their turn, each student should return the question to the bottom of the pile and the next student has their turn. As the game progresses, if a student chooses a question they have already answered, then they should take another card.
- The winner is the first to freach the FINISH.

# Unit 5

## Activity

Whole-class communicative activity

## Aim

To practise using *will* for prediction and speaking about Speaking Part 3

## Grammar and lexis

Practise *will* for predictions

## Preparation

Make copies of the cards (cut up, one card per student).

## Time

20 minutes

## Student's Book link

Unit 5, after the Speaking on page 62.

## Procedure

- Give each student a card. Explain that there are four different cards in the room, A, B, C and D.
- Read the first statement from one of the cards out loud and ask one of the students whether they agree or not. Keep asking individual students until you find someone who agrees. When you find someone who agrees, ask them why they agree. Write down their name and reason on the card, making it clear to the students what you are writing and where.
- Tell students they have ten minutes to find someone who agrees with each statement on their card and to find out their reasons. Remind students to write down a name and reason. Encourage students to move around the room, speaking to as many people as possible. They should try to speak to people with A, B, C and D cards.
- Once students have found someone who agrees for all of their statements and completed their cards, ask them to sit in groups of four. Each group should have all cards A, B, C and D in it. Ask each student to choose two points from their card and to discuss in their group whether they agree with the statements or not and why.

- Elicit some feedback from each group on the statements that caused the most discussion.
- As an extension, have each group write their own additional 'Find someone who ...' cards containing other issues. Repeat the activity.

# Unit 6

## Activity

Card ordering activity (class activity)

## Aim

To practise analysing and describing processes

## Grammar and lexis

Describing sequences

## Preparation

For groups of 18, make one set of all cards and cut up. For smaller groups, choose one process and then add cards from the other process as distractors.

## Time

25 minutes

## Student's Book link

Unit 6 – describing sequences, end of page 81

## Procedure

- Give each student in the class a cut up card.
- If you have used all 18 cards, explain that they have two different processes between everyone. If you have used one process and some cards from the other, explain that they have 10 cards from one process and other cards from a different process.
- Tell students that they have 10 minutes to try to put the stages into the correct order. If need be, they should also decide which cards are not part of the process. It would be a good idea to get students physically moving around the room to stand in the correct order.
- Check students have stood in the correct order and, if necessary, that they have left out the the steps that do not belong in this process.
- As an extension, you could ask students to write 140 words describing one of the processes. Students should try to use the vocabulary for describing sequences on page 81 of the Student's Book.

ANSWERS

**Set 1**
1  Initially, raw materials are delivered to the factory.
2  The raw materials are then crushed.
3  Next, the raw materials are batched and mixed to create the mixture for the bricks.
4  Following that the material is taken to the brick-making machine where water is added and sludge and air are removed.

5   Next, textures and coating are applied to the material which is called slug.

6   Wires now cut the slug into individual bricks.

7   The last step is to cook the bricks in a kiln.

8   Finally, bricks are held in a holding room before being packed and unloaded.

**Set 2**

1   The process of traditional cheese making starts with the use of raw milk.

2   The raw milk is curdled and produces curds and whey.

3   After this, the curds and whey are cut with a rake.

4   Next, the mixture is cooked and stirred.

5   The whey is drained off and the curds are left in the container.

6   The curds are then milled and made into a finer product.

7   Afterwards, this finer product has salt added to it.

8   Next, the salted mixture is poured into moulds to create the shape necessary.

9   Then these moulds are pressed to create a firmer cheese.

10  Finally, the cheese is ripened over time on shelves.

# Unit 7

## Activity

Group game (groups of three)

## Aim

To practise using collocations

## Grammar and lexis

Collocations

## Preparation

Copy and cut up one set of 15 dominoes for every group of three students. Copy and cut out one 'Possible collocations' answer sheet per group.

## Time

20 minutes

## Student's Book link

Unit 7, end of the Vocabulary on page 97

## Procedure

- Put students into groups of three. Give each group a cut up set of dominoes.
- Draw these two of the dominoes onto the board: *take + opportunity / once-in-a-lifetime + success*. Ask students whether two of the words on the different halves can go together to make a collocation or not.
- Tell students to divide their dominoes within their group so that each person has five. Tell them that the aim of the game is to be the first one with no dominoes left.
- One student should put down a domino. The person to their left should try to match one

of their dominoes to this to form a correct collocation. The game continues with each student taking a turn one after the other.

- Let the students play the game and monitor to check the correct collocations are being used.
- More than one solution is possible. When groups have finished the game and have no more dominoes to place, give them the 'Possible collocations' answer sheet to check their answers.

# Unit 8

## Activity

Pairwork communicative description

## Aim

To practise describing maps and changes in a maps over time for Writing part 1

## Grammar and lexis

Describing maps

## Preparation

Make copies of the A and B maps so that each student has one map.

## Time

25 minutes

## Student's Book link

Set at end of unit 8

## Procedure

- Put students into pairs. Give each pair one Student A and one Student B sheet. Explain to students that one of them has two maps, Barrow in 2005 and Barrow in 2016. The other only has Barrow in 2005 and will draw Barrow in 2016.
- Brainstorm language with the students to describe location and types of change. Add them to the board, along with any they forget.
- Tell students to work in pairs. Using the language on the board, Student A describes the changes that have taken place while Student B takes notes on his/her sheet. Student B then draws Barrow 2016 in the blank space using his/her notes.
- Once Student B has completed the map, he/she can compare it to Student A's version for accuracy.
- As an extension, ask students to write 140 words describing the changes in the map.

# Unit 9

## Activity

Group game (groups of four)

## Aim

To revise the target language of Unit 9 and practise for Speaking Part 2 and 3

## Grammar and lexis
Vocabulary for description and evaluation

## Preparation
Make one copy of the board on page 142 and the cards (cut up) for each group of four students.

## Time
20–25 minutes

## Student's Book link
Set at end of unit 9

## Procedure
- Organise students into groups of four. Give each group a set of cut up cards and a board game. Divide each group into A and B pairs.
- Write one of the cards on the white board. Ask students to think about how they can explain each word without saying it. Tell them they cannot use other forms of the target word e.g. say *the adjective of hate*. After 30 seconds, ask one student to explain the words without saying any of them.
- Tell the students to place the cards face down in the middle of the table and that they have to describe words to their partner. While one pair is describing the words the other pair should time one minute and monitor that the student speaking does not use the words on the card.
- Tell students that they can skip words they do not know, but only one per card. Students should discard cards once they have described them. Monitor the students making a note of any skipped words. You can explain these later.
- Students should describe as many words as possible in one minute. The number of words correctly described and guessed is how many squares the students can move around the board.
- The pairs should then swap roles so that Student Bs are timing and monitoring while Student As are describing and guessing.
- Students should rotate roles until all the cards are used, or one pair reaches the end of the board.
- As an extension, you could ask students to work in pairs to complete these Part 2 and 3 tasks:

## Part 2 questions:

Describe a building you admire. You should say:
- where it is and what it is
- what it looks like
- why you admire it

and why you think it's important to protect buildings like these.

## Part 3 questions:

How does the appearance of a city affect people's emotions?
Do you think it's important to preserve historic buildings?
Would you rather live in a historic or modern city?

# Unit 10

## Activity
Pairwork matching

## Aim
To practise paragraph matching task

## Grammar and lexis
Synonym matching

## Preparation
Make one copy of cards (cut up).

## Time
15 minutes

## Student's Book link
Unit 10, after exam reading questions

## Procedure
- Cut the paragraph headings up and place on the walls around the classroom.
- Tell students to use the reading passage from pages 143–144 of the Student's Book.
- Ask students to make notes in their notebook about the main point of each paragraph, *excluding* the short two-lined paragraph. Monitor and check the students' notes. Ask students to compare their notes with a partner.
- Put students into pairs. Tell students that they have to find the matching headings for each paragraph around the classroom as quickly as possible. Give students a maximum of 8 minutes. Explain that the fastest and most accurate team wins. Write the points available on the board:
  *5 minutes = 10 points        6 minutes = 8 points*
  *7 minutes = 6 points         8 minutes = 4 points*
  Teams will then get one extra point for every correct match and lose one point for every incorrect match.
- Check the answers as a class and award points. When different pairs have different headings, ask them to explain the reasons for their choice.
- As an extension, ask students to match any synonyms in their notes to the paragraph headings.

ANSWERS

A – Paragraph 3   B – Paragraph 6   C – Paragraph 1
D – Paragraph 4   E – Paragraph 7   F – Paragraph 5
G – Paragraph 2 [Note: 2-line paragraph excluded]

**Notes for photocopiable activities**

# Unit 11

## Activity
Whole-class listening activity

## Aim
To practise recognising commonly confused letters/numbers. Listening – form, note and table completion

## Grammar and lexis
Letters and numbers

## Preparation
Make a copy of enough bingo cards so that each student has one.

## Time
15 minutes

## Student's Book link
Unit 11. Set this task after the Listening section.

## Procedure
- Give each student one of the bingo cards. Ask them whether they know how to play bingo. If anyone does, ask them to explain it.
- You will need to say each entry twice. First, read item one out loud at a natural pace. Ask students to cross it out if they have it on their card. The second time you say it, you should spell it out if it is a word that is similar, e.g., Eliot and Elliott.
- Read out each of the pieces of information in the table in order. Continue until one of the students shouts 'bingo'. Check the student's card. If they have made a mistake start again from the point they made a mistake.
- As an extension, ask students to write down ten similar pieces of information. They then read them out loud to a partner, who writes them down.

# Unit 12

## Activity
Group speaking activity (groups of three)

## Aim
To practise adjectives and describing travel experiences for Speaking Part 2.

## Grammar and lexis
Adjectives with multiple meanings.

## Preparation
Make a copy of both sets of cut up cards for each group of three students.

## Time
15 minutes

## Student's Book link
Unit 12 after vocabulary on pages 164–165.

## Procedure
- Put students into groups of three. Give each group a set of both cards. Students should place both sets face down on the table in front of them.
- Take one card from each pile. Read the cards out loud to the students. Use card A for the setting and card B as the word you need to include. Close your eyes and describe the place using the word from the set B pile.
- Students should work in their groups and take turns to take a card from each pile and show them to the group. They should then close their eyes and try to describe the experience using the word from pile B. The other two students should time 30 seconds. They get a point for using the word and a point for speaking for 30 seconds. Students should recycle the A cards until they

| 1 | Call 08453906211 | 16 | June 12<sup>th</sup> 1984 | 31 | www.soul-roze.com |
|---|---|---|---|---|---|
| 2 | Flight PS 921 | 17 | £861.21 | 32 | 12 Elliot Close |
| 3 | £681.21 | 18 | Card 7879 4350 3205 6912 | 33 | MN19 6VY |
| 4 | June 21<sup>st</sup> 1984 | 19 | www.saul-roze.com | 34 | Call 08453906221 |
| 5 | Card 7879 4530 3205 6912 | 20 | 12 Elliott Close | 35 | Reference AP91S03 |
| 6 | www.sole-rose.com | 21 | NM91 6VY | 36 | June 24<sup>th</sup> 1984 |
| 7 | 12 Eliot Close | 22 | Reference PA91S03 | 37 | Card 7879 4530 3502 6912 |
| 8 | MN19 6YV | 23 | June 31<sup>st</sup> 1948 | 38 | NM19 6YV |
| 9 | Reference AB19S03 | 24 | Flight PZ 921 | 39 | Flight SS 912 |
| 10 | June 1<sup>st</sup> 1948 | 25 | £688.31 | 40 | £671.21 |
| 11 | Flight BZ 912 | 26 | 12 Eliott Close | 41 | Call 08453960211 |
| 12 | £618.12 | 27 | Reference AB91Z03 | 42 | 12 Eliot's Close |
| 13 | Call 08543906211 | 28 | June 1<sup>st</sup> 1984 | | |
| 14 | www.soul-rose.com | 29 | Flight FS 291 | | |
| 15 | Reference AP19S03 | 30 | Card 7897 4530 3205 6912 | | |

have run out of B cards. The winner is the one with the most points once all cards have been used. While students are speaking make a note of any errors and feedback as a whole class.
• As an extension, you could ask students to complete this Part 2 task in pairs:

> Describe a holiday you enjoyed. You should say:
> • where this holiday was
> • what you did on the holiday
> • why you enjoyed it so much
>
> and explain who you would recommend it to.

# Unit 13

## Activity
Group game (groups of four to six)

## Aim
To practise Speaking Parts 2 and 3

## Grammar and lexis
Nouns related to systems and language of concession

## Preparation
Make one copy of the cut up cards for every group of 6 students.

## Time
25 minutes

## Student's Book link
Unit 13, end of Speaking Part 3 on page 190

## Exam link
Speaking Part 2 and 3

## Procedure
• Divide the class into groups of 4 to 6 people. Give each group a set of cards. Tell students to read their card.
• Choose one of the cards and prepare to speak on the topic for 1 to 2 minutes. Before you speak, write the words for concession on the board. Try to include these in your answer. Tell students to listen for these words as you speak. Afterwards, ask students if you used at least 3 of these words. Then ask students to rank the persuasiveness of your talk on a scale of 1 to 5, with 5 being the most persuasive
• Tell students that they have 2 minutes to prepare their talk of 1 to 2 minutes. After each talk students should award marks out of 5 for persuasiveness and a bonus point for using at least 3 expressions for concession.

• Give students 2 minutes to prepare their talk. Move around the room and help with ideas and vocabulary as they prepare.
• Students should then take turns to give their talk and award points.

As an extension you could ask each group to vote on the most persuasive talk and then ask those students to deliver their talk to the whole class.

# Unit 14

## Activity
Group game (groups of three or four)

## Aim
To practise giving extending sentences connected to Part 3 speaking topics

## Grammar and lexis
Recycle money and values vocabulary

## Preparation
Make one copy of cards (cut up) for every group of three or four students.

## Time
15 minutes

## Student's Book link
Unit 14, set at end of of Speaking Part 3, page 201

## Exam link
Speaking Part 3

## Procedure
• Divide the class into groups of three or four. Give each group a set of cards.
• Choose one of the cards and extend it with your own opinion. You can decide to tell the truth or a lie. When you have finished, ask the students to decide whether you were telling the truth or a lie.
• Tell students that they have to prepare their own answers that can either be true or false. Once they have decided, they should write true on the card if they are going to tell the truth and false if they are going to tell a lie.
• Give students 1 minute to prepare their answer.
• Students should then take turns to give their answer for a maximum of 30 seconds. The other students should decide whether they are telling the truth or a lie. If they are correct they win a point. The person with the most points is the winner.

As an extension you could allow students to interrogate each other after they have given their opinion.

# Progress Test 1: Units 1–3

## Listening

**Questions 1–4**

*Complete the form below.*

*Write **NO MORE THAN THREE WORDS AND/OR A NUMBER** for each answer.*

| HOLIDAY BOOKING FORM | |
| --- | --- |
| **Example** | |
| Size of group | .........6........ |
| Accommodation chosen | Villa **1** ................................... |
| Dates of stay | 19–26th **2** ................................... |
| Cost | **3** £................................... per week. |
| Deposit payable | **4** £................................... |

**Questions 5–8**

*Complete the notes below.*

*Write **NO MORE THAN THREE WORDS AND/OR A NUMBER** for each answer.*

| To do list |
| --- |
| Need to **5** ................................... immediately. |
| Check everyone is **6** ................................... |
| Ask everyone if they'd like to hire a private **7** ................................... |
| Pay deposit. |
| Remember to pay the balance of the cost by **8** ................................... May. |

**Questions 9 and 10**

*Choose **TWO** letters, **A–E**.*

*Which **TWO** activities would Alice and her friends like to do on their holiday?*

A  Lying on the beach

B  Wind surfing

C  Walking

D  Mountain biking

E  Dolphin watching

# Reading

## READING PASSAGE

*You should spend about 20 minutes on **Questions 1–13**, which are based on the Reading Passage below.*

### Questions 1–5

The Reading Passage below has seven sections, **A–G**.

*Choose the correct heading for sections **C–G** from the list of headings below.*

| List of Headings |
| --- |
| **i** How privacy concerns can affect public attitudes to the IoT |
| **ii** Different equipment that can be linked within the IoT |
| **iii** Other possible issues that might deter people from adopting the IoT |
| **iv** The use of barcodes for connecting different devices |
| **v** The question of compatibility |
| **vi** What has made the IoT possible |
| **vii** The benefits of fast connection speeds for IoT linked objects |
| **viii** The main benefits of IoT |

1  Section **C**

2  Section **D**

3  Section **E**

4  Section **F**

5  Section **G**

**A** The human race has always sought control of its environment, but the global rush to connect every device possible to the internet should be setting alarm bells ringing. The issue is whether people are in danger of surrendering control of their immediate environment and privacy, to the so-called *Internet of things* (IoT). The concept of IoT can be traced back to the 80s when a Coca Cola machine at Carnegie Mellon University reported back the quantity of Coca Cola bottles in the machine and their temperature.

**B** The number of connected devices, in recent years, has grown rapidly and will continue to do so in the coming decades, as connectivity spreads. Connections between offices and home appliances are now commonplace with computers, smart devices such as TVs, smartphones and printers interacting with each other. But people's lives are about to be revolutionised by the connection of billions of objects. According to Gartner Inc., by 2020, there will be over 25 billion interconnected objects, excluding smartphones, laptops and computers, creating a vast market worth hundreds of billions of dollars a year, as numbers of the latter also increase, but at a much slower rate.

**C** The IoT is made possible as the result of two major developments. Without the internet and the recent developments in wi-fi and mobile technology, talking to connected objects would not be feasible. The second is manufacturers' ability to embed electronic software, including barcodes or identifiers, in objects like kettles or heating systems to enable connectivity. These, in turn, allow individuals and manufacturers to talk to, i.e. exchange data, with other devices such as a smartphone or remote control.

**D** The range of objects that can be connected is endless. Smartphones can already exchange data with laptops or tablets, and refrigerators can exchange information about their contents and temperature, sending messages to a smartphone when, for example, certain items such as milk or eggs are running low or are past their use-by date. This, of course, means that the stored food also needs to be fitted with software to enable connectivity with the refrigerator. Other household objects such as lights, air-conditioning and microwaves can also be switched on and off via a smartphone, even when the user is away from home, no matter the distance. Security, including internal and external cameras, doors and alarms, can also be monitored.

**E** The most obvious advantage of a connected world is that of convenience. Having devices inside, such as those above, and outside the home, such as vehicles like cars, linked to a single device such as a smartphone is hugely liberating. As well as freeing people up for other tasks in the home and at work, where greater productivity and creativity should ensue, the IoT should ensure more time for leisure activities.

**F** The advantages are clearly appealing, but there are obstacles that need to be overcome before a true IoT exists. The greatest, perhaps, is making sure all the devices and systems from a wide range of manufacturers and internet providers, including software producers and search engines, are completely compatible on a global scale. Such a situation may not be easy to accomplish.

**G** In addition to the difficulty of achieving compatibility, there are other clear challenges. The general public, for example, may not be ready for the development of the IoT, nor sufficiently aware of its potential for investment of their time and money. This may lead to lack of sales of internet connected objects, which, in turn, will keep the costs high, and consequently lead to not just urban and rural divide, but also between individuals, and possibly nations. The obvious concerns about privacy apart, the main challenge may come from a public who are not quite ready for the development of technology in this direction. Nor may they be aware enough of the possibilities to carry the process forward.

Other concerns that might put people generally off using the IoT are that, as with machines, the connection may break down or malfunction. People are likely to be stressed, not just by such eventualities, but also by the amount of data that they need to control as ever more objects that they own are connected. There is already increasing concern among parents, employers and educators that people are being deskilled by technology in general. This is a concern that is certain to increase, as the world surrenders control, and privacy, to a vast army of objects.

## Questions 6–12

Do the following statements agree with the information given in the Reading Passage?

Write:

| | |
|---|---|
| **TRUE** | *if the statement agrees with the information.* |
| **FALSE** | *if the statement contradicts the information.* |
| **NOT GIVEN** | *if there is no information on this.* |

6 The idea of having an IoT first appeared in the early 1980s.

7 The IoT will bring about considerable change to the way people live.

8 The IoT will limit people's freedom.

9 Workers will be more productive and creative as a result of the IoT.

10 The worldwide compatibility of IoT-ready objects is easily achieved.

11 The development of IoT may be hampered by people's attitudes.

12 The educational establishment will be increasingly worried by the effect of IoT on people's skills in the future.

## Question 13

*Choose the correct letter, A, B, C or D.*

Which of the following is the most suitable title for the Reading Passage?

A The benefits of the introduction of the IoT

B How the IoT has changed people's lives

C Obstacles to the development of the IoT

D The IoT – benefits and issues for concern

# Grammar

**1** Underline the correct verb form for **1–12**

Few inventions **1** (*have had/has been had*) as much impact on the world as the smartphone, introduced to the world in about 2008, **2** (*has had now/is now having*). Since then, it **3** (*has been adopted/was adopted*) by people at a faster rate than many other inventions and **4** (*is now owned/is now being owned*) by a sizeable proportion of the population. This speedy adoption rate **5** (*compares/is now comparing*) well with the impact of other inventions such as the car. According to recent research, for example, the car **6** (*takes/took*) about 85 years before it **7** (*has been owned/was owned*) by over 50% of the population in the USA.

New inventions **8** (*arrived/arrive*) on the market on a regular basis. Some **9** (*become/are becoming*) instantly popular and then **10** (*go/are going*) out of fashion. Currently, companies **11** (*are investing/invested*) huge sums of money on advertising new products, but, as always, the success of adoption of any new product often **12** (*depends/is depending*) on luck.

**2** Correct the grammatical errors in the sentences below. Some sentences are correct.

**1** Even until recently, the majority of the world's population would live in rural areas.

.......................................................................................................................................

**2** Twice as much smart TVs were sold last year, compared to this.

.......................................................................................................................................

**3** Some people can't stand watching films on their phones, but I love it.

.......................................................................................................................................

**4** Snowboarding is one sport that I don't find very excited.

.......................................................................................................................................

**5** The Shard in London is currently highest building in Europe.

.......................................................................................................................................

**6** It's much more difficult to achieve high scores in practical exams.

.......................................................................................................................................

**7** E-books never will replace real books.

.......................................................................................................................................

**8** I have never spoken German to anyone, but I learnt it at school.

.......................................................................................................................................

**9** Since the beginning of the 21st century, the population doubled.

.......................................................................................................................................

**10** I was amazing by the range and quality of the products on offer.

.......................................................................................................................................

**11** Business has been effected slightly by the very hot weather.

.......................................................................................................................................

**12** I have to admit that I was boring as I listened to the lecture.

.......................................................................................................................................

**13** Furniture sales did not rise as quickly as other products.

.......................................................................................................................................

**14** The use of the technology is not always a positive thing for people.

.......................................................................................................................................

**15** Always I am not sure what to do for the best.

.......................................................................................................................................

# Vocabulary

**1** Circle the most appropriate answer **A**, **B**, **C** or **D** below.

**1** He always did his homework because he was very .............. .

   **A** dynamic       **B** talented       **C** conscientious       **D** respected

**2** Unfortunately, the economic situation .............. rapidly, before a slight recovery.

   **A** deteriorated       **B** destroyed       **C** harmed       **D** improved

**3** I'm very interested .............. anything to do with the environment.

   **A** with       **B** by       **C** at       **D** in

**4** She faced many challenges in life. .............., she managed to become a successful athlete.

   **A** Moreover       **B** In addition       **C** Nevertheless       **D** Although

**5** Tennis is a(n) .............. sport which can be played indoors and outdoors.

   **A** field       **B** racquet       **C** equestrian       **D** track

**6** Our tutor's very .............., as he always makes an effort to talk to students outside class.

   **A** considerate       **B** sociable       **C** reliable       **D** practical

**7** Flying has recently become much cheaper. .............. more people are travelling abroad.

   **A** For example,       **B** However,       **C** As a result,       **D** Nevertheless,

**8** I'd like to talk about something I'm really addicted ..............: chocolate!

   **A** by       **B** to       **C** with       **D** on

**9** I live near the railway station, which is very .............. for commuting to work.

   **A** appropriate       **B** necessary       **C** inspiring       **D** convenient

**10** When I started playing golf, I needed .............. .

   **A** a rod       **B** some clubs       **C** a saddle and bridle       **D** a pitch

**11** What I'm mad .............. most is old black and white films!

   **A** about       **B** to       **C** in       **D** with

**12** Some people couldn't live without a smartphone, .............. I really don't need one.

   **A** however       **B** in spite of       **C** despite       **D** but

**2** Choose the best phrase **i–viii** to describe each graph **A–H** below.

Prices …

  **i** fell slightly and then levelled off.

 **ii** remained flat.

 **iii** plummeted.

 **iv** rose gradually.

  **v** fell gradually.

 **vi** soared.

**vii** dipped.

**viii** fluctuated.

PHOTOCOPIABLE

**3** Now match the phrases **i–viii** with a description below which has a similar meaning.

**1** stayed low

**2** took a headlong dive

**3** slowly increased

**4** took a sharp jump

**5** declined over time

**6** experienced an insignificant drop before recovering

**7** suffered a small drop before stabilizing

**8** was erratic

# Writing

**WRITING TASK 1**

You should spend about 20 minutes on this task.

> *The graph below shows the number of people employed in sport in thousands in selected EU countries between 2011 and 2014.*
>
> *Summarise the information by selecting and reporting the main features, and make comparisons where relevant.*

Write at least 150 words.

**Employment in sport**

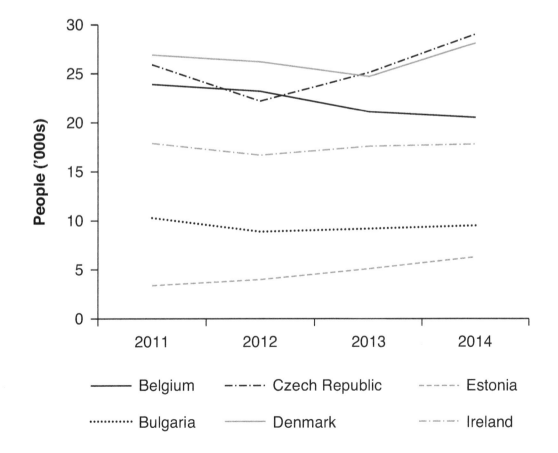

# Progress Test 2: Units 4–6

## Listening

**SECTION 2**  *Questions 11–20*

*Questions 11–14*

Label the map below.

Write the correct letter, *A–J*, next to Questions **11–14**.

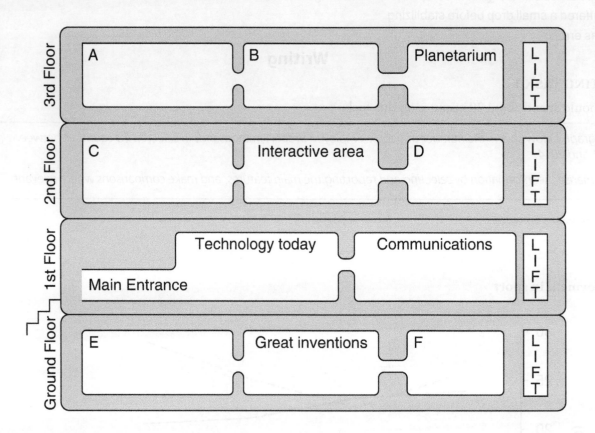

**11** Transport Gallery        .............

**12** People of the Past      .............

**13** The Human Body        .............

**14** Refreshments Area      .............

*Questions **15–17***

*Choose the correct letter, **A**, **B** or **C**.*

**15** When did domestic fridges first start to sell in large numbers?

    **A** 1934

    **B** 1922

    **C** 1748

**16** How much did a vacuum cleaner cost in 1900?

    **A** £2,000

    **B** £12,500

    **C** £350

**17** The Present Day Galleries particularly attract children of a younger age, because

    **A** they follow the school curriculum and are very educational.

    **B** there are lots of activities the children can take part in.

    **C** they use fun, music and lighting designed to appeal to children.

*Questions **18–20***

*Complete the sentences below.*

*Write **NO MORE THAN THREE WORDS AND/OR A NUMBER** for each answer.*

**18** The guide advises that children should have some ...................... in the water play area.

**19** The Future Gallery is aimed at children ...................... .

**20** The Planetarium is under different management, so there is an ...................... .

# Reading

**READING PASSAGE**

*You should spend about 20 minutes on **Questions 1–13**, which are based on the Reading Passage below.*

## Bamboo – a miracle plant

Bamboo, a member of the grass family, is native to various regions of the world, including sub-Saharan Africa, northern Australia, parts of the Americas with a tropical climate and to most of Asia, where it grows in abundance. Bamboo is noted for its strength, but it has one extraordinary characteristic: it grows at a phenomenal rate, with some species achieving around 120 centimetres growth in a day, but the average growth rate in a 24 hour period is about 60 centimetres. Some species can grow up to 46 metres in about 6 weeks. The bamboo can reach its full maturity in one three-four month season.

Natural bamboo plantations involve little use of virgin forests, but bamboo does escape from plantations into surrounding areas. In bamboo plants, the part of the bamboo underground binds the soil together so it can grow even in damaged or overused soil. No pesticides are generally needed. The growth rate is spectacular. The bamboo plant produces shoots for the first year, and starts to sprout branches and leaves, which dry and harden. In the third year, these shoots harden further, shedding the outer layers and becoming mature plants. After the fifth year, the shoots decay and die. When the plant is harvested, the bamboo is not killed. It just begins growing again. Bamboo that is suitable for construction can be harvested in three to five years. A bamboo pole that is suitable for the market can be replaced in a matter of a few months, whereas it may take oak trees more than 40 years to produce the equivalent amount.

Bamboo can be exploited in a myriad of ways, including musical instruments, fuel, as a decorative domestic indoor and outdoor plant, as well as cosmetics and household items such as bamboo towels, which are much more absorbent than cotton. New bamboo shoots, called *culms*, are used in Asian cooking. They are sweet tasting and nutritious, being a low-calorie source of potassium, but not all types of bamboo are edible with many containing toxins that need to be removed by boiling before consumption. It is famously a food for pandas, who consume nearly 20 kilograms of bamboo shoots a day, and also for the golden Bamboo lemur for whom the toxins are not harmful.

Bamboo also has medicinal uses, being used in Chinese medicine for the treatment of infections. It is also used as a treatment of fever and in the relief of inflammation of the lungs, as well as for the treatment of respiratory diseases.

The impressive growth rate has also led to its popularity in the construction industry. Its short life-cycle means that it is an easily renewable natural resource whose harvesting has little impact on its immediate surroundings. Bamboo is an increasingly valuable material in the construction industry. Treated bamboo, a very hard material that is used in the construction industry because of its flexibility and light weight, has been used as a building material in scaffolding, house frames and even as reinforcement in concrete buildings. In some countries, it is also used as a material for flooring. As an eco-friendly material that is sustainable, bamboo has become popular outside Asia as an alternative construction material for fences and garden furniture, etc.

The growth in the use of bamboo as a construction material for worldwide consumption has led to a number of concerns. One is the overharvesting of the crop and the other is the impact on the surrounding environment from the need to treat and transport the bamboo.

There are also concerns about the popularity of bamboo as a product leading to the destruction of virgin forests and increased release of carbon into the atmosphere, but with the spectacular growth rate of bamboo, which is much faster than trees, and the amount of carbon dioxide sequestered or bound up in bamboo, they are more efficient at storing carbon dioxide even though forests store more carbon dioxide at any one time. The carbon is only released back into the atmosphere when the bamboo decomposes or is burnt. So its potential for storing carbon dioxide is considerable.

PHOTOCOPIABLE

*Questions 1–5*

*Complete the flow-chart below.*

*Choose* **NO MORE THAN TWO WORDS** *from the passage for each answer.*

**Harvesting Bamboo**

**1** _____ sent up by the plant in first year

↓

Branches and leaves produced; they **2** _____ and _____

↓

In third year, outer layers shed; bamboos become **3** _____

↓

Once harvested, bamboo not dead – it starts **4** _____

↓

For construction grade bamboo, the harvesting can take place after three to five years compared to **5** _____ , which require over 40 years.

*Questions 6–10*

Do the following statements agree with the information given in the Reading Passage?

*Write:*

**TRUE** *if the statement agrees with the information*

**FALSE** *if the statement contradicts the information*

**NOT GIVEN** *if there is no information on this*

6 The main feature of bamboo is its rapid growth rate.

7 Bamboo has a wide range of uses.

8 Bamboo shoots do not contain any harmful substances.

9 In the construction industry, bamboo is valued for its flexibility and lightness.

10 The transport and treatment of bamboo raises environmental concerns.

*Questions 11–13*

*Answer the questions below.*

*Choose* **NO MORE THAN THREE WORDS AND/OR A NUMBER** *from the passage for each answer.*

11 Where has bamboo's popularity as an environmentally-friendly material increased?

12 What may the appeal of bamboo be destroying?

13 What is bamboo more efficient at storing over its lifetime than any other plant?

# Writing

**WRITING TASK 2**

You should spend about 40 minutes on this task.

Write about the following topic.

> *Even with the constant improvements in health care, many countries are struggling to provide adequate health provision for all their citizens.*
>
> *What do you think are the main causes of this situation? What might be effective in tackling the problem?*

Give reasons for your answer and include any relevant examples from your own knowledge or experience. Write at least 250 words.

# Vocabulary

**1** Complete the gaps with a form of the word in brackets.

Ireland has always been an **1** .................. (importance) part of Europe. It is less well known for its **2** .................. (industry) centres such as Belfast, where the famous ocean liner, the Titanic, was built, and is, perhaps, more celebrated for having a **3** .................. (beauty) countryside, with a spectacular coastline, along with famous glens and rivers. Ireland also has a highly regarded **4** .................. (agriculture) tradition. Overall, the **5** .................. (nation) economy remains relatively successful. Throughout recent history, Ireland has seen huge demographic changes, with many people having migrated to other English-speaking parts of the world, notably the UK and the USA. Ireland is sometimes viewed as a very **6** .................. (tradition) country, but recent **7** .................. (technology) developments have changed the economic map creating thousands of new jobs. In fact, **8** .................. (predict) have indicated that this part of the economy is set to expand over the next few decades. This **9** .................. (project) is based on a combination of factors including the number of international companies in Ireland, especially in the tech-focused economy around Dublin. Ireland is not the most **10** .................. (population) country in Europe, with a population density of 68 per square km, but the population is set to expand into the middle of the century.

**2** Delete the adjective which does not collocate with the noun in each sentence.

**1** This is clearly a(n) (effective/dangerous/difficult) situation for everyone involved.

**2** I'm going to describe a (significant/ festive/memorable) occasion when I was quite young.

**3** It is sometimes difficult to find the (perfect/ideal/golden) solution to a problem.

**4** People should see redundancy as a (golden/perfect/happy) opportunity to do what they really wanted to do.

**5** The economy is now a(n) (unfavourable/burning/major) issue for everyone.

**3** Decide which answer, **A**, **B**, **C** or **D** best fits each space.

**1** There was a very strange ................. on the bus home last night.

   **A** incident       **B** crisis       **C** outcome       **D** dilemma.

**2** Since the factory opened, the town has become a(n) ................. community.

   **A** indigenous       **B** governing       **C** dominant       **D** thriving

**3** I had the ................. that he had not prepared for the exam at all.

   **A** possibility       **B** impression       **C** opportunity       **D** issue

**4** The settlers rarely respected the traditions of the ................. people.

   **A** modern       **B** urban       **C** current       **D** indigenous

**5** ................. , I didn't understand the flow-chart on future predictions, but then suddenly I did.

   **A** Initially       **B** Before       **C** At last       **D** As soon as

# Grammar

**1** Some of the sentences below contain grammatical errors. Correct the sentences with errors.

**1** It has been predict that bees will disappear in the future.

**2** By 2030, sales will have reached 5 million items a year.

**3** Bags or any luggages can be left at reception.

**4** I'm planning to leave for the field trip very early tomorrow.

**5** The accommodations in cities can be expensive.

**6** My grandfather gave me an excellent piece of advice.

**7** People should be fined for dropping litters on the street.

**8** Young children need to be careful with tablets and smartphones or they are breaking them.

**9** Next June, I'll have lived here for ten years.

**10** Small businesses are particularly vulnerable to an economic downturn.

**11** The length of prison sentences appears to have no affect on crime levels.

**12** According to informations on climate, global weather patterns are changing.

**13** Something ought to be done about problems such as pollution.

**14** Sorry, I'm being really busy next week, so I can't have a chat about our seminar paper.

**15** In the past, people used to pass furnitures on to their children, not throw it away.

**2** Choose the correct active or passive form of the verb in brackets.

**The tears of frankincense**

The trees from which the frankincense resin **1** ................. (extract) **2** ................. (grow) in cool conditions, and **3** ................. (find) in fairly remote, harsh locations in Oman, Somalia and India. The production of the resin **4** ................. (involve) a lengthy process where it **5** ................. (harvest) from the trees anything up to three times a year. At the first stage in the process, a vertical cut **6** ................. (make) in the tree bark with a hatchet, which **7** ................. (expose) the milky sap that **8** ................. (lie) beneath the bark. This wound on the bark **9** ................. (then allow) to bleed and the sap **10** ................. (form) tears of frankincense as it **11** ................. (flow) down. These tears **12** ................. (leave) to harden on the tree for a few weeks. The resin which **13** ................. (form) at the third harvest **14** ................. (produce) the best resin. Once the resin **15** ................. (collect), it **16** ................. (sort and grade). The most opaque resin **17** ................. (prize) above all others.

# Progress Test 3: Units 7–9

## Listening

*Questions 21–25*

*Complete the notes below.*

Write **ONE WORD AND/OR A NUMBER** *for each answer.*

| University Skills Certificate | | |
|---|---|---|
| | **Focus of Modules taken:** | **Total credits earned:** |
| Lucy | • Preparing for job interviews<br>• Benefiting from work **21** ..................<br>• Personal Development | **22** .................. credits |
| Jon | • Personal Development<br>• Team **23** ..................<br>• **24** ..................Skills | **25** .................. credits |

*Questions 26–28*

*Answer the questions below.*

Write **NO MORE THAN TWO WORDS AND/OR A NUMBER** *for each answer.*

**26** How many main learning outcomes did the Personal Development Module have? ......................

**27** What does Jon say is the first thing for people to do when they are criticised? ......................

**28** According to the personality questionnaire, what was Lucy good at being? ......................

*Questions 29 and 30*

*Choose* **TWO** *letters , A–E.*

Which **TWO** types of coursework are required for the Personal Development module?

**A** an assignment

**B** a survey

**C** a case study

**D** an online blog

**E** a literature review

# Reading

## READING PASSAGE

*You should spend about 20 minutes on **Questions 1–13**, which are based on the Reading Passage below.*

### Learn what you want

**A**  At the Lumiar school in Sao Paulo, there are no classrooms, homework or playtime. In place of teachers, there are full-time mentors to impart 'love, wisdom and values', and part-time experts who teach singular skills such as piano, painting or Japanese culture. Learning is based on the Confucian principle: 'I listen and I forget, I see and I remember, I do and I learn.' The school is the latest project of the unorthodox business guru Ricardo Semler. The Brazilian achieved worldwide fame a decade ago with his million-selling book *Maverick!*, in which he described how he revitalised his family firm by giving employees the power to set their salaries and working hours and to choose their bosses.

**B**  Semler has set about the school system with similar revolutionary gusto. Armed with University of Chicago statistics showing that 94 per cent of what we learn in school is never used in later life, he decided to ditch what he calls the 'unsuccessful teaching methods' used in millions of schools around the world. 'The fact that kids learnt Ulan Bator was the capital of Mongolia back in school is not making them learn constellations or how to weld or how to use a completely new computer system any faster,' Semler says. 'We are trying to prove that by giving kids freedom, they will in the end be better educated, with much more residual knowledge than the kids in the disciplined schools. They can have a much happier existence and be much more prepared for life if we don't teach them the stupid things that traditional schools do.'

**C**  The realisation that schools were turning out dysfunctional adults came to Semler in 1982 after he took over his father's company and found himself having to 'deprogramme' the employees. The 24-year-old expected the workers at the marine pump manufacturer to use their initiative, but few knew how. He fired two thirds of the senior managers on his first day. Although he continued to shake things up, the serious reforms came at the start of the 1990s, when political upheaval almost forced the company to the wall. Redundancies appeared inevitable until the unions presented him with a novel proposal. They agreed to take a wage cut if management did, too, and if they got a larger share of the profits and power of veto over company expenditure. Semler agreed, and when it became clear that the workers were every bit as committed to saving the firm as he was, he gave them more and more responsibility.

**D**  One group of 150 employees branched off to form an autonomous manufacturing unit; it was so successful that Semler split the entire company into small, self-managed divisions. When he went even further and abolished secretaries, working hours and titles, gave employees the freedom to set their own salaries and turned over all decisions to special workers' committees, business experts pronounced him mad and predicted the company would go bust within months. In fact, the opposite happened. The changes helped turn Semco into an agile and modern business whose sales rose from $30 million in 1988 to $212 million last year. The company now has operations in four countries and makes a third of its money from managing the non-core businesses of multinationals such as Wal-Mart and Carrefour. Employee turnover is less than one per cent a year.

**E**  Having satisfied himself that adults thrive on responsibility, Semler set out to show that children would react the same way. 'Playing at this age is the fundamental aspect of learning,' says Semler. 'One of the things that is very silly – and I hear from educators all the time – is that schools essentially teach kids to learn. They don't need school for that. Learning is what they do best. We kill it for them.' Although many students spend their first weeks testing the limits of their newfound freedom – Semler admits some do nothing but play video games and eat McDonald's food – the novelty soon wears off and they start demanding to learn new skills.

**F**  Semler wholeheartedly believes the experiment will work – he even sends his four-year-old son to Lumiar – and state schools in nine Brazilian cities have asked him to transform their classrooms into democratic ones, with more toying with the idea. 'When we started with the same assumptions at the company, everybody said, you can be sure it does not work, and that wasn't our experience at all,' he says. 'Our assumptions about human beings – that they are basically honest and interested and ready for gratifying work – were not wrong anywhere along the line. We have the same assumptions here and what we've seen so far corroborates what we thought.'

**Questions 1–5**

The Reading Passage has six paragraphs, **A–F**.

Which paragraph contains the following information?

Write the correct letter, **A–F.**

*NB You may use any letter more than once.*

1 the impact of changes on Semco's business sales

2 what often happens when students first attend the Lumiar school

3 a transformation that made people predict Semco's collapse

4 the irrelevance of information of traditional schooling to pupils' future lives

5 early business decisions made by Semler

**Questions 6–10**

*Classify the following features as characterising:*

**A** the Lumiar school

**B** the company Semco

**C** both the Lumiar school and the company Semco

**D** neither the Lumiar school nor the company Semco

6 It gives people more freedom.

7 It teaches people how to learn.

8 It sets up small groups which manage themselves.

9 It uses mentors as role models.

10 It allows people to decide on their own rewards and punishments.

**Questions 11–13**

*Choose **THREE** letters, **A–H**.*

*Which **THREE** of the following reforms that Semler made at Semco are mentioned in the text?*

**A** The management led special workers' committees.

**B** Employees' salaries at all levels were increased.

**C** The use of job titles was ended.

**D** Employees were given control of how much they wanted to be paid.

**E** The management got a larger slice of the profits.

**F** Employees could decide who should be made redundant.

**G** Workers were given greater authority in the company .

**H** The management were given new responsibilities and job titles.

# Writing

**WRITING TASK 1**

You should spend about 20 minutes on this task.

> *The plans below show the changes to a cottage between 1950 and the present day.*
> *Summarise the information by selecting and reporting the main features, and make comparisons where relevant.*

Write at least 150 words.

**1950 house**

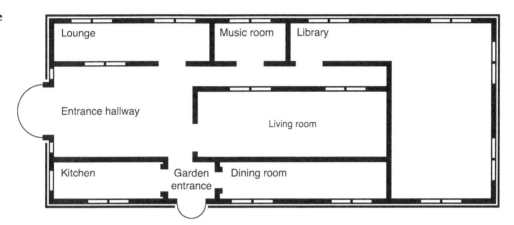

**1970 language school**

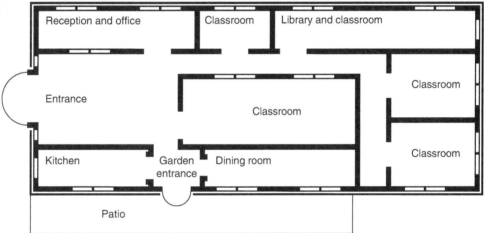

**The present day museum**

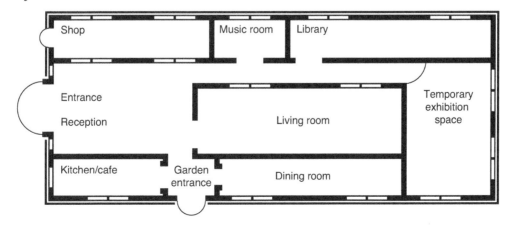

# Vocabulary

**1**  For each set of three sentences, use each noun from the box once only.

**1** Last year I changed my ................. so I didn't have to commute so far.

**2** I really hate having to go to ................. at the weekend.

**3** The new supermarket will threaten the ................. of the local shop-keepers.

| job | livelihood | work |
|---|---|---|

**4** It is harder to climb the ................. ladder, once you have children.

**5** She is a lawyer by ................. , but also writes children's books in her spare time.

**6** He went back to college to gain new ................. .

| profession | qualifications | career |
|---|---|---|

**7** Studying at university is a once-in-a-lifetime ................. , so it's important not to miss it.

**8** The deal could be of financial ................. to us in the future.

**9** Making such a good profit is an impressive ................. in the current circumstances.

| benefit | opportunity | achievement |
|---|---|---|

**10** The ................. is definitely up and coming as house prices have doubled in recent years.

**11** There have been some changes in the ................. of the main station.

**12** The area definitely benefits from its central ................. .

| neighbourhood | location | vicinity |
|---|---|---|

**13** The job is not very well paid, but it has excellent ................. .

**14** You should take this ................. , as you may not get the opportunity again.

**15** Recently, she has enjoyed a great deal of ................. .

| prospects | success | chance |
|---|---|---|

**2**  Complete each sentence with a word made from the item in brackets.

**1** Machu Picchu in Peru is one of the most ................. Inca sites. (impress)

**2** We had a ................. holiday in the Himalayas. (memory)

**3** Some of the African exhibits in the museum are absolutely ................. . (price)

**4** There are various ................. to be found in American National Parks . (attract)

**5** The view of the ruins was so beautiful I felt quite ................. . (emotion)

**6** An ................. to the museum is planned for next year. (extend)

**7** The art gallery has recently undergone a complete ................. . (transform)

**8** Our new apartment couldn't be in a better ................. for facilities like schools and shops. (locate)

**9** Returning to my home town, after so long, made me very ................. . (nostalgia)

**10** The new office is much more ................. than the previous one. (space)

# Grammar

**1**  Choose the correct alternative in italics below.

## 1  The importance of architecture

Architecture plays a crucial role in people's lives, mainly because **1** *its/their* influence is felt by all on a daily basis. First of all, **2** *it/this* can have a huge impact on the physical, but also mental health of **3** *these/those* who live in urban environments. **4** *It/This* is because the internal and external design of buildings can influence people's mood considerably, which also makes **5** *it/them* a crucial consideration in the construction of office and public buildings. **6** *They/Those* need to be appealing to the eye as well as being functional.

## 2  A career in programming

I think that nowadays there is such a wide range of jobs available compared to **1** *these/those* on offer to previous generations. **2** *Its/This* situation is the direct result of new professions such as computer engineers and software programmers that have been created since the advent of the internet. The attraction of jobs like **3** *them/these* to young people is enormous, because **4** *they/those* offer **5** *them/these* the opportunity to develop their own careers in cutting edge professions. That does not make job hunting easier compared to the past, however.

## 3  Studying history and geography

Another way to help develop an awareness of the world is to promote the study of the history and geography of the ancient world at secondary level. **1** *It/This* would help to broaden children's knowledge of the world, but **2** *it/this* would put pressure on the school curriculum, and it is likely **3** *it/this* would face some resistance from businesses and educators. Nevertheless, despite **4** *these/those* objections, studying such subjects is now more vital than **5** *it/this* has ever been.

**2**  Choose the correct alternative in italics in each sentence.

 **1**  It is vital for young people to obtain a good education; *unless/otherwise*, their employment prospects may be affected.

 **2**  The Student Union *used to/would* be in a different place in 2010.

 **3**  *Was/Were* the minister to invest more in the arts, it would increase employment.

 **4**  *If/Unless* I had worked a little harder, I would have achieved more.

 **5**  The exhibition *could/must* be very popular, as the queues outside the museum are enormous.

 **6**  *Unless/If* something is done about training in technology, some countries will lack skilled workers.

 **7**  The company *must/should* have given the student more feedback about their performance during work experience than they did.

 **8**  If universities *are not/will not be* properly funded, they will not produce world-class research.

 **9**  If more money were invested in public transport, people *had/would* make more use of the service.

**10**  *Unless/If* we leave now, we'll miss the start of the lecture on modern cartography.

**11**  If the neighbourhood *had not been/would not have been* transformed, there would not have been so many public amenities like theatres and parks.

**12**  I think I *could deal/could have dealt* with the presentation on career development more effectively than I did.

**13**  The government *should/might* definitely subsidise more apprenticeships in engineering.

**14**  The essay was very thorough. You *should/must* have worked really hard.

**15**  Were more emphasis *put/not put* on education in the arts, it would not be so undervalued.

# Progress Test 4: Units 10–12

## Listening

**SECTION 4** *Questions 31–40*

### Questions 31–37

*Complete the table below.*

Write **ONE WORD AND/OR A NUMBER** *for each answer.*

**Australian Art**

| Period | Artists | Notes |
|---|---|---|
| 18th century | Sydney Parkinson | Drew pictures of Australian **31** ................. which met with some disbelief |
| 19th century | John Lewin | Settled in Australia in **32** ................. . Painted nature pictures and also **33** ................. of famous figures |
| | Heidelberg School artists | Focused on the difference in the nature of Australian **34** ................. |
| 20th century | Grace Cossington Smith | Noted for pictures of Sydney Harbour Bridge when not yet **35** ................. |
| | Emily Kame Kngwarreye | Became a professional painter when she was almost **36** ................. |
| | James Gleeson | A surrealist |
| | Ian Fairweather | Influenced by Western and **37** ................. art |

### Questions 38–40

*Choose **THREE** letters, **A–G**.*

According to the speaker, which **THREE** of the following has John Dalhsen used to make art?

**A** footwear

**B** sand

**C** clothes pegs

**D** plastic bags

**E** shells

**F** seaweed

**G** nylon rope

# Reading

## READING PASSAGE

*You should spend about 20 minutes on **Questions 1–14**, which are based on the Reading Passage below.*

### First, middle or last: what's the difference?

Scientists have long believed that birth order plays a large part in determining one's character traits and career choices.

Now we have the proof. Norwegian scientists have released a study that shows that first-borns enjoy, on average, an IQ advantage of three points over the next in line. The second child, in turn, they discovered, is a point ahead of the third. The differences may seem small but the effect, they say, can be enormous. Just two or three IQ points can correlate to a 15-point difference in SAT scores.

And the differences don't stop there. In the Philippines, studies show that last-born siblings tend to be shorter and weigh less than their taller first-born siblings, and tend to go into less prestigious professions.

The statistics seem to suggest that there is more than a little truth in the findings. In a recent poll of 1,583 chief executive officers in America, 53 per cent were first-borns.

This higher achievement is probably caused partly by the amount of attention paid to first-borns by their parents while still an only child, and partly because the eldest devotes time to mentoring their younger siblings.

Dr Richard Woolfson, a Glasgow-based child psychologist, acknowledges that parents put their all into their first child. 'By the time the others come along they are more relaxed, knowing what is important and what isn't and, it has to be said, they have less time.'

Dr Woolfson is a firm believer in the theory that birth order is partly responsible for certain characteristics. 'But this doesn't mean that all first-borns share the same ones,' he says. 'Only that the tendencies are there.' The challenge for parents, he says, is to ensure that their offspring are not constrained by such tendencies. Some first-borns are brighter because, unconsciously, there are more expectations of them. 'Parents need to recognise that each child is individual, with its own strengths and weaknesses. It is about encouraging them to achieve what they can achieve.' He recommends ensuring that each child has a role. For example, if the older child gets to choose an outing, then another should choose the meal out and another is allowed to choose something else. Some parents, who perhaps have a good sense of injustice, do this naturally. Others need to make the effort.

Professor Richard Wiseman, a psychologist at Hertfordshire University, is much more sceptical about the effect of birth order than many of his colleagues. 'If push came to shove, I would say there is something in it, but there are also many other factors at play, for instance a child's attractiveness,' he says. 'The bottom line is that the relevance of birth order is a very inexact science.'

As a youngest child himself, Dr Woolfson recalls readily his most common utterance: 'It isn't fair.' All of us, he believes, remain very conscious throughout life where we come in the family pecking order.

'Certainly, I do,' says Gill Marshall, 43, a mother of three. 'I was the eldest and, while my parents were wonderfully supportive, I felt more was expected of me. If I got an A-minus, I was told I'd done really well but could have done better. My younger sister, who was generally a B-plus, was told she had done fabulously.'

Mrs Marshall has twin boys of nine, Eddie and George, and a six-year-old daughter, Phoebe. Interestingly, Eddie should have been born first, because of his position in the birth canal. But when Mrs Marshall needed an emergency Caesarean, doctors discovered that his twin was trapping his foot and so George arrived five minutes ahead of Eddie. Yet, astonishingly, the twins divide strictly along who should have been born first lines. Eddie displays all the characteristics of a first-born, while George behaves as a second-born.

Eddie is academic and more mature, but lacks self-esteem. By contrast, George struggles at school, but has a well-developed imagination and is more creative. Eddie obeys every rule at school while George believes they exist to be broken. Similarly, while Eddie wants to read what his class list suggests George is happier with magazines filled with pictures. And that difference is marked in how they play. 'If I take them to the woods, George will say: "Let's play Robin Hood." Eddie will want to do something much more conventional like run a race.

'Phoebe has benefited from having such vastly different siblings. With George she will play make-believe. With Eddie she is happy to bowl a ball to him.' And the mother admits, her expectations of her youngest are lower. 'I definitely do say: "You do what you want, love," more often to Phoebe.'

## Questions 1–4

*Complete the table.*

*Choose **NO MORE THAN TWO WORDS AND/OR A NUMBER** from the passage for each answer.*

| Typical features of different birth orders | | |
|---|---|---|
| **First born** | **Middle** | **Last born** |
| IQ exceeds that of middle child by 1 ................. | IQ is 2 ................. higher than next child | Frequently 3 ................. and lighter than siblings<br><br>Also often have 4 ................. occupations |

## Questions 5–11

*Complete the summary using the list of words, **A–O**, below.*

### Suggested reasons for birth order characteristics

First-born children usually receive 5 ................... because of the time spent as 6 ................... children. Then, as other children are born, the eldest also learns from 7 ................... them. With younger siblings, parents do not have the 8 ................... . Inevitably, parents now also 9 ...................

Dr Woolfson believes in the effect of birth order, but not that all first-borns have 10 ................... . Professor Wiseman thinks that the impact is 11 ................... .

| | | | | | |
|---|---|---|---|---|---|
| **A** | playing with | **B** | more material goods | **C** | different hopes |
| **D** | same expectations | **E** | good behaviour | **F** | individuals |
| **G** | teaching | **H** | lack time | **I** | more attention |
| **J** | more complex | **K** | more money | **L** | identical traits |
| **M** | learning from | **N** | only | **O** | just |

## Questions 12–14

*Look at the following children mentioned in the text and the list of descriptions below.*

*Match each child with the correct description, **A–F**.*

12  Eddie

13  George

14  Phoebe

### List of descriptions

A  does not like to go against norms

B  is far more ambitious and ruthless

C  receives less pressure from parents

D  has a more attractive personality

E  receives more praise from parents

F  has more original and unusual ideas

# Writing

**WRITING TASK 2**

You should spend about 40 minutes on this task.

Write about the following topic:

> *Some people think that the arts, such as ballet and opera, should not be subsidised by public money. Others believe they play a vital role in maintaining our culture and should receive financial support from the government.*
>
> *Discuss both these views and give your opinion.*

Give reasons for your answer and include any relevant examples from your own knowledge or experience.

Write at least 250 words.

# Vocabulary

1   Decide which answer, **A**, **B**, **C** or **D** best fits each space.

1   Some students are too shy to act in plays, but they can take part in painting the ..................... .
   **A** back                  **B** scenes                  **C** scenery                  **D** curtains

2   Many people are extremely ..................... of art installations – they feel that they are not really art.
   **A** approving             **B** in favour               **C** critical                 **D** unfavourable

3   After so many years working closely together, there is a ..................... relationship between the companies.
   **A** specialist            **B** special                 **C** specialised             **D** specific

4   Mozart ..................... his first symphony at the age of eight.
   **A** designed              **B** showed                  **C** composed                **D** expressed

5   London has a very culturally ..................... population.
   **A** diverse               **B** different               **C** dissimilar              **D** unusual

6   When famous people retire, they often write their ..................... .
   **A** mementos              **B** memorabilia             **C** memories                **D** memoirs

7   The person I admire most is my uncle, who is my closest living ..................... .
   **A** parent                **B** relative                **C** ancestor                **D** sibling

8   What I'd like to describe is a performance of *Hamlet*, which is, I think, Shakespeare's best ..................... .
   **A** play                  **B** stage                   **C** master work             **D** act

9   Most young people are very interested ..................... music.
   **A** for                   **B** on                      **C** in                      **D** –

10  There's nowhere quite like it anywhere else in the world; it's ..................... .
   **A** unusual               **B** unique                  **C** unexpected              **D** unfamiliar

11  When my aunt's husband died, she was left a(n) ..................... .
   **A** widower               **B** ancestor                **C** descendant              **D** widow

12  My grandfather started work at the age of 12 and experienced considerable ..................... .
   **A** hardship              **B** difficult               **C** inconvenience           **D** comfort

13  She ..................... the whole story! Lies from start to finish!
   **A** made                  **B** fabricated              **C** designed                **D** developed

14  I went to see a play because the ..................... loved it, but I found it disappointing.
   **A** criticism             **B** critics                 **C** criticising             **D** critical

15  By discussing issues in the tutorial group as they arise, we ..................... a good relationship.
   **A** maintain              **B** keep                    **C** save                    **D** show

# Grammar

**1** Complete each gap with *a/an, the* or the *zero article*.

Travelling is one of **1** .......... best ways to learn about **2** .......... world. By **3** .......... travelling to **4** .......... country like Russia or Japan, **5** .......... people encounter **6** .......... new languages and **7** .......... cultures as well as **8** .......... experiences and food. Such contact can encourage **9** .......... visitor to these countries to learn more about **10** .......... communication in **11** .......... Russian or Japanese, as well as improving **12** .......... understanding of their own language. When people, especially **13** .......... young, have **14** .......... dealings with **15** .......... new culture as well as its language, it is **16** .......... very exciting experience and can broaden their horizons and improve their personal development. As well as finding out more about **17** .......... different types of **18** .......... cultural activities like **19** .......... theatre and festivals, it is also interesting to see **20** .......... way of life and enjoy **21** .......... food of other countries.

**2** Some of the sentences below contain a grammatical error. Find and correct the sentences which are incorrect.

**1** The place which I liked it the best was Rio de Janeiro.
**2** If it weren't for the fact that I obtained a good degree in art, I don't know what I have done.
**3** Exeter University in the southwest of England has a beautiful campus.
**4** If only I hadn't waited so long to start doing my reading for my paper on street art.
**5** Paris? That's the city where I used to live in.
**6** Even I had remembered to include the data, I wouldn't have been able to persuade the audience.
**7** People which drive to work should be encouraged to car share.
**8** Provided students study hard, they will have a good chance of passing the exam.
**9** He went to university in New York, there is a variety of entertainment venues.
**10** The art form, that appeals to young people most, is possibly contemporary art.
**11** If I were you, I will start writing up your psychology project as soon as you can.
**12** I'll lend you the books that I bought for the essay if you would not write in them .
**13** I'm going to describe a friend, Peter, who is someone whom I trust completely.
**14** Unless the department had been given more money, it can't invest more in community development.
**15** Beijing is a city I will never forget.

# Progress Test 5: Units 13–14

## Listening

*Questions 31–35*

*What does the speaker say about each form of money or barter?*

*Choose **FIVE** answers from the box and write the correct letter, **A–F**, next to Questions **31–35**.*

**Early forms of money and barter in the United States**

| |
|---|
| **A** used when large sums needed to be paid |
| **B** replaced with documents |
| **C** given as payment to construction workers |
| **D** banned for a short time |
| **E** used as an offering to the Gods |
| **F** kept in transparent containers |

**31** gold dust      ...........

**32** cocoa beans    ...........

**33** potlatch       ...........

**34** wampum         ...........

**35** tobacco leaves ...........

*Questions 36–40*

*Complete the summary below.*

*Write **ONE WORD AND/OR A NUMBER** for each answer.*

**The development of money in the United States**

- In 1690, paper money was introduced in Massachusetts to pay **36** ................... .

- Other colonies copied the idea, resulting in a rise in **37** ................... .

- British government response: ban on paper money in colonies in **38** ................... .

- In 1790, the dollar first became a **39** ................... currency.

- Apart from silver dollar coins, until 1930s, there were ten dollar coins, known as **40** ................... .

# Reading

**READING PASSAGE**

*You should spend about 20 minutes on* **Questions 1–13**, *which are based on the Reading Passage below.*

## Windcatchers – a cool tale

The ancient world is full of inventions and discoveries from which modern professionals, such as architects, engineers and scientists, have learnt much and have much to learn. The field of air-conditioning is no exception. Just as the quest for ways to keep warm has been a focus of human endeavour throughout human history, before there was even basic air-conditioning, keeping cool in hot weather, ranging from seeking shelter from the elements in caves and trees to temporary structures such as tents and more permanent constructions such as mud and brick buildings, also exercised the human race.

In the ancient world, wealthy Romans had a sophisticated form of air-conditioning with water circulating inside the walls of their houses to help regulate the temperature. Likewise, the Egyptians used various techniques that were early forms of air-conditioning. They had supposedly, for example, a simple form of air-conditioning, which used the power of evaporation to cool rooms by hanging wet sheets in doorways and windows. As the air passed through the sheets, it carried off the moisture, cooling the air. A more sophisticated form of air-conditioning from the middle of the third millennium BC, which is not fully understood, was found in the so-called *Solar Ships* or *Cheops Ships* that are buried near the pyramids in Egypt. The ships contain a wooden framed structure with a canvas roof to trap moisture and cool the structure. Ancient Egyptian frescos also demonstrate another evaporative technique employed, with slaves fanning pots of water that cooled the air.

Ancient Egypt also had an early example of a windcatcher from the latter part of the second millennium BC. These windcatchers, now found in Iran and other parts of the Middle East, are a simple yet sophisticated form of environmentally-friendly air-conditioning that have been cooling and providing ventilation for buildings for hundreds of years.

The city of Yazd in Iran is famous for its skyline marked by the outline of these majestic towers soaring above the cityscape, with one of the tallest being the windcatcher of Dowlatabad. Windcatchers are also found in other countries in the region, such as Bahrain with the windtower of Isa bin Ali House in Muharraq, and in UAE, Pakistan and Afghanistan.

A windcatcher, or *badgir* as it is known in Persian (*bad* meaning 'bad wind' and *gir* meaning trap/catcher), is a tower which functions among the tightly packed buildings with thick walls and small windows in very hot environments to keep living quarters and courtyards cool. It works on the basic principle of harnessing the greater air movement at the top of buildings, a natural phenomenon which can be witnessed in the winds at the top of modern day skyscrapers or tower blocks anywhere in the world.

The basic windcatcher has various features. It consists of a four- or eight-sided tower. The top of the tower is covered and not open like a chimney. It typically has four or eight adjustable grills at the top, one on each side depending on the number of sides on the tower. They are uni-, bi- and multi-directional depending on the nature of the prevailing winds locally. The primary function of the windcatchers is to catch cooler air higher up above the buildings it seeks to cool and then direct it down into the rooms and courtyards at a lower level. When the wind blows in one particular direction, the other openings are closed, so the cooler air is pushed down the shaft inside the tower to the living quarters below. To ensure that the ambient temperature at the lower levels is kept low, the area where people live is completely sealed to prevent hot air from coming into the building from outside. As well as catching the cooler breeze, the windcatcher also has a facility to let the hotter air escape from the lower levels.

Windcatchers also function in another way. The air is caught not just with the open grill or port facing the prevailing wind, but also with it facing away from the wind, relying on the Coanda effect, which reduces the amount of dust that is brought into the buildings below.

Modern windcatchers can now be found in various locations around the world. The Kensington Cricket club in Barbados in the Caribbean has an aluminium windcatcher that captures wind from different directions and is, therefore, much more efficient. The Zénith in Saint-Etienne in France, an indoor arena, designed by the British architect Norman Foster, has an aluminium roof that catches the wind and provides natural ventilation. Perhaps, in future cityscapes, we will see more beguiling structures like windcatchers.

## Questions 1–5

*Choose **FIVE** letters, **A–I**.*

Which **FIVE** examples of air-conditioning practices from the ancient world are mentioned in the Reading Passage?

**A**  Windows were never opened during the day.

**B**  A device that traps moisture was built on a boat.

**C**  People lived in tents in hot weather.

**D**  Caves with their cool interiors were used as shelters.

**E**  Houses were built close together in narrow streets.

**F**  Fans were used to drive air over water in containers.

**G**  Windows and doors were covered with wet material.

**H**  A windcatcher was used to ventilate buildings.

**I**  Water was passed inside the walls of buildings

## Questions 6–10

*Label the diagram below.*

*Choose **NO MORE THAN THREE WORDS AND/OR A NUMBER** from the passage for each answer.*

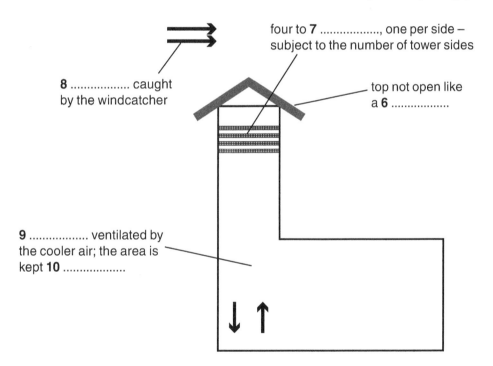

## Questions 11–13

Do the following statements agree with the information given in the Reading Passage?

*Write:*

| | |
|---|---|
| **YES** | *if the statement agrees with the claims of the writer* |
| **NO** | *if the statement contradicts the claims of the writer* |
| **NOT GIVEN** | *if it is impossible to say what the writer thinks about this* |

**11**  Windcatchers work on the basis that air moves faster at different levels above ground.

**12**  Windcatchers work only if the opening at the top of the tower faces into the wind.

**13**  The indoor arena by Norman Foster is more effective than the windcatcher at the Barbadian cricket club.

# Writing

## WRITING TASK 1

You should spend about 20 minutes on this task.

> *The charts below show the purchases made over the internet by age group in the UK in 2014.*
>
> *Summarise the information by selecting and reporting the main features and make comparisons where relevant.*

Write at least 150 words.

### Purchases made over the internet in the UK by age group, 2014

Travel arrangements

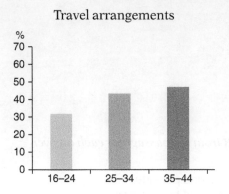

Film, music including downloads

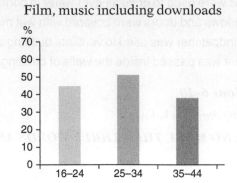

Video games software and upgrades

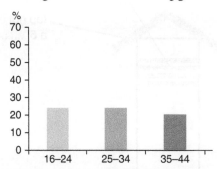

# Vocabulary

**1** For explanations **1–10**, write a noun relating to systems. Begin with the letters given and write one letter for each space.

| | |
|---|---|
| **1** i _ _ _ _ _ _ _ | a system that allows access to websites and email |
| **2** v _ _ _ _ _ _ | a type of bridge that carries trains on high arches, often across a valley |
| **3** s _ _ _ _ _ | a computer that controls all the computers or similar devices in a network |
| **4** p _ _ _ _ | a tall metal structure which supports wires carrying electricity |
| **5** s _ _ _ _ _ _ _ _ | an object sent into space to transmit and receive data and information |
| **6** g _ _ _ | a network such as one that supplies electricity |
| **7** t _ _ _ _ _ | an underground passage through which vehicles or trains can pass |
| **8** w _ _ _ | a deep hole dug in the ground to access oil or water |
| **9** c _ _ _ _ | a thick plastic-covered wire used for carrying electricity |
| **10** r _ _ _ _ _ _ _ | a factory where natural substances such as oil are processed |

2 Match each word in the left-hand column with a word in the right-hand column to make three compound nouns in each box. You may use each item only once.

**1–3**

| money | income |
| cash | reserves |
| investment | box |

**4–6**

| savings | expenditure |
| education | plan |
| spending | power |

**7–9**

| debt | expenditure |
| credit | mountain |
| consumer | limit |

**10–12**

| currency | war |
| government | spending |
| price | reserves |

**13–15**

| personal | customs |
| traditional | morals |
| mineral | wealth |

PHOTOCOPIABLE

# Grammar

**1**  Rewrite the sentences using a modal verb.

**1**  In some cities, people are not allowed to drive in the centre without paying a charge.

In some cities, people ...................... drive in the centre without paying a charge.

**2**  The broadband infrastructure is likely to improve with more government investment.

The broadband infrastructure ...................... improve with more investment.

**3**  All staff in the department of the built environment are obliged to wear an ID badge at all times.

All staff in the department of the built environment ...................... wear an ID badge at all times.

**4**  It is possible for people to be seen by a doctor even if they don't have medical insurance.

People ...................... be seen by a doctor even if they don't have medical insurance.

**5**  It was a bad idea to wait so long before going to see your supervisor.

You ...................... waited so long before going to see your supervisor.

**6**  It is essential for new high-speed rail links to be funded by the government.

New high-speed rail links ...................... to be funded by the government.

**7**  It would've been possible for my tutor to help me with my transport project, had he wanted to.

My tutor ...................... helped me with my internet project, had he wanted to.

**8**  The conductor made me miss my drama tutorial because she stopped the train, even though it wasn't necessary.

The conductor ...................... stopped the train. It made me miss my drama tutorial.

**9**  The new skyscraper is predicted to be the tallest in the world.

The new skyscraper ...................... the tallest in the world.

**10**  The best thing for people to do is to write to the head of the economics department.

People ...................... write to the head of the economics department.

**2**  Decide if you can delete each item **1–20** in brackets. In four places, the items can be kept or removed.

## The pursuit of money

The pursuit of money is considered by some (**1** people) as causing more harm than good, but there are many circumstances where (**2** the pursuit of) it does not (**3** cause as much harm as it is thought to cause). There is no doubt that (**4** money) can corrupt people and their relationships with (**5** others) in their family and (**6** those people) at work. Profit (**7** made from the pursuit of money) can be pursued for the benefit of large companies to the detriment (**8** of society) in general. For example, family homes can be knocked down to make way for apartments and factories. Doing (**9** so) only benefits rich (**10** organisations) and not local communities. Likewise, small family businesses can be driven from an area to make way for expensive shops (**11** to benefit rich people and not local communities).

Although (**12** all of) this is true, money is not always the root of all evil that people imagine (**13** it to be). Government investment in the improvement of local facilities like shops and infrastructure can lead to the regeneration of neighbourhoods. (**14** Doing) this can enhance local people's lives by bringing new jobs (**15** to the area). The knock-on effect (**16** of this) is clear. As more (**17** money) is brought into an area, local people have more (**18** money) to spend, thus increasing the benefit (**19** to the community). So the pursuit of money is not all as bad as it seems (**20** to be).

# Final Test

## Listening

### SECTION 1 *Questions 1–10*

#### Questions 1–4

*Complete the notes below.*

*Write **NO MORE THAN THREE WORDS AND/OR A NUMBER** for each answer.*

---

**Weston Leisure Centre**

***Example***

Facilities: Swimming Pool, Gym and <u>Fitness Classes</u>.

Classes available: Pilates, circuit training, **1** ..............................

Opening hours: Mon–Sat **2** ......... am to ......... pm

Induction session: tests members' fitness, creates a **3** ............................. and instruction of gym use

Personal training: available with an **4** .............................

---

#### Questions 5–8

*Complete the table below.*

*Write **NO MORE THAN THREE WORDS AND/OR A NUMBER** for each answer.*

**Contract Options**

| Option | Details | Price |
|---|---|---|
| **Yearly Membership** | Unlimited use of all gym facilities and two **5** ................ with an instructor. | £300<br>For certain groups, a discount of **6** ................ |
| **Six-month contract** | Unlimited use of all facilities with induction session. | **7** £................ for whole period. |
| **Casual Member** | Pay each time you visit. | Annual membership fee: **8** £................<br>£8.00 per visit. |

#### Questions 9 and 10

Complete the sentences below.

Write **NO MORE THAN TWO WORDS** for each answer.

**9** The man is booked for an induction session on .............................. at 3pm.

**10** For the induction, the man should NOT wear ............................. .

### SECTION 2 *Questions 11–20*

#### Questions 11–13

*Choose the correct letter, **A**, **B** or **C**.*

**11** According to the speaker, volunteering is

    **A** viewed in a positive light by employers and universities.

    **B** regarded as delaying young people's career development.

    **C** thought of as something done abroad before starting university.

**12** The speaker says that volunteering can help people

    **A** obtain a good place at the university of their choice.

    **B** obtain a better job in accountancy or banking.

    **C** think about what career they want to do.

**13** Two former students from the school are returning to

    **A** run a month-long summer programme for teenagers.

    **B** volunteer during the summer for a month.

    **C** organise a summer course to train volunteers.

### Questions 14 and 15

*Choose* **TWO** *letters,* **A–E.**

What **TWO** farm-related activities can volunteers take part in?

**A** collecting eggs

**B** preparing garden produce for sale

**C** giving horse-riding lessons

**D** keeping the farm tidy

**E** feeding the animals

### Questions 16 and 17

*Answer the questions below.*

*Write* **NO MORE THAN THREE WORDS** *for each answer.*

**16** What does the speaker say the farm wants young minds to help with?

    ...................................................................................................................

**17** What does the speaker say they are attempting to improve?

    ...................................................................................................................

### Questions 18–20

*Choose* **THREE** *letters,* **A–G.**

Which **THREE** things does the speaker say the farm can help volunteers with?

**A** paying for work insurance

**B** finding work experience placements.

**C** subsidising future university courses.

**D** providing references for jobs

**E** reduced fares to place abroad

**F** funding visits to other projects

**G** finding work with other organisations

## SECTION 3   Questions 21–30

### Questions 21–27

*Complete the summary below.*

*Write* **NO MORE THAN THREE WORDS AND/OR A NUMBER** *for each answer.*

---

**Findings on campus tours**

- Data collected using a post-tour **21** .............
- People asked about the information they received via **22** .............
- Asked if it had arrived **23** ............. and it was helpful
- Content of the tour: an average score of **24** ............. on the scale, but a problem with the **25** ............. of the tour
- Tour guides considered **26** ............. and people really appreciated the **27** .............

---

**Questions 28–30**

Which steps for improving the way the research is conducted are mentioned by the people below?

*Choose **THREE** answers from the box and write the letters, **A–F**, next to Questions **28–30**.*

| Steps |
| --- |
| **A** Include more yes/no questions. |
| **B** Change the grading scale for the tour to 1–10. |
| **C** Ask for feedback straightaway. |
| **D** Leave more space on the form for comments. |
| **E** Interview the prospective students in person. |
| **F** Provide a freepost envelope. |

**Steps**

28 Sonya ...................

29 Maurice ...................

30 Tutor ...................

## SECTION 4  *Questions 31–40*

**Questions 31–36**

*Complete the summary below.*

*Write **NO MORE THAN THREE WORDS AND/OR A NUMBER** for each answer.*

- Short chronology theory – human settlement in the New World, at the most **31** ........................ ago
- The landbridge theory – generally accepted since **32** ........................ – migration of people from Siberia into Alaska
- People who came over the landbridge – thought to have been **33** ........................
- Pacific coastal model – people arrived by boat from **34** ........................
- Suggested that first people crossed from Australia/Polynesia
- No **35** ........................ that people came to America from Australia
- DNA from Alaskan tooth suggests that people spread **36** ........................ around 10,000 years ago

**Questions 37–40**

*Choose **FOUR** answers from the box and write the correct letter, **A–C**, next to Questions **37–40**.*

Which Californian tribe can be described in the following ways?

| |
| --- |
| **A** The Chumash |
| **B** The Tongva |
| **C** Both the Chumash and the Tongva |

37 have a sea-faring tradition

38 have two different names

39 have a name which means 'people of the earth'

40 have been in California for at least 8,000 years

# Reading

## READING PASSAGE 1

*You should spend about 20 minutes on Questions 1–13, which are based on the Reading Passage below.*

## Internet access and different uses

Information and communications technology (ICT) has become widely available to the general public, both in terms of accessibility as well as cost. A boundary was crossed in 2007, when a majority (55%) of households in the EU-28 had internet access. This proportion continued to increase and in 2014 reached 81%, rising by an additional two percentage points compared with 2013.

Widespread and affordable broadband access is one of the means of promoting a knowledge-based and informed society. In the EU-28 in 2014, broadband was by far the most common form of internet access in all EU Member States: it was used by 78% of the households, an increase of 36 percentage points since 2007.

### Internet usage

As of the beginning of 2014, just over three quarters (78%) of all individuals in the EU-28, aged between 16 and 74 years, used the internet at least once within the previous three months. At least 9 out of every 10 individuals in Denmark, Luxembourg, the Netherlands, Sweden, Finland and the United Kingdom used the internet. By comparison, less than two thirds of all individuals aged 16 to 74 used the internet in Portugal, Greece, Italy, Bulgaria and Romania. The proportion of the EU-28's population that had never used the internet was 18% in 2014, down two percentage points from the year before and down from 30% in 2009.

### Internet usage on the move

The use of the internet while on the move means using the internet away from home or work, and using the internet on a portable computer or handheld device via mobile or wireless connections. In 2012, 36% of individuals aged 16 to 74 within the EU-28 used a mobile device to connect to the internet, compared to 2014, by which time this share had risen to 51%. The most common mobile devices for internet connections were mobile or smart phones, laptops, notebooks, netbooks or tablet computers. Sweden, Denmark and the United Kingdom recorded the highest proportion of mobile internet use in 2014, with around three quarters of individuals aged 16 to 74 using the internet while on the move. By comparison, around one quarter of individuals in Bulgaria, Romania and Italy used the internet away from home or work.

One of the most common online activities in the EU-28 in 2014 was participation in social networking. Nearly half (46%) of individuals aged 16 to 74 used the internet for social networking, for example, using sites such as Facebook or Twitter.

### Using cloud computing for saving and sharing files

Despite the increase in internet use and access, a considerable part of the population had not yet become aware of the existence of cloud services despite being internet users, by 2014. Services based on cloud computing technology allow users to store files or use software on a server run over the internet. Cloud services are a relatively new phenomenon compared with web applications for social networking, listening to music or watching films. One of the main challenges faced when measuring the usage of cloud services is being able to make a clear distinction between these and other online services. In 2014, one in five (21%) individuals aged 16 to 74 in the EU-28 saved files on internet storage space, in other words, using cloud services. More than one third of individuals in the Netherlands, Sweden, Luxembourg, the United Kingdom and Denmark used internet storage space for saving files, while in Lithuania, Poland and Romania these services were used by less than 1 in 10 individuals for this purpose.

Compared with other ways of electronic file sharing, internet storage space was less often used for this purpose as more detailed results show. While 15% of the EU-28 population used internet storage space for sharing files in 2014, a greater proportion used e-mail applications (44%), USB sticks, DVDs or Bluetooth (30%) or personal websites and social networking sites (28%). Most individuals who were cloud users appreciated the ease of accessing files from several devices or locations. Among those internet users who were aware, concerns about security and privacy were a major factor that prevented them from using such services.

### Ordering goods and services

The proportion of individuals aged 16 to 74 in the EU-28 who ordered goods or services over the internet for private use has risen and in 2014 reached 50%, an increase of six percentage points compared with 2012. As such, the EU digital target to have 50% of the population buying online by 2015 was achieved a year early. More than two thirds of individuals in the United Kingdom, Denmark, Sweden, Luxembourg, the Netherlands, Germany and Finland ordered goods or services over the internet, whereas the proportion was nearer one person in five in Italy and Bulgaria and around 1 in 10 in Romania. In percentage point terms, the largest increase between 2012 and 2014 was observed in Estonia, jumping 26 percentage points from 23% in 2012 to 49% in 2014. The next largest increase, among the EU Member States, was in the Czech Republic (11 percentage points); in Iceland an increase of 12 percentage points was observed.

## Questions 1–5

Do the following statements agree with the information given in Reading Passage 1?

*Write:*

| | |
|---|---|
| **TRUE** | *if the statement agrees with the information* |
| **FALSE** | *if the statement contradicts the information* |
| **NOT GIVEN** | *if there is no information on this.* |

1 After the year 2007, most households in the EU-28 were able to access the internet.

2 Having a cheap and extensive access to broadband is the only way to create an informed society based on knowledge.

3 In 2014, the proportion of people accessing the internet exceeded all expectations.

4 The difference between the proportion of those in the EU-28 who had never used the internet in 2009 and 2014 was surprising.

5 Swedes were among the top users of the internet while away from home, at the beginning of 2014.

## Questions 6–10

*Complete the notes below.*

*Choose **NO MORE THAN THREE WORDS** AND/OR **A NUMBER** from the passage for each answer.*

### Individuals aged 16 to 74 within the EU-28 in 2104

**Mobile device to connect to the internet**

– About 75% of people in Sweden, Denmark and the UK accessed the internet **6** ................... .

– About 25% in Bulgaria, Romania and Italy used the internet in the same way.

**Social networking**

Almost **7** ................... used the internet for this.

**Cloud computing**

In 2014, one in five used cloud services on the internet for **8** ................... :

– over one **9** ................... for those in the Netherlands, Sweden, Luxembourg, the UK and Denmark

– in Lithuania, Poland and Romania – 1 out of every **10** ...................

## Questions 11–13

*Complete each sentence with the correct ending, **A–E**, below.*

11 The rise in people buying online in Estonia was

12 The goal of having half of the population making online purchases was

13 About one fifth of Italians

A reached ahead of schedule.

B avoided using the internet away from home.

C placed orders for merchandise or services.

D proportionately greater than other countries.

E received with great satisfaction.

## READING PASSAGE 2

*You should spend about 20 minutes on Questions 14–27, which are based on the Reading Passage below.*

### The legacy of Krakatoa

**A** One hundred and twenty-five years ago this Wednesday occurred the biggest bang the inhabited world has ever known. Indonesia's Krakatoa volcano erupted. It did so with the force of 13,000 Hiroshima atom bombs, propelled a trillion cubic feet of rock, pumice and ash into the air, and made a noise loud enough to be heard 1,930 miles away in Perth. The explosions, fallout and resulting tidal wave (130 feet high in places) killed 36,417 people in Java and Sumatra, destroyed 165 villages and towns, and two-thirds of the island. Wind streams blew the fine ash as far away as New York; sea levels were raised in the English Channel, and over the following year, global temperatures were reduced by 1.2 °C.

**B** Today, the remains of one of Indonesia's most active volcanoes continue to spit and bubble. Now part of Ujung Kulon National Park, it is known as Anak Krakatoa, or Krakatoa's child, a post-collapse cone which has emerged from within the caldera of the original volcano over the past half-century and now stands about 600ft above sea level.

**C** During the approaching anniversary of the 1883 eruption, locals and tourists will remember the catastrophe when they visit Anak during the annual Krakatoa Festival – not exactly a celebration, more of a cultural memorial dedicated to one of history's most momentous natural disasters.

**D** Richard Arculus, a professor of geology at the Australian National University in Canberra, will be sorry not to be there. He is among what he calls a 'specialised gang' that traverses the world in search of the Earth's more unstable crusts and underwater volcanoes. Anak Krakatoa is a must. 'It's got a kind of status. You can go to the lip and sometimes, if it's not erupting, you will see an active vent with smoke and steam coming out of it,' he said. While it is not the most orthodox of tourist attractions, it pulls a steady stream of visitors excited by the Hollywood version of events, immortalised by the 1969 film *Krakatoa, East of Java*.

**E** What they see is that there is very little greenery on Anak Krakatoa itself apart from some stunted vegetation around the perimeter. Professor Arculus added, 'If it stopped erupting, if ash stopped coming out of it, it would be colonised by tropical vegetation very quickly.' But at the moment, it appears to be more of a barren rock.

**F** The national park it is part of, roughly the size of Bedfordshire, is home to Java's largest remaining area of lowland rainforest, and became a UNESCO World Heritage Site in 1992. It is known for its Javan one-horned rhino, the rarest large animal on Earth with only 50 left, 250 species of birds, and, possibly, the Javan tiger, although this has not been sighted since 1950.

**G** Krakatoa has provided writers and film-makers with a feast of stories. There is the account of the steamship thrown nearly two miles by the giant tidal waves that engulfed many nearby islands. But the most extraordinary tale involved a German quarry manager who told how he was swept off the roof of his three-storey office, only to be saved by a passing crocodile. As he cascaded through the jungle propelled by the giant wave, he spotted the croc beside him and leapt on its back. Safely aboard, he dug his thumbs into the creature's eye sockets and was carried along for the next few miles until he was dumped on the jungle floor.

**H** Myth or not, it is part of the folklore of Krakatoa, which sits astride the same faultline responsible for the 2004 earthquake off the coast of Sumatra. Surprisingly, the volcanic eruption of 1883 was not as severe as this more recent seismic movement. Professor Arculus said the total amount of water displaced by the Krakatoa volcano was much less. 'The problem around Krakatoa was that there was a big population living around the Sumatran and Javan shores, and because they were only a few kilometres away they copped a lot of it, but the tsunami was relatively trivial in size.'

**I** Professor Arculus also corrects the misspelling of the volcano's name, which is officially Krakatua. 'It was wrongly spelt on the telegraph when the news was sent to London and it's been corrupted by the Brits ever since,' he pointed out. While Anak Krakatua – or Krakatoa – is largely dormant, tourists can still witness wisps of smoke erupting from the emerging cone. But there is no real reason to worry, at least for the moment. It'll take several thousands of years before it gets to the same size and has the potential to erupt and collapse again.

PHOTOCOPIABLE

*Questions 14–19*

Reading Passage 2 has nine paragraphs, **A–I**.

Which paragraph contains the following information?

*NB You may use any letter more than once.*

**14** how someone stayed alive with the help of a wild animal

**15** the fact that the spelling of Krakatoa is incorrect

**16** a list of the global events caused by the eruption at Krakatoa

**17** a reference to rare wildlife that may be extinct

**18** a prediction about future volcanic activity on Anak Krakatoa

**19** the reason behind Anak Krakatoa's appeal to sightseers

*Questions 20–24*

*Complete the sentences below.*

*Choose* **NO MORE THAN THREE WORDS** *from the passage for each answer.*

**20** The Krakatoa eruption led to the island being reduced in size by .......................... .

**21** What is left of the island is now called Anak Krakatoa, which translates as .......................... .

**22** Little plant life exists on Anak Krakatoa, because it has not yet .......................... .

**23** No-one has seen .......................... for over half a century.

**24** Professor Arculus assessed the size of the tsunami following the eruption of Krakatoa as .......................... .

*Questions 25–27*

Do the following statements agree with the information given in the Reading Passage?

*Write:*

**TRUE**        *if the statement agrees with the information*

**FALSE**       *if the statement contradicts the information*

**NOT GIVEN**    *if there is no information on this.*

**25** The 2004 oceanic earthquake was less powerful than the 1883 eruption on Krakatoa.

**26** The heavy death toll from the Krakatoa eruption resulted from the impact of a tidal wave on a sizeable population living nearby.

**27** Anak Krakatoa's dormant state is under constant observation.

## READING PASSAGE 3

*You should spend about 20 minutes on **Questions 28–40**, which are based on the Reading Passage below.*

It was once accepted currency among neuroscientists that the physical development of the brain stopped in very early childhood – save for a gradual loss of brain cells. However, in recent years all that has changed. Scientists now realise that the teenage brain undergoes the same sort of radical re-development seen in the rest of the body. The appearance of adult characteristics during puberty, such as facial hair in boys, appears to be paralleled inside the head with some equally dramatic changes in the physical structure and layout of the brain. It was not until the advent of brain scans – which allowed scientists to study the living brain in real time – that the true scale of the changes in teenage brain circuitry became fully apparent.

Two main changes are now known to take place during adolescence. The first involves the growth of fatty insulation around the electrically charged neurons – the message-transmitting cells of the brain. This extra insulation increases the speed of transmission a hundredfold. The second change concerns the growth and then deliberate pruning back of the synapses, which link neurons to one another. This re-shaping of the brain is considered a critical part of intellectual maturity. Tests show that there is a marked change in the way the adolescent brain handles information and deals with problems – a sign of growing maturity. 'There seems to be a qualitative shift in the nature of thinking such that adolescents are more self-aware and self-reflective than prepubescent children,' says Dr Blakemore. 'Adolescents develop a capacity to hold in mind more multi-dimensional concepts and are thus able to think in a more strategic manner.'

It was a 1999 study that laid much of the groundwork for the recent reappraisal of the teenage brain. Judith Rapoport, a child psychiatrist at the US National Institute of Mental Health in Washington DC, studied the brain development of 145 children using magnetic resonance imaging. Dr Rapoport found a phase of overproduction of grey matter in the frontal cortex – the 'thinking' part of the brain – just prior to puberty. The brain's grey matter is made of nerve cells, or neurons, and their connections. It was already known that an earlier growth of grey matter in the womb was followed by a general pruning back of cells in the first few years of life. Now it became apparent that there was a second wave of growth and pruning during puberty.

Even more interesting was the discovery that this time it was focussed primarily on the brain's pre-frontal cortex, the part of the outer cortex responsible for 'higher' functions such as decision-making, planning, the control of emotions, empathy and the understanding of other people's facial expressions. One of the key roles of the pre-frontal cortex, for instance, is understanding and interpreting the facial expressions of others. Adults rely on the frontal cortex to interpret faces. Teenagers are not very good at this, or at least they seem to be not very good. Take the expression of fear. When taking part in psychological tests, young teenagers are notoriously bad at detecting fear in the faces of others. Brain scans show why. In early adolescence, teenagers use a part of the brain called the amygdala to interpret fear in a facial expression. This is an evolutionary ancient part of the brain and it forms part of the primitive 'gut reactions' – instincts that do not involve much thought. During adolescence, possibly because of the reshaping of the brain, adolescents shift from relying on the amygdala to using the pre-frontal cortex.

It may, at first glance, seem rather odd that cutting back on nerve connections is a critical part of achieving intellectual maturity. But in fact, it is not a good thing to have too much grey matter. 'We need to prune it back, to get rid of the excess,' Dr Blakemore explains. It seems, then, that teenagers go through a period when their pre-frontal lobes are 'learning' to work more efficiently. This is the part of the brain that distinguishes man from the rest of the animal kingdom. It's what makes us – and teenagers – human. So the next time a teenager behaves badly, spare a thought for the 'work in progress' still taking place between their ears.

### Questions 28–33

*Complete each sentence with the correct ending, **A–F**, below.*

**28** It used to be thought that the brain ceased to develop at a very early stage of

**29** The changes that occur in the body of teenagers is also seen in the

**30** Scans gave scientists the opportunity to see teenagers'

**31** Scientific discoveries have shown there are changes to the body and brain in

**32** The speed of message transmission in the teenage brain is increased by

**33** The changes in the brain in adolescence is thought of as important for

**A**  intellectual maturity.

**B**  childhood.

**C**  puberty.

**D**  neuron insulation.

**E**  brain circuitry.

**F**  brain.

### Questions 34–39

Classify the following descriptions as relating to the brain.

**A**  in childhood

**B**  in early adolescence

**C**  in adulthood

**34** Its state of self-awareness has yet to begin to mature.

**35** Nerve connections are cut back primarily from the pre-frontal cortex.

**36** Nerve connections are cut back from the whole brain.

**37** The brain cannot understand the emotions expressed in people's faces effectively.

**38** The brain uses the pre-frontal cortex to interpret expressions.

**39** The understanding of fear shown in people's faces is done by the amygdala.

### Question 40

*Choose the correct letter, **A**, **B**, **C** or **D**.*

**40** Which of the following is the most suitable title for Reading Passage 3?

    **A**  The teenage brain: how it differs from a baby's brain

    **B**  The teenage brain: a scientific analysis of the changes

    **C**  The teenage brain: the potential dangers of brain scans

    **D**  The teenage brain: how it distinguishes man from the animals

# Writing

## WRITING TASK 1

You should spend about 20 minutes on this task.

> *The bar chart below shows the value of UK e-commerce sales by industry sector between 2009 and 2015.*
>
> *Summarise the information by selecting and reporting the main features and make comparisons where relevant.*

Write at least 150 words.

**Value of UK e-commerce sales by industry sector, 2009 to 2015 (excluding micro-enterprises)**

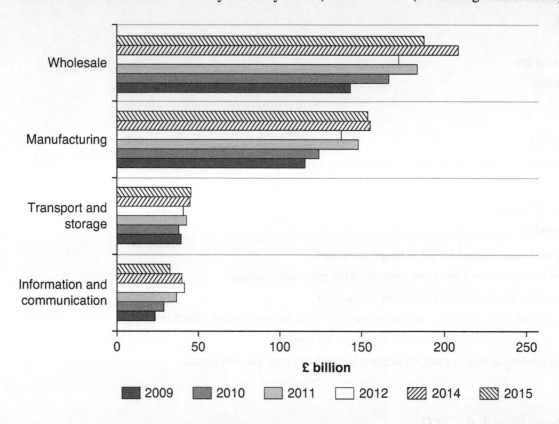

## WRITING TASK 2

You should spend about 40 minutes on this task. Write about the following topic:

> *People today seem to be increasingly buying consumer goods such as the latest domestic appliances, clothes and electronic gadgets.*
>
> *Do you think this is a positive or negative development?*

Give reasons for your answer and include any relevant examples from your own knowledge or experience.

Write at least 250 words.

# Speaking

## PART 1

The examiner asks the candidate about him/herself, his/her home, work or studies and other familiar topics.

*EXAMPLE*

**Games**

- What kind of games do children like playing where you live? Why?
- Do you enjoy playing games like video games? Why/Why not?
- Tell me something that you don't like about games.
- Do you think playing all types of games are good for children? Why/ Why not?

## PART 2

You will have to talk about the topic for one to two minutes. You have one minute to think about what you are going to say. You can make some notes to help you if you wish.

*EXAMPLE*

> Describe a market near where you live that you sometimes use.
>
> You should say:
>
>   what kind of produce or services the market sells
>
>   what the market looks like
>
>   where the market is located
>
> and explain why you like to use this market.

## PART 3

*Discussion topics:*

**Shopping in markets**

*EXAMPLE QUESTIONS:*

What types of markets are there in your neighbourhood? Do any of them sell street food, electrical goods, clothes, for example?

How do large shopping complexes like shopping malls affect local markets and businesses?

Some people say that it is important to keep places such as street markets alive? Do you agree or disagree?

**Sport**

*EXAMPLE QUESTIONS:*

Why do you think people like to shop on the internet?

Are there any disadvantages to shopping on the internet? What is the most serious?

Do you think people's shopping habits on the internet will affect how people live in the future? In what way?

# Answer key to tests

## Progress Test 1

### Listening

**Section 1**

| | | | |
|---|---|---|---|
| 1 | Toledo | 2 | July |
| 3 | 1,600 | 4 | 400 |
| 5 | book (the) flights | 6 | insured |
| 7 | chef | 8 | 17<sup>th</sup> |

**9 and 10** IN EITHER ORDER  C, E

 **Listening script**

**Section 1**

**V = Villa owner ; A = Alice**

**V:** Hello? How can I help you?

**A:** Well, I'd like to book a villa for a short holiday for myself and five other friends, so six in total.

**V:** How many bedrooms would you like?

**A:** Er … three would be fine – we don't mind sharing.

**V:** Well, there's Villa Rosada, which has three bedrooms, or Villa Toledo, which has two bedrooms that can both take three people. That one's obviously a bit cheaper.

**A:** Mm, I think the cheaper one, <u>Villa Toledo</u>, please. How do you spell that?

**V:** T–O–L–E–D–O

**A:** And how much is that for a week?

**V:** That depends on the time of year you want to come.

**A:** Say the end of July, beginning of August?

**V:** Well, up to the 15th June is mid-season, and er after that it's the high season.

**A:** What about <u>19th–26th July</u>, then?

**V:** Er yes, … the villa is free then, at the moment.

**A:** And how much would that be?

**V:** That would be er <u>£1,600 for the villa for the week</u>, not per person.

**A:** That sounds great. Can I book it now?

**V:** Yes, of course. You'd need to pay a 25% deposit to secure the booking, so that's £440.00. Mm no, sorry, it's <u>£400.00</u> of course. I can take your card details now …

..........................................................

**A:** Could you give me some advice about organising the flights and so on?

**V:** Well, the first thing is to make sure you book the flights straightaway. Faro's a very popular destination and flights can get booked up very quickly.

**A:** OK, yes, think I'd better make a list of things to do. So <u>book flights</u>, right away.

**V:** And are you going to hire a car?

**A:** Yes, er we can all drive and have driven in Spain before.

**V:** Well, just make sure everyone is <u>insured</u>.

**A:** Er good point, I'll check that.

**V:** What are you planning to do about food?

**A:** Mmm I take it the villa has a kitchen.

**V:** Mmm yes, there's quite a large one with an outside dining area, but you don't want to be doing too much cooking on holiday, do you? We can offer you a private chef at a very reasonable rate. It won't cost any more than going out to eat, and you can have your meals in the comfort of your own place.

**A:** Mmm … that sounds interesting, I'll talk to the others and see if they'd like to hire a <u>chef</u>. Can I get back to you on that?

**V:** Of course. Just don't forget that you need to pay the balance of the rent by the <u>17th April</u>.

**A:** No, I won't … oh, just one more thing. Are there any particular places or activities you'd recommend?

**V:** Well, er there's the beach, which is very popular, but it's very long and where the villa is, it doesn't get crowded.

**A:** That sounds good, but we're looking for something more thrilling than lying on the beach.

**V:** Well, if you like walking, there's some beautiful countryside just away from the coast. Or you could go mountain biking …

**A:** Mmm <u>I think we'd all rather go walking than biking.</u> It's a bit less tiring, I think.

**V:** Do you play golf?

**A:** Oh no, not at all.

**V:** Er you could also go out on a boat to watch dolphins. <u>There are usually lots of schools of dolphins around.</u>

**A:** <u>Really? That sounds great, I think that's one thing we'd all like to do</u>. How would we go about arranging a trip?

**V:** There are several boats that do it. You can book in advance or when you come.

**A:** Oh sounds fantastic.

### Reading

| | | | | | |
|---|---|---|---|---|---|
| 1 | vi | 2 | ii | 3 | viii |
| 4 | v | 5 | iii | 6 | Not Given |
| 7 | True | 8 | False | 9 | True |
| 10 | False | 11 | True | 12 | True |
| 13 | D | | | | |

### Grammar

**1**

| | | | |
|---|---|---|---|
| 1 | have had | 2 | is now having |
| 3 | has been | 4 | is now owned |
| 5 | compares | 6 | took |
| 7 | was owned | 8 | arrive |
| 9 | become | 10 | go |
| 11 | are investing | 12 | depends |

**2**

1 Even until recently, the majority of the world's population used to live in rural areas.

2 Twice as many smart TVs were sold last year, compared to this.

3 Correct

4  Snowboarding is one sport that I don't find very exciting.

5  The Shard in London is currently the highest building in Europe.

6  Correct

7  E-books will never replace real books./Never will E-books replace real books.

8  Correct

9  Since the beginning of the 21st century, the population has doubled.

10  I was amazed by the range and quality of the products on offer.

11  Business has been affected slightly by the very hot weather.

12  I have to admit that I was bored as I listened to the lecture.

13  Correct

14  The use of technology is not always a positive thing for humankind.

15  I am not always sure/I am never sure what to do for the best.

## Vocabulary

**1**

| | | | | | |
|---|---|---|---|---|---|
| 1 | C | 2 | A | 3 | D |
| 4 | C | 5 | B | 6 | B |
| 7 | C | 8 | B | 9 | D |
| 10 | B | 11 | A | 12 | D |

**2**

| | | | | | |
|---|---|---|---|---|---|
| A | vi | B | iv | C | vii |
| D | viii | E | iii | F | ii |
| G | v | H | i | | |

**3**

| | | | | | |
|---|---|---|---|---|---|
| 1 | ii | 2 | iii | 3 | iv |
| 4 | vi | 5 | v | 6 | vii |
| 7 | i | 8 | viii | | |

## Writing TASK 1

*Model answer*

The chart provides information about employee numbers in sport in various countries in the EU from 2010 to 2014. It is clear that the trends in employment numbers in sport are mixed with Estonia showing the greatest rise proportionately.

While the volume of workers employed in sport was low in Estonia over the period, there was an almost twofold rise in numbers from about 3,400 workers in 2012 to 6,300 in 2014. By contrast, the trend in Ireland was flat with a negligible fall from around 17,900 to 17,800 and a dip to about 16,700 in 2012. In Belgium, employment numbers in sport declined from approximately 23,900 to 20,500, whereas those in Bulgaria experienced a drop from about 10,300 to about 8,900 in 2012 before recovering to around 9,500 in 2014. In Denmark, meanwhile, employment numbers in sport climbed from about 26,900 to 28,100 with a fall to about 24,700 in 2013.

Despite a rise from about 25,900 to 29,000 in employee numbers in sport in the Czech Republic over the period, there was a dip to about 22,200 in 2012.

*Word count: 181 words*

**COMMENTS**

The answer is divided into three clear paragraphs with a paraphrase of the rubric in the introduction followed by a clear overview, which comments on the trends and highlights a noticeable feature of the data. The response uses a range of structures, mixing noun phrases, e.g. *there was an almost twofold rise in numbers/ the trend in Ireland was flat*; verbs, e.g. *employment numbers in sport declined*; and various linking devices, e.g. *while, by contrast, meanwhile* to indicate comparison.

# Progress Test 2

## Listening

| | | | | | |
|---|---|---|---|---|---|
| 11 | E | 12 | F | 13 | C |
| 14 | A | 15 | A | 16 | A |
| 17 | B | 18 | protective clothing | | |
| 19 | over 12/twelve | 20 | extra charge | | |

 **Listening script**

**Section 2**

Hello, everyone and welcome to the Time Capsule, which is an interactive museum, where we don't just look at things from the past, but also explore the present and the future. The museum has four spacious floors of exhibits, and ten different galleries, so, first of all, let's orientate ourselves.

We're currently standing at the main entrance, which is actually on the first floor. If you look at your map, you'll see that the first gallery houses an exhibition called 'Technology Today'. Passing through that gallery, you'll find yourself in the 'Communications' gallery, opposite the lifts. In this area, we look at lots of different forms of communication, particularly new types of communication. If you then take the lifts down to the ground floor, there are three galleries. The furthest one from the lifts is the 'Transport' gallery, where we have a fine collection of old trams and buses. Next is the gallery devoted to 'Great Inventions', which is a very interactive area where you can try all sorts of things out, and finally, on the far right as you look at the map, is the gallery called 'People of the Past'.

The ground floor is, as you can see, completely given over to an exploration of the past, while the first and second floors concentrate on the present. Looking at the second floor, as you come out of the lift there is a gallery about 'Life on Earth', and on the far left as you look at the map is a fascinating exhibition called 'The Human Body'. In between these two exhibitions is our interactive children's area, aimed particularly at the under-eights. If you get hungry or thirsty, you just need to go up to the top floor, where the refreshments area is to the left of the 'Futures' gallery, which is next to the Planetarium.

••••••••••••••••••••••••••••••••••••••••••••••••

OK, now you've got your bearings, let me tell you a little more about the galleries and exhibits. As I mentioned, our exhibitions divide into past, present and future. Starting with the past, perhaps the most interesting exhibition is 'Great Inventions'. The theme here is everyday inventions, such as the fridge. Although the first refrigerator was invented in 1748, and domestic fridges were first launched in the 1920s, they didn't become a popular household item until 1934, when it was so hot that people found they couldn't otherwise keep their food fresh. Did you know that one of the first vacuum cleaners on the market, in 1900, would have cost a vast sum in today's money, around $2000. Time Capsule also pays considerable attention to the present day, with exhibits which're directly relevant to modern life. These present day galleries are especially appealing to younger children, as the displays are very interactive. For example, you can walk through a reconstruction of different habitats in our 'Life on Earth' exhibition, experiencing the jungle, or the polar regions. Or, in 'The Human Body', you can play with a giant digestive system and see exactly what does happen to your food mm … The play area's extremely innovative, and if you have children, you may find it hard to get them out of there again! A particular favourite is the water play area – just make sure your children wear some protective clothing!

On the top floor, you can find our 'Future' gallery and the Planetarium. The gallery looks at developments in space and technology, and is especially suitable for those over 12. Younger children can of course visit as well, but I should point out that there's an extra charge for the Planetarium, as it's run by a separate group from the Time Capsule.

Okay, I hope that covers everything. Mmm, … any questions? … Oh, yes? …

## Reading

1  Shoots
2  dry, harden
3  mature plants
4  to grow
5  oak trees
6  Not Given
7  True
8  False
9  True
10  True
11  outside Asia
12  virgin forests
13  carbon dioxide

## Writing TASK 2

### Model answer

Providing satisfactory health care is a global challenge despite the latest advances in the medical field. This situation is the result of several factors, but there are various approaches to help ease the problem.

The primary reason is, perhaps, population growth around the world. The impact of the advances in medical provision is being reduced by the rising number of people seeking medical care. This is not just through a rise in the number of children being born, but also through increased life expectancy as medical science and improvements in greater prosperity generally lead to longer lifespans, but not necessarily in good health. Moreover, the number of people suffering from costly, affluent diseases such as diabetes is increasing. Another reason is the cost of modern medicines, treatment and procedures is rising, further adding to the problem.

It may not be possible to deal with the rising population numbers directly, but it is possible to reduce the cost of medical treatments by encouraging people of all age groups to adopt healthier lifestyles and better diets, as well as engaging in greater physical activity such as walking, throughout their lives, but especially as they become older.

In addition to the adoption of healthier ways of living, more efficient use of resources and greater emphasis on reducing the cost of treatments could be achieved by governmental and private investment. For example, greater international collaboration on tackling illnesses like obesity and infectious diseases could lead to quicker and more cost-effective solutions than at present.

As we have seen, there are some important reasons behind the difficulties faced by countries worldwide as they try to provide adequate heath care, but the problem can be tackled in a variety of ways.

*Word count: 285 words*

**COMMENTS**

The response is divided into five clear paragraphs. The introduction paraphrases the rubric and states what the response will discuss. The second paragraph details various causes and the next two body paragraphs offer solutions with a conclusion linked to the essay and the task. There is a range of vocabulary, e.g. *on balance, impact, life expectancy, lifespans, adopt lifestyles, collaboration, tackling*, as well as structures and linking devices.

## Vocabulary

**1**

| | | |
|---|---|---|
| 1  important | 2  industrial | 3  beautiful |
| 4  agricultural | 5  national | 6  traditional |
| 7  technologica | 8  predictions | 9  projection |
| 10  populous | | |

**2**

| | | | | | |
|---|---|---|---|---|---|
| **1** | effective | **2** | significant | **3** | golden |
| **4** | happy | **5** | unfavourable | | |

**3**

| | | | | | |
|---|---|---|---|---|---|
| **1** | A | **2** | D | **3** | B |
| **4** | D | **5** | A | | |

## Grammar

**1**

1  It has been predicted that bees will disappear in the future.
2  Correct
3  Bags or any luggage can be left at reception.
4  Correct
5  The accommodation in cities can be expensive.
6  Correct
7  People should be fined for dropping litter on the street.
8  Young children need to be careful with tablets and smartphones or they will break them.
9  Correct
10  Correct
11  The length of prison sentences appears to have no effect on crime levels.
12  According to information on climate, global weather patterns are changing.
13  Correct
14  Sorry, I'm/will be really busy next week, so I can't have a chat about our seminar paper.
15  In the past, people used to pass furniture on to their children, not throw it away.

**2**

| | | | | |
|---|---|---|---|---|
| 1 | is extracted | 2 | grow | |
| 3 | are found | 4 | involves | |
| 5 | is harvested | 6 | is made | |
| 7 | exposes | 8 | lies | |
| 9 | is then allowed | 10 | forms | |
| 11 | flows | 12 | are left | |
| 13 | is formed | 14 | produces | |
| 15 | is collected | 16 | is sorted and graded | |
| 17 | is prized | | | |

# Progress Test 3

## Listening

21  experience
22  20/twenty
23  building
24  communication
25  30/thirty
26  5/five
27  listen carefully
28  a shaper
29 and **30**  IN EITHER ORDER  A, D

 **Listening script**

**Section 3**

**T = tutor; L = Lucy; J = Jon**

**T:**  Hello, everyone. Jon and Lucy, it's your turn to give feedback on how you've been getting on with the University Skills Certificate. Could you tell us which modules you decided to take and why, and which of these you found most useful, and why? Lucy would you like to go first?

**L:**  Well, I really wanted to focus on skills that I might need after I graduate, so I mostly went for three business-oriented modules. First of all, I took a module on techniques on getting ready for job interviews as I thought that might be useful, and the second one I did was on getting the best out of work experience. And I also had to take the core module on personal development. But I think it was a bit of a waste of time, that one …

**T:**  And how many credits did you earn? Did you get the full certificate?

**L:**  Well, I would have done, if it hadn't been for the Personal Development Course. You see, it was a core module, which meant I had to complete it to finish the course. I didn't though, so I only got 20 credits. I might go back and do a different core module though and get my 30 that way.

**T:**  And Jon. What about you?

**J:**  Like Lucy, I took the personal development course but two other modules were different. My second one was on team building, which was really practical. And I think they'll both make me more employable. So, I can't agree with Lucy on the Personal Development Module.

**T:**  So, what was your third module?

**J:**  Communication Skills. Each of my modules was 10 credits, so I had 30 credits in total, which gave me the certificate.

**T:**  You seemed to disagree on the Personal Development Module. Can you tell us a bit more about it?

••••••••••••••••••••••••••••••••••••••••••••••••••••••••••••

**J:**  Yes, well, I thought it was really useful. There were five main learning outcomes, erm, defining assertive behaviour, understanding how that is expressed, dealing with criticism, drawing up personal development plans and improving our own interpersonal behaviour.

**T:**  Which of those did you personally find most useful?

**J:**  Mmm, I think, probably, dealing with criticism. I used to find it really hard when people criticised me for anything, but they gave us some strategies for dealing with it better.

**T:**  Such as?

**J:**  Well, first of all, what you need to do is listen carefully to the criticism, rather than being too defensive. It sounds obvious.

**L:**  Well, it is obvious, isn't it? That's what I didn't like about the course. It was all a bit too obvious. I just didn't feel I was learning anything.

**T:** Was there anything positive you felt you got out of the course?

**L:** Well, I did enjoy doing the personality questionnaire. I found out some useful things about my style as a member of a group. Apparently, I'm a good 'shaper'.

**T:** What does that mean?

**L:** That I'm a high achiever.

**T:** And what about you, Jon?

**J:** The questionnaire showed I was a good networker.

**T:** What did the coursework consist of?

**L:** Well, I thought we might need to do a lot of reading … you know, read around the subject and then produce a review of the literature, but it wasn't like that at all.

**J:** No, that's right, it was more personal than that. We had to keep an online journal reflecting on our personal development on a weekly basis, and the tutors read it and wrote comments.

**T:** Wasn't there any kind of formal assessment? A case study or something?

**J:** It was formally assessed through an assignment. We had to write 5,000 words on assertive behaviour and how it is expressed, looking at things like body language.

**T:** Mmm right, that all sounds pretty interesting …

## Reading

| | | | | | |
|---|---|---|---|---|---|
| **1** | D | **2** | E | **3** | D |
| **4** | B | **5** | C | **6** | C |
| **7** | D | **8** | B | **9** | A |
| **10** | D | **11–13** | IN ANY ORDER C, D, G | | |

## Writing TASK 1

*Model answer*

The plans show the transformation of the ground floor of a cottage from 1950 to the present.

It is clear that the function of the space and the various rooms changes over the period with slight modification of the latter. For example, the lounge left of the entrance in 1950 had become a reception and office in the language school by 1970, while the music room had been turned into a classroom. By 1970, the part of the library at the back on the left had been kept, but the rest was divided into two classrooms. The living room in the centre of the plan had also been converted into a classroom with the kitchen and the dining room to the left of the entrance keeping the same functions.

At present, the space is a museum with the original lounge now a shop. The classrooms next to the reception and office and in the middle of the plan have reverted to their original functions, while the classrooms created from the library for the language school have become a temporary exhibition space.

*Word count: 181 words*

**COMMENTS**

The response describes all the changes with a range of structures, including appropriate tenses, e.g. the present simple for the introduction and the overview, the past perfect indicating changes by 1970 and the present perfect for the present day, and vocabulary, e.g. *functions, modification, had been turned into/converted into, have reverted to*. There is a clear overview at the beginning of the second paragraph and the answer is paragraphed clearly.

## Vocabulary

**1**

| | | | |
|---|---|---|---|
| **1** | job | **2** | work |
| **3** | livelihoods | **4** | career |
| **5** | profession | **6** | qualifications |
| **7** | opportunity | **8** | benefit |
| **9** | achievement | **10** | neighbourhood |
| **11** | vicinity | **12** | location |
| **13** | prospects | **14** | chance |
| **15** | success | | |

**2**

| | | | |
|---|---|---|---|
| **1** | impressive | **2** | memorable |
| **3** | priceless | **4** | attractions |
| **5** | emotional | **6** | extension |
| **7** | transformation | **8** | location |
| **9** | nostalgic | **10** | spacious |

## Grammar

**1**

**1**

**1** its **2** it **3** those **4** this **5** it **6** they

**2**

**1** those **2** this **3** these **4** they **5** them

**3**

**1** This **2** it **3** it **4** these **5** it

**2**

| | | | |
|---|---|---|---|
| **1** | otherwise | **2** | used to |
| **3** | Were | **4** | If |
| **5** | must | **6** | unless |
| **7** | should | **8** | are not |
| **9** | would | **10** | unless |
| **11** | had not been | **12** | could have dealt |
| **13** | should | **14** | must |
| **15** | put | | |

# Progress Test 4

## Listening

**31** wildlife

**32** 1800

**33** portraits

**34** light

**35** completed

**36** 80/eighty

**37** Asian

**38–40** IN ANY ORDER A, D, G

**Listening script**

**Section 4**

In the first of this series of talks on Australian culture, I'd like to give you an overview of Australian art. I'll be focusing on the 18th century to the present day and then there'll be a separate lecture on Aboriginal art, which will kick off a new exhibition on modern Australian art opening to the public in two weeks' time.

As you know, James Cook first charted the coastline of Australia in 1770, and on board his ship was Sydney Parkinson, a botanical illustrator. The drawings he made of <u>Australian wildlife</u> were taken back to Europe, where they were not always taken very seriously. Famously, a great many people thought that his drawing of a platypus was a hoax, … they couldn't believe that such a creature could exist!

In the early 19th century, a professional artist from England, John Lewin, settled in Australia in <u>1800</u>, though he had originally intended to return to England, using the proceeds he made from his paintings of wildlife. Unfortunately for him, these had gone out of fashion, and so he set himself up in business as a <u>painter of portraits</u> of well-known people in Sydney.

In the 19th century, Australian art moves from a more European perspective towards developing a uniquely Australian identity. Artists such as Tom Roberts and Arthur Streeton were part of the so-called Heidelberg School, whose attention was directed to the very different properties of <u>Australian light</u>, representing the much brighter, vibrant colours of the landscape. Incidentally, the school wasn't named after the German city, but after a farm near Melbourne where the painters came together to paint.

By the 1850s, art exhibitions had started to increase in popularity and the first Australian art gallery, the National Gallery of Victoria, as it's now known, was founded in 1861.

But it wasn't until the 20th century that the first well-known women artists began to emerge. At the beginning of the century, one well-known female artist was Grace Cossington Smith, whose work has been exhibited at the National Gallery. Cossington Smith is perhaps best known for paintings of Sydney Harbour Bridge, <u>before it was completed</u>. She was drawn to the image of the two sides straining to meet in the middle.

More recently, Emily Kame Kngwarreye, a prominent indigenous artist, who didn't begin painting professionally <u>until she was nearly 80</u>, has become one of the most commercially successful Australian artists ever. Her work is highly valued and fetches huge sums of money.

Other notable artists and movements of the 20th century would have to include James Gleeson, Australia's foremost surrealist, and Ian Fairweather, a Scottish painter who spent most of his life in Australia, whose paintings are clearly inspired by a combination of <u>Western and Asian</u> art.

In the present day, of course, artists continue to be influenced by the great movements of the past, but also by 21st century influences. The digital age is making its mark, as is the environment. One artist that is particularly well known for his eco-art is John Dahlsen. His artwork is made up from things that he finds on the beach, but not from things like seaweed and seashells as you might expect. Dahlsen, who loves walking on the beach, started to notice the volume of rubbish that was being washed-up on the sand. He started collecting it to bring home, and noticed how, when sorted into colours, it could seem almost beautiful. In the year 2000, he won the Wynne Prize for his work, Totems, <u>which are tall totem poles made entirely of rubber beach sandals that he found washed-up on the beach. Another of his works, Blue Rope, has layers of different colours – blue and green. It looks like the sea, but is made from old nylon rope, fishing nets and plastic bags.</u> Not surprisingly, the environmental movement has taken him to their hearts as not only is he actually picking up a great deal of rubbish, he is also doing a lot to raise awareness of the problem …

## Reading

| | |
|---|---|
| **1** 3/three points | **2** a point/1 point |
| **3** shorter | **4** less prestigious |
| **5** I | **6** N |
| **7** G | **8** D |
| **9** H | **10** L |
| **11** J | **12** A |
| **13** F | **14** C |

## Writing TASK 2

*Model answer*

Funding for the arts from the public money is considered by some as unacceptable. By others, however, it is argued that subsidies for cultural events such as ballet and opera ought to be provided as they play an important part in keeping culture alive. My personal view is that these activities should be funded provided access is available to the wider public.

On the one hand, financial support from the government for the arts is criticised, because people believe that it benefits only a small number of people rather than the public at large. Another criticism is that the money could be spent on other areas such as education and health, which would have a greater impact on the well-being of society.

On the other hand, it is maintained by others that funding of arts such as ballet and opera helps to improve cultural awareness and therefore deserves public support financially. They also argue that such activities are a valuable means of keeping culture alive, while at the same time providing valuable job opportunities and developing creative abilities.

Having examined both views, I feel there is a clear need to support the above art forms through government subsidies. Certain types of activity such as ballet and opera could not survive without public support, as they are expensive to produce. If subsidies are given, however, access to performances should be made available to the wider public through cheaper seats. This would ensure that public money is targeted at everyone while keeping it alive.

As we have seen, there are differing views as to financial subsidies for the arts, but I personally believe that such support is perfectly valid to maintain the culture of a country.

*Word count: 284 words*

**COMMENTS**

The response paraphrases the rubric in the introduction. Each of the two views is given a separate paragraph, as is the writer's opinion. The structure of the body paragraphs follows the introduction and the conclusion reflects both these aspects of the response.

## Vocabulary

| | | | | | |
|---|---|---|---|---|---|
| 1 | C | 2 | C | 3 | B |
| 4 | C | 5 | A | 6 | D |
| 7 | B | 8 | A | 9 | C |
| 10 | B | 11 | D | 12 | A |
| 13 | B | 14 | B | 15 | A |

## Grammar

**1**

| | | | |
|---|---|---|---|
| 1 | the | 2 | the |
| 3 | zero article | 4 | a |
| 5 | zero article | 6 | zero article |
| 7 | zero article | 8 | zero article |
| 9 | a | 10 | zero article |
| 11 | zero article | 12 | the/zero article |
| 13 | the | 14 | zero article |
| 15 | a | 16 | a |
| 17 | zero article | 18 | zero article |
| 19 | zero article/th | 20 | the |
| 21 | the | | |

**2**

1 The place which I liked the best was Rio de Janeiro.
2 If it weren't for the fact that I obtained a good degree in art, I don't know what I would have done.
3 Correct
4 Correct
5 Paris? That's the city where I used to live.
6 Even if I had remembered to include the data, I wouldn't have been able to persuade the audience.
7 People who drive to work should be encouraged to car share.
8 Correct
9 He went to university in New York, where there is a variety of entertainment venues.
10 The art form that appeals to young people most is possibly contemporary art.

11 If I were you, I would start writing up your psychology project as soon as you can.
12 I'll lend you the books that I bought for the essay if you don't write in them
13 Correct
14 Unless the department is given more money, it can't invest more in community development.
15 Correct

# Progress Test 5

## Listening

| | | | | | |
|---|---|---|---|---|---|
| 31 | F | 32 | A | 33 | D |
| 34 | C | 35 | B | 36 | soldiers |
| 37 | inflation | 38 | 1764 | 39 | national |
| 40 | eagles | | | | |

 **Listening script**

**Section 4**

Good morning, everyone, my talk today is about the early history of money in the United States. And I'd like to start by looking at how trade was conducted before the early settlers arrived. Most people agree that there wasn't money in the sense we understand it today. In most cases, there were different sorts of barter systems. However, we know that elsewhere in the Americas, in Mexico, for example, the Aztecs did sometimes use gold as … mmm … a kind of currency. Basically, they would barter different goods and use the gold dust, which was <u>kept in see-through quills</u> and so it was visible, … to make up the difference if one item to exchange was worth significantly more. Another form of payment was cocoa beans, which were used in sacks with thousands of beans by the Aztecs <u>to make very large payments</u>.

In North America and Canada, a system called *potlatch* existed among Native Americans. Essentially, a potlatch was a kind of party where the host would demonstrate his wealth by giving away as much of it as possible. People took it in turns to host the potlatch and competed to give their possessions away, so in the end everyone in the community was provided for. Potlatch was, in fact, <u>temporarily made illegal</u> in Canada as it was not thought to contribute to the work ethic. But doing so had exactly the opposite effect because it removed people's motivation to earn money.

*Wampum*, which was later adopted as a currency by the settlers, wasn't a currency to begin with. Wampum are beads made from seashells, and they were certainly very valuable among American Indians. The right shells were not easy to find and the beads were time-consuming and difficult to make, so this gave them a commodity value. They would certainly have been used in bartering. The settlers, however, used them as a form of money. In fact, <u>the workers who built the city of New York were paid in</u> *Wampum*. There were many alternative currencies used in the past.

Another form or currency was tobacco. Tobacco leaves were used as currency in and around the colony of Virginia for about 200 years. They were not the most practical of currencies though, as the leaves tended to fall apart quite quickly, and gradually, <u>certificates representing tobacco held in warehouses started to be used instead</u> – in effect, a kind of paper money.

In later years, other forms of paper currency started to be issued. <u>In 1690, Massachusetts was the first colony to issue notes to pay soldiers</u>. The notes could be exchanged for gold or silver, but were also accepted as legal tender. Other colonies followed suit, and, as time went on, the British government tried to prevent the colonies from issuing paper money.

That was partly because they didn't want to lose control, <u>but also because some colonies were issuing so much that it was causing very high inflation</u>. This obviously worried the British government. In fact, it culminated in the complete banning of all colonial paper money in <u>1764</u>, which was one of the main reasons behind the American Revolution. During the Revolution, America produced a flood of paper money, which was worth less and less, and although in the short-term it did provide the necessary finance, it inevitably led to hyperinflation. By the end of the war, American finances were in chaos and in 1790, <u>the dollar was established for the first time as a national currency</u>. The hope was that by replacing all the different states' currencies, some stability could be achieved. However, there was a great shortage of gold and silver and the government was forced to accept the use of foreign gold and silver coins, particularly Spanish dollars, as legal tender as well. Gradually these were phased out, but American silver dollars are still legal currency, though you don't see many of them around these days. <u>There were also ten dollar coins, known as eagles</u> because of the bird printed on them, which were in circulation right up until the 1930s …

## Reading

**1–5** IN ANY ORDER  B, F, G, H, I
**6** chimney
**7** 8/eight adjustable grills
**8** cooler air
**9** living quarters/lower levels
**10** completely sealed
**11** Yes
**12** No
**13** Not Given

## Writing TASK 1

*Model answer*

The data provides information about items purchased online by different age groups in the UK in 2014.

Generally speaking, there seems to be a correlation between age and purchases with the younger age

groups more likely than the older to make purchases online. This is clearly illustrated by purchases of clothes and sports goods, with over 60% of those 16–44 and 40% in the 55–64 group, compared to 20% in the 65+ age group doing so. A similar pattern is seen regarding films and music, including downloads, with online purchasing declining with age from about 45% for those aged 16–24 to under 10% for the 65+ age group. Meanwhile, about half of those aged 25–34 purchased these items online.

Regarding household goods there is also a clear age relationship with those aged 16–24 and 65+ making online purchases, about 30% and 20% respectively. The 24–34 age group constituted the main group, about 60% purchasing household items online, with this falling to about 40% for the 55-64 age group.

*Word count: 173 words*

COMMENTS

The response clearly reflects the data with the overview at the beginning of the second paragraph summarising the relationship between the various charts. All of the relevant data to support the overview is mentioned with a range of structures and vocabulary.

## Vocabulary

**1**
**1** internet  **2** viaduct  **3** server
**4** pylon  **5** satellite  **6** grid
**7** tunnel  **8** well  **9** cable
**10** refinery

**2**
**1** money box  **2** cash reserves
**3** investment income  **4** savings plan
**5** education expenditure  **6** spending power
**7** debt mountain  **8** credit limit
**9** consumer expenditure  **10** currency reserves
**11** government spending  **12** price war
**13** personal morals  **14** traditional customs
**15** mineral wealth

## Grammar

**1**
**1** cannot/can't  **2** should
**3** must/have to  **4** can
**5** shouldn't have  **6** need/have
**7** could have  **8** needn't have
**9** will be  **10** should/ought to

**2**
**1** Yes  **2** Yes  **3** Yes
**6** Yes  **7** Yes  **11** Yes
**12** Yes, but it can also be kept
**13** Yes, but it can also be kept
**14** Yes, but it can also be kept
**16** Yes, but it can also be kept
**18** Yes  **20** Yes

# Answer key to tests

## Final Test key

### Listening

**Section 1, Questions 1–10**

1 exercise to music
2 8, 10
3 personalised programme/program
4 extra charge
5 free sessions
6 40%/percent/per cent
7 180
8 50
9 Sunday
10 outdoor shoes

---

 **Listening script**

**Section 1**

**R = receptionist; C = male customer**

**R:** Good morning, Weston Leisure Centre. Can I help you?

**C:** Hi, I'm ringing to find out some information about the fitness facilities you have.

**R:** Yes. We have quite a range … We have a pool with sauna and spa area, a gym with all the latest fitness equipment and various fitness classes. What do you think you might be interested in?

**C:** Well, mmm … probably not the pool, I'm not that keen on swimming. So erm probably the gym, or maybe some of the classes. What classes do you offer?

**R:** Er we have a wide range that changes regularly. Er let's see. There's Pilates, yoga, circuit training, exercise to music, … . They're mostly held during the day only.

**C:** Mmm, I can only come evenings or weekends.

**R:** Well, there's a Pilates class on a Tuesday evening and circuit training on Wednesday and Friday in the evening . Mmm … and <u>there's an exercise to music class</u> on Saturday mornings.

**C:** Er what are the opening hours of the gym?

**R:** <u>That's open 8am to 10pm Monday to Saturday,</u> 9 to 6pm on Sundays.

**C:** And would I get any instruction on how to use the gym?

**R:** Well, all new members have to have an induction session with an instructor. <u>He or she checks how fit they are and then creates a personalised programme</u> and shows them how to use the gym.

**C:** And then I'm on my own?

**R:** Mmm, there are personal trainers available for one-to-one sessions, <u>but there is an extra charge for this.</u>

..............................................................

**C:** How much does it cost to join the gym then?

**R:** Well, we offer different packages. The cheapest one is our Yearly Membership, which entitles members to unlimited use of the gym, including

swimming, use of the sauna and fitness classes <u>and two free sessions with a personal trainer.</u> It's £300 for the year, <u>but there are concessions for students, the unemployed or those over 60 with a reduction of 40%.</u>

**C:** Mmm. Er what other packages are available?

**R:** Well, the next cheapest is a six-month contract again with unlimited use of all facilities but no one-to-one sessions with a personal trainer except for an induction session. <u>That's £180 for six months.</u>

**C:** Oh that doesn't sound too bad.

**R:** Or you can be a casual member and pay for each session you come. Mmm <u>for this there's an annual membership fee of £50</u> and then you can just pay £8 every time you come. That's a good option if you don't think you'll use the gym that often.

**C:** Mmm it's quite a bit more expensive.

**R:** Mmm, you can come any time you like, whereas with the other two, you're locked in for six months or a year.

**C:** Mmm, OK. I think I'll be more likely to come if I pay for a period of time – I want to get my money's worth! Mmm, I think I'll go for the six-month membership.

**R:** OK, mmm , if you want to book an induction session, you can do all the paperwork at the same time. When would be a good time?

**C:** Er do you have anything on Saturday?

**R:** Mmm no, sorry, we're really busy … perhaps Sunday at 3pm?

**C:** <u>On Sunday?</u>

**R:** <u>Yes. Would that be okay?</u>

**C:** <u>Yes, great, thanks.</u> And er what should I wear?

**R:** Mmm, a T-shirt, shorts or tracksuit trousers, nothing special, <u>but you must wear some indoor trainers, not outdoor shoes of any kind.</u> That's really quite important …

---

**Section 2, Questions 11–20**

11 A
12 C
13 B
14 and 15   IN EITHER ORDER  D, E
16 office technology
17 (The) farm website
18–20  IN ANY ORDER  A, D, F

---

 **Listening script**

**Section 2**

Hi, my name's Andy Lodge and I'd like to thank the headmaster for inviting me to come and talk to you about volunteering over the summer months at our city farm. Many of you, no doubt, have been planning to go to university or start work, and have perhaps thought about what you're going to do over the summer months.

Volunteering's a good way to gain valuable experience and helps to develop a wide range of skills such as teamwork, socialising and time-management. Any volunteer work, however minimal, is regarded very favourably by universities and employers. Increasingly it's being recognised that volunteering can help young people to develop their independence and maturity.

Volunteering in the city farm's a worthwhile experience, and might even help you think about your particular career choice or university course in a new light. For instance, last year we had a number of students from the school who had applied for accountancy and banking courses, and after volunteering for two months with us several postponed their courses for a year so they could do more volunteering here, along with part-time work. And two university students, also from the school, who were with us last year, are coming back to volunteer for a month on a summer programme for school children we are running for the first time.

There are different types of farm work that you can get involved in. For example, if you're not afraid of hard work and enjoy meeting and working with other people, there's helping to keep everything in the farm in good order and helping to look after the animals including feeding them. We have various farm animals like cows, goats, sheep, lambs, donkeys, rabbits, horses and ponies and we also have a llama as well chickens, ducks and geese. All the animals are very popular, especially as we have riding lessons for local children at very low cost. Working with the animals is an area that attracts a lot of volunteers, who come back to see how the animals are getting on.

We also have several gardens and an orchard, which require a lot of help from volunteers such as weeding and picking the fruit and vegetables. We grow everything from lettuce to tomatoes, carrots to cabbages as well apples, pears and plums in our orchard. We use some of these to feed the animals, but some of the produce we sell and we need volunteers to help with packaging and distribution.

If all this doesn't appeal to you, there's the shop and café where we also take volunteers, and the office where we need young minds to help us with erm office technology. Erm … at the moment, we're trying to upgrade the farm website and design a virtual interactive trail around the farm site, so if you are into software engineering and you want to get a step up into the virtual world, this is something you might want to help out with.

⋯⋯⋯⋯⋯⋯⋯⋯⋯⋯⋯⋯⋯⋯⋯⋯⋯⋯⋯⋯

Finally, we also take care of all insurance issues for you while you are on and off the premises while doing any volunteer work with us. And a couple of other things that will be of help to you – we can provide references for any future work or courses you plan to do. Mmm … our references have helped a huge number of young people get work and get on courses. Also, we have some funds to help suitable applicants to visit other volunteer projects in various parts of the world, including New York and Venezuela. You can take some of your experience with you and bring back new ones to help out farm

projects here. You won't be going on your own on these trips as there's always at least one adult from the farm project to accompany any group.

Now we're going to watch a short 5-minute video about the farm showing volunteers at work and being interviewed and then afterwards, I'll take questions and you can …

**Section 3, Questions 21–30**

21 feedback/feed-back form
22 e(-)mail
23 in good time
24 four/4
25 length
26 (very) knowledgeable
27 free gifts
28 E
29 D
30 C

 **Listening script**

**Section 3**

**T = Tutor; S = Sonya; M = Maurice**

**T:** Hi, come in. How are you Sonya? Maurice?

**S:** Hello, Dr Kumar. Fine thanks.

**M:** Yes, fine.

**T:** So, you looked at the impact of the new campus tours that have recently been set up for people who'd like to come and study here.

**S:** Yes, we thought it would be good to do something that might have some tangible benefit for the university itself and also help improve the service offered.

**T:** Yes, it's now a well-established idea taking groups of people round the campus regularly to give an overview of what's on offer. So, it's always worth reviewing such practices. How did you go about collecting data?

**M:** After they'd taken the tour, we gave out a feedback form to prospective students to fill in. First of all, we asked some questions about the information which had been sent by email to them before the tour. We had been told that a lot of people don't actually turn up for the tours and we wanted to know why.

**T:** So, what did you ask them?

**S:** We looked at whether people had received information about the tour in good time before the visit.

**T:** That's a good question.

**S:** And if they had found the information helpful.

**T:** Hmm … . I think there's a bit of a problem with that question.

**M:** Quite a lot of people said they didn't and although we knew there was a problem, we still didn't know what the problem was.

**S:** Yes, we should've asked a more open question, like: 'What information did you find most helpful or least useful?' Most people said they did, though.

**T:** Who did you give the feedback form to?

**M:** People who'd been on the tour.

**T:** So they were the people who had actually turned up. Maybe, you'd need to think about talking to the people who didn't turn up?

**S:** I suppose so, but that could be difficult though. Mmm … then we asked them about the content of the tour itself. We asked people to rate various things on a scale of 1–5, with 1 being the lowest and 5 the highest.

**M:** The content of the tour generally came out quite high, about 4 on average, so we know that people are seeing what they need to, though I guess we could find out a bit more about this … However, there's one thing … the length was marked down at an average of 2. We're not sure though if this means the tour was too short or too long.

**T:** Or both!

**M:** Yes, I suppose so. Everyone thought the people leading the tours, who are mostly current students, were very knowledgeable.

**S:** And mmm … visitors were very pleased with the mmm … free gifts they were given at the end.

...........................................................

**T:** So, how do you think you could improve the research methodology and find out a bit more? Sonya?

**S:** Well, I think it would be a good idea to move away from the yes/no questions and even the grading 1–5 and ask more open questions. Perhaps, we could actually talk to people face to face? What do you think, Maurice?

**M:** I think that might be quite difficult to set up. I agree with you about the open questions, but I think we should just leave more spaces on the feedback form for people to write comments on. We could ask people to answer why/why not questions.

**T:** I think both approaches are possible, but if you do what Sonya's talking about, it will probably reduce the number of people you can get feedback from.

**S:** Well … yes, but we might get some much more detailed information. I don't think people like writing pages and pages on a feedback form.

**T:** I think you also need to think about when you ask for feedback. You might get more responses if you ask for the feedback immediately, rather than asking people to post it back to you. Even with a freepost envelope or email, a lot of people won't bother.

### Section 4, Questions 31–40

**31** 16,000/sixteen thousand years
**32** (the) 1930s/nineteen thirties
**33** nomadic hunters
**34** north-east/northeast Asia
**35** genetic evidence
**36** down the coast
**37** C
**38** B
**39** B
**40** C

**Listening script**

### Section 4

Today I'd like to give you a brief overview of the different theories and models of migration to the New World, or the Americas. I should point out that there is not complete agreement as to how people settled in the Americas, and so there won't be any answers, just a selection of popular theories.

First of all, there are two general theories. One is that the first people arrived in the so-called New World no longer than 16,000 years ago. This idea is known as *short chronology*. The other is called *long chronology*, which states that the first people arrived much longer ago than that, perhaps as much as 40,000 years ago.

There is also some argument as to how the first people reached the Americas. The longest standing theory, widely accepted since the 1930s, is the *landbridge theory*. This suggests that people migrated from Siberia into Alaska, and across the Bering Strait, which then contained a landbridge linking the two continents. According to this theory, the people migrating were nomadic hunters.

Spearheads of a particular shape have been found throughout North and Central America, supporting the landbridge theory and dating the migration at between 17,000 and 10,000 years ago – a short chronology. By contrast, the long chronology school of thought argues that, although people definitely crossed the Bering Strait at that time, they were not the first people to arrive. Some evidence exists of earlier inhabitation, especially in the south of the current United States and Central and South America. The question is where they came from. A number of theories have been put forward. The Pacific coastal model suggests that people arrived by boat from northeast Asia, following the coastline. However, some anthropologists suggest that the first people crossed from Australia or Polynesia. There are some apparent similarities between the Australian Aborigines and some of the tribes of Southern Patagonia. However, genetic evidence does not support this theory.

Genetic evidence is actually starting to make some headway in understanding migration patterns. Recently, the DNA was extracted from a 10,300-year-old tooth found in a cave in southern Alaska. Researchers discovered descendants with the same DNA all along the Pacific coast from California to Tierra del Fuego. This strongly indicates that some of the first inhabitants may have dispersed down the coast, though it is thought that this was no more than about 10,000 years ago.

...........................................................

Several of the descendants found by this study were descendants of Chumash Indians, living in California. Similarities have been found between their DNA and that of people living in Japan and north-east Asia, perhaps supporting the Pacific coastal model.

The history of the Chumash and other neighbouring Californian tribes is interesting and may provide further evidence of their ancestry. Along with the Tongva, a tribe found to the south, they regularly went out into the ocean fishing. This is unusual amongst New World peoples, and may indicate that this is how their ancestors originally arrived.

The boats used by the Chumash are called 'tomols' and there may be a linguistic link with a similar word used by the Polynesians. Tongva boats are called 'ti-ats'.

The Tongva are also known as Gabrielenos, after the tradition of naming tribes after nearby Spanish missions. The original name of the Tongva means 'people of the earth'. Plenty of Chumash and Tongva places names are still used in California, such as 'Malibu' in Los Angeles County.

Settlements prove that the Chumash were in the area at least 10,000 years ago, and archaeologists have uncovered a prehistoric Tongva site, estimated to be 8,000 years old. This, of course, still fits very comfortably within the 'short chronology' theory I mentioned earlier.

## READING

### Reading Passage 1, Questions 1–13

| | | | |
|---|---|---|---|
| 1 | True | 2 | False |
| 3 | Not Given | 4 | Not Given |
| 5 | Not Given | 6 | on the move |
| 7 | 50%/fifty per cent | 8 | saving files |
| 9 | ⅓/one third | 10 | 10/ten |
| 11 | D | 12 | A |
| 13 | C | | |

### Reading Passage 2, Questions 14–27

| | | | |
|---|---|---|---|
| 14 | G | 15 | I |
| 16 | A | 17 | F |
| 18 | I | 19 | D |
| 20 | two thirds/⅔ | 21 | Krakatoa's child |
| 22 | stopped erupting | 23 | the Javan tiger |
| 24 | trivial | 25 | False |
| 26 | True | 27 | Not Given |

### Reading Passage 3, Questions 28–40

| | | | | | |
|---|---|---|---|---|---|
| 28 | B | 29 | F | 30 | E |
| 31 | C | 32 | D | 33 | A |
| 34 | A | 35 | B | 36 | C |
| 37 | B | 38 | C | 39 | B |
| 40 | B | | | | |

## Writing TASK 1

*Model answer*

The chart compares the amount of e-commerce sales in billions of pounds generated from various areas of industry in the UK from 2009 to 2015. Overall, it is clear that despite the general sales trend in the sectors being upward, the patttern of the rise in each varies, with wholesale accounting for the largest amount throughout the period.

As regards wholesale, for example, there was an incease in the value of online sales from approximately £140 blliion in 2009 to around £180 billion in 2015. By comparison, while the amount of online sales in manufacturing also climbed over the period, from about £130 billion to about £160 billion, the overall rise was very small in the last four years with a dip to about £145 billion in 2011.

The volume of sales in the transport and storage and information and communictions sectors, meanwhile, were much smaller, as the former went up only slightly from about £40 billion to £45 billion over the period and the latter from about £25 billion to about £35 billion.

*Word Count: 175 words*

**COMMENTS**

The answer satisfies the requirements of the task. The introduction paraphrases the rubric and there is a clear overview in the second senence. The data for the four sectors is summarised and the specific data supplied as supporting evidence.

## Writing TASK 2

*Model answer*

People in the modern world appear to be more materialistic compared to the past with a greater focus on the acquisition of the most up-to-date household, clothing and technological items. Such a trend clearly has a positive impact economically, but, on balance, I feel it is primarily negative.

The growth in the purchase of consumer goods such as those above is certainly good for the economy. As people make new purchases to replace old items, like the latest fashions in white goods like washing machines, more jobs are created directly in shops and factories, and indirectly as people in new jobs spend more money. As a result, living standards are raised, leading to a virtuous circle.

However, the increase in consumerism is harmful, because it makes people focus on acquiring objects rather than on relationships and improving their lives generally. Moreover, as society becomes more materialistic, for example, through pressure from peers and from advertising, people can be driven to debt, which, in turn, can lead to depression, family break-ups and loss of homes.

# Answer key to tests

The focus on buying more and more consumer goods also creates huge amounts of waste. Many items are purchased like new versions of smartphones or clothes or domestic appliances when they come on to the market irrespective of whether they are needed. E-waste, for example, has increased phenomenally in recent years, as has the volume of discarded clothes, which are discarded without being worn out. The mountains of white goods such as refrigerators TVs and functioning washing machines that have been discarded in the pursuit of the latest fashionable items compounds the problem.

In conclusion, while there are clearly some financial benefits, increase consumerism is harmful for society.

*Word count: 285 words*

### COMMENTS

The response is divided into clear paragraphs with the introduction paraphrasing the rubric. A clear position is maintained throughout with the introduction giving the writer's stance, the second paragraph examining the positive aspect of the development, and the third and fourth paragraphs explaining the writer' position. The conclusion reflects the organisation of the body paragraph and the introduction, and, hence, the task.

# IELTS strategies for students

## Introduction

Below are some of the strategies that need to be automatic for you to be able to develop your confidence as you prepare for the academic version of the IELTS examination. You can add other strategies to the list as you progress through the course. Note that you learn skills and techniques; and strategies are what you choose to use as you read, write, speak and listen.

**Activating schemata**: you activate schemata to help you predict as you read by focusing on nouns and verbs so that you build up 'a theme or picture' as you read or listen. It is *also* important for you to help listeners and readers to activate their own schemata as they listen to you and read what you've written. It is, therefore, vital that you use words and phrases that create a consistent theme and that are relevant to the topic that you are writing or speaking about. To help readers and listeners further, you can give examples and reasons to develop the context you're presenting and thus help with schemata activation.

**Nominalisation:** you use the process of nominalisation to talk about abstract ideas and concepts and to summarise. In this process, you build information around nouns rather than verbs. For example, in Writing Task 1, you can turn *'Attendances at the cinema rose dramatically by 50% over the period'* into *'There was a dramatic 50% rise in attendances at the cinema over the period'*. In the latter sentence, the information is added before (adjective/percentage) and after (prepositional phrases) the noun (*rise*).

In all four skills in the IELTS exam, you need to be able to notice and process the exact meaning of noun phrases, which can, for example, be between 9–12 words long, e.g.:

- in paragraph headings, *the effect of rising sea levels on certain island communities*
- in Writing Task 2 *Some people think that the cost of the preservation of old buildings in major cities is …*
- in Listening Section 4, *the _____ of the use of plastic in cosmetic products on the environment*
- in Speaking Part 3, *Do you think that the cost of the preservation of old buildings in major cities is a good use of scarce funds?*

**Noticing:** you need to be able to develop your noticing skills when you read, write and listen. For example, in the Reading test, it is important to be able to notice elements in the texts such as causes, effects, examples, general statements/conclusions, problems, reasons, solutions, etc.; linking devices such as *for example, such as, although, but, however,* etc.; general and specific information in a text, the organisation of the text from titles, subheadings and questions; general patterns that you have met in previous reading tests or other parts of the IELTS examination. Things like this will help you develop your speed and accuracy and, hence, competence in performing in the exam.

**Paraphrasing**: you use paraphrasing to avoid repetition as you write and speak. For example, it is important to paraphrase the rubrics in both Writing tasks. This shows the range of your knowledge of grammatical structures as well as vocabulary. You also need paraphrasing skills to avoid repetition as you develop your answers as you write and speak. In the Reading and Listening tests, you need to be able to recognise/notice paraphrasing in the questions and the reading passages, etc. You need, therefore, to have knowledge of a wide range of language, e.g., for expressing cause and effect, measures and solutions, etc.

**Predicting**: you use predicting skills in the Reading and Listening tests to help you answer the questions. It is important to distinguish guessing from predicting. Guessing means that you give an answer without thinking, whereas predicting means that you use your knowledge and the information given to work out possible answers and the general meaning of answers as well as the organisation of a Reading Passage or Listening test. You can do the latter from titles and headings as well as the questions.

Predicting effectively involves using the skills and experience you already have to answer questions without actually imposing your opinion, etc., when giving the answers.

You also use predicting skills to think about the organisation of a Reading Passage or paragraph using the title before you start reading. If you do not do so, then you are wasting valuable information and time. See also *activating schemata* and *navigating a text* and *noticing*.

**Managing time**: you need to be able to manage your time extremely carefully and efficiently in preparation for the IELTS examination. It is important to be able to complete the tasks given in each component within the allocated time and not to do more than is necessary. For example, in Writing Task 1, you are advised to write your answer in 20 minutes. It is advisable, therefore, to spend about two minutes planning and two minutes checking, leaving you with 16 minutes for writing. It is worth thinking about all the components of the exam and reflecting on the time you need to complete the tasks. Use a stopwatch and look at the time as you read or write so that you *feel* what 20 minutes, and 40 minutes, in the Writing test is like. The same applies to the Reading test.

# IELTS strategies for students

**Organising and planning**: you need to develop efficient organisational and planning skills so that you can operate accurately and effectively in all parts of the examination. For example, in the Reading test you need to allocate the appropriate time for each Reading Passage, bearing in mind that one of the passages has 14 questions. You need, therefore, to adjust your time accordingly. You also need the above skills when you write your answers for Writing Tasks 1 and 2. You need to organise your ideas and their development so that they are clear to the examiner. The same applies in the Speaking test. See *activating schemata*.

**Questioning**: you can examine exam questions, or information, in Reading or Listening by using questions. For example, when you are asked to fill a gap in sentences such as *Recycling has a positive _____ on the environment*, you can ask yourself questions. Examples of questions are:

● *Is the missing word a noun, verb, adjective, adverb or number?*
● *Are there any clues before and after the blank space?*
● *Is the pattern of words in the sentence familiar?*
● *Is there a clear relationship between the different parts of the sentence?*
● *Is this relationship to do with cause and effect?*

You won't have time to ask all these questions in the exam, but you can practise as you prepare so that you can trigger possible answers. Remember, you need to develop this so that the questions are automatic and fast by the time you take the exam.

**Reading closely**: you read the text closely to examine information carefully after you have located it in a Reading Passage. When you find the information you are looking for, remember to read the text either side of the information and also note that the context of the paragraph will influence the meaning.

**Reflecting**: you can reflect on, or think about, each unit or several units as you progress through the Student's Book. You can use this reflection for revision purposes, thinking about the language or the skills you have learnt. You can also discuss these with your friends and colleagues. If you have time, you can write a brief summary of the unit in your own words in list form, and keep and refine the summaries as you progress through the course. If your colleagues are also doing this, it is useful for you to compare the process you use for reflection.

**Scanning**: you can use scanning to look for words and paraphrases of words. How you find the words does not matter. If you scan them from left to right, it is difficult to stop your brain from reading. Try the methods below, using a pencil to guide your eye.

1  Scan a paragraph, or part of a text, from the bottom to the top or the top to the bottom, looking left to right, or right to left.
2  Scan a paragraph, or part of a text, in a zigzag from left to right, or right to left.
3  Scan a paragraph, or part of a text, diagonally looking from left to right or right to left. Start from the top or bottom on the left to the right.

**Skimming**: you use skimming to get the gist or general meaning of a paragraph or whole text, including the questions. You should aim to skim a Reading Passage and questions in an IELTS Reading test in about two minutes. In the exam, you do not have time to read the whole passage closely. In order to increase your skimming speeds, learn to look at the words that give you the general meaning or gist so that you can *build a picture* of the passage. To do this, skim a paragraph looking mainly at the nouns and verbs. This is called *activating schemata*. See *activating schemata*. Compare this with *reading closely* and *scanning*.

**Summarising**: you need to be able to summarise efficiently to write answers for Task 1. You also need to be able to notice/recognise summaries in the Listening and Reading tests. For both of these you need to be able to paraphrase and recognise/notice paraphrases. You also need to be able to use and understand processes such as *nominalisation*.

**Surveying**: You survey the whole of the Reading test before you begin. This should take you no more than 30–60 seconds. You look at the titles of the passage and any subheadings and the questions. This helps you plan your time and pace.

**Transferring knowledge/skills:** you need to make a conscious effort to transfer knowledge, language and skills from one part of the test to another. For example, if you learn cause and effect language such as *result from/in, lead to, because of*, etc, in your preparation for the Writing test, it is also applicable in the Reading, Listening and Speaking tests. The same applies to factual knowledge and skills.

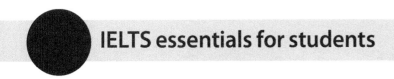

## Introduction

Below is a selection of essential elements you will come across in the academic version of the IELTS exam.

It is important to keep examples of the elements below as you study for your own development and revision purposes.

**Cause and effect:** these two elements often go together, and sometimes occur with problem and solution. You can express causes in many different ways, e.g., *as a result of, because of, resulting from* and effects, e.g., *leads to, causes, produces, results in,* etc. You can use causes and effects to explain/develop ideas/concepts and arguments in the Speaking and Writing tests and you also need to be able to notice/recognise them in all their variations in the Listening and Reading tests. See *Navigating* and *Predicting* in IELTS strategies.

**Classification:** you can classify information in order to compare or evaluate it more easily. You are asked to classify information in the Reading test, e.g., events relating to dates, items relating to classes, etc. You also encounter classification when you have to complete information in tables in the Listening and Reading tests. In Writing Task 1, you can use classification to group data to compare and contrast it, and in writing Task 2, you classify/group/sort ideas into, e.g., causes, effects, example, general statements/conclusions, problems, reasons, solutions, etc., in order to write about them.

**Comparison and contrast:** you can use comparison and contrast language structures for Task 1 to compare and contrast the size of various items. You can also use such language to express you opinion/position/stance. You need to recognise when people are comparing ideas.

**Evaluation:** you can evaluate or say what you think about something such as an item, an event, an idea/concept, etc., in different ways. You can use: adjectives, e.g., (it is) important/harmful/essential; comparisons and contrasts, e.g., more/less important/beneficial than. You do not always have to say *I think/In my* opinion, etc.

**Exemplification:** you can give examples in many ways, e.g., *For example/For instance, in Germany, … like Germany, … in countries such as Germany.* You do not always have to use devices like *for example,* etc. You can say: *In Germany, people* ….

It is essential to use examples in writing and in speaking in order to make things more concrete, e.g., *currency such as dinars or dollar/infrastructure such as roads and bridges*, and give a context for your ideas. It helps the reader/listener to: activate their own schemata; clarify what you are saying and give a point of reference. As you use examples

yourself, you can begin to notice/recognise where they are likely to appear in a sentence or paragraph.

**General vs. specific statements:** you use general statements to state what you are going to write or talk about and to summarise what you have written or talked about.

In Writing Task 1, for example, you need to write an overview of the data, etc., and in Writing Task 2, you need to be able to write topic sentences to introduce a paragraph. In Writing Task 1, the overview is followed by specific information as proof of the overview or leads to a conclusion regarding the specific data. In Writing Task 2, the topic sentence is followed by an explanation or proof of the topic sentence, i.e. *state and prove.* Note that general statements are also used to: conclude paragraphs, summarise ideas/concepts within paragraphs and to conclude essays and articles. It is necessary to notice/recognise both kinds of statements and where they are likely to occur in all parts of the exam. See *Navigating* and *Predicting* in IELTS strategies.

**Opinion/Position/Stance/View:** you can express your views in many ways, e.g., *I think/believe, In my opinion*, but you can also express your opinion by using adjectives, e.g., *important* and by comparison and contrast, e.g., i*s a better way, the best way to.* See *Evaluation* and *Comparison and Contrast.* You also need to be able to use and notice/recognise opinions, etc., in all aspects of the exam, e.g., in Writing Task 2 and in the Reading test. For the latter, see *Navigating* and *Predicting* in IELTS strategies.

**Problem and solution**: these two elements often go together. Problems may be presented in many forms, e.g., *the cost of living is increasing/Living standards are decreasing.* You come across problems in all aspects of the IELTS examination, e.g., Writing Task 2, the Listening test and Speaking Part 3. Solutions can be expressed in many ways as well, e.g., *The government should/can/could reduce taxes/The best way is for the government to reduce taxes.* Measures, suggestions, proposals and recommendations can be used to present solutions. Being able to recognise the two elements of this relationship is important in navigating reading, writing and spoken discourse. It is important to recognise the location of solutions relative to problems. See *Prediction* in IELTS strategies

**Process:** a process involves steps/stages and phases, which you can highlight using words and phrases like *then, next, at this stage.* You can encounter processes in Writing Task 1, Listening and Reading. For Writing Task 1, you need to describe the stages, etc., in a process and highlight them. In Reading and Listening tests, you need to be able to notice and recognise the stages in a process, which may not always be highlighted as clearly as in your own writing.

**Purpose:** you can express a purpose by using linking devices such as: *to, in order to, so as to, so* and *so that.* You use a purpose to show the result you want to achieve. A purpose is different from a result, which can happen whether you want it or not. It is important to state purposes to show why your ideas/concepts or suggestions are important.

**Reasons:** you can express a reason by using linking devices, e.g., *because, since, as, for;* the preposition *with,* e.g., *with the change in weather.* You can also use phrases like *this is because,* and by expressing a purpose, e.g., *to, in order to, so as to, so* and *so that.*

Reasons are used in writing and speaking to explain and support ideas. You need to use them in Writing Task 2 and also in all parts of the Speaking test. You need to be able to notice/recognise reasons given by writers in the Reading and Listening tests. See *Navigating* and *Predicting* in IELTS strategies.

**Time:** you can express time relationships using dates, e.g., *in 2017, Up to 2017, prior to 2017, it wasn't until 2017, it was only after 2017, between 2000 and 2017.* You use them when describing data, etc., in Writing Task 1, and you use them to highlight time in Writing Task 2, e.g., *Until recently, Before 2008.* In the Reading test, you have to be able to notice/recognise and process the occurrence of events relative to each other. You may, for example, have to classify events, etc., into periods. See *Classification, Navigating* and *Predicting* in IELTS strategies.

# Listening answer sheet

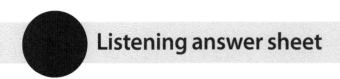

 BRITISH COUNCIL

 idp IELTS AUSTRALIA

 CAMBRIDGE ENGLISH
Language Assessment
Part of the University of Cambridge

IELTS Listening and Reading Answer Sheet

Centre number:

Pencil must be used to complete this sheet

Please write your full name in CAPITAL letters on the line below

Then write your six digit Candidate number in the boxes and shade the number in the grid on the right

Test date (shade ONE box for the day, ONE box for the month and ONE box for the year):

Day: 01 02 03 04 05 06 07 08 09 10 11 12 13 14 15 16 17 18 19 20 21 22 23 24 25 26 27 28 29 30 31

Month: 01 02 03 04 05 06 07 08 09 10 11 12     Year (last 2 digits): 13 14 15 16 17 18 19 20 21

## Listening   Listening   Listening   Listening   Listening   Listening

| | | | | |
|---|---|---|---|---|
| 1 | | 21 | | |
| 2 | | 22 | | |
| 3 | | 23 | | |
| 4 | | 24 | | |
| 5 | | 25 | | |
| 6 | | 26 | | |
| 7 | | 27 | | |
| 8 | | 28 | | |
| 9 | | 29 | | |
| 10 | | 30 | | |
| 11 | | 31 | | |
| 12 | | 32 | | |
| 13 | | 33 | | |
| 14 | | 34 | | |
| 15 | | 35 | | |
| 16 | | 36 | | |
| 17 | | 37 | | |
| 18 | | 38 | | |
| 19 | | 39 | | |
| 20 | | 40 | | |

Marker 2 Signature

Marker 1 Signature

Listening Total

IELTS L-R v1.0

denote Print Limited 0121 520 5100

DP787/394

# Reading answer sheet

Please write your **full name** in CAPITAL letters on the line below:

_____

Please write your Candidate number on the line below:

_____

Please write your three digit language code in the boxes and shade the numbers in the grid on the right.

0 1 2 3 4 5 6 7 8 9
0 1 2 3 4 5 6 7 8 9
0 1 2 3 4 5 6 7 8 9

**Are you:** Female? ▭   Male? ▭

Reading   Reading   Reading   Reading   Reading   Reading

**Module taken** (shade one box):   Academic ▭   General Training ▭

| # | Answer | Marker use only | # | Answer | Marker use only |
|---|--------|-----------------|---|--------|-----------------|
| 1 | | ✓ 1 ✗ | 21 | | ✓ 21 ✗ |
| 2 | | ✓ 2 ✗ | 22 | | ✓ 22 ✗ |
| 3 | | ✓ 3 ✗ | 23 | | ✓ 23 ✗ |
| 4 | | ✓ 4 ✗ | 24 | | ✓ 24 ✗ |
| 5 | | ✓ 5 ✗ | 25 | | ✓ 25 ✗ |
| 6 | | ✓ 6 ✗ | 26 | | ✓ 26 ✗ |
| 7 | | ✓ 7 ✗ | 27 | | ✓ 27 ✗ |
| 8 | | ✓ 8 ✗ | 28 | | ✓ 28 ✗ |
| 9 | | ✓ 9 ✗ | 29 | | ✓ 29 ✗ |
| 10 | | ✓ 10 ✗ | 30 | | ✓ 30 ✗ |
| 11 | | ✓ 11 ✗ | 31 | | ✓ 31 ✗ |
| 12 | | ✓ 12 ✗ | 32 | | ✓ 32 ✗ |
| 13 | | ✓ 13 ✗ | 33 | | ✓ 33 ✗ |
| 14 | | ✓ 14 ✗ | 34 | | ✓ 34 ✗ |
| 15 | | ✓ 15 ✗ | 35 | | ✓ 35 ✗ |
| 16 | | ✓ 16 ✗ | 36 | | ✓ 36 ✗ |
| 17 | | ✓ 17 ✗ | 37 | | ✓ 37 ✗ |
| 18 | | ✓ 18 ✗ | 38 | | ✓ 38 ✗ |
| 19 | | ✓ 19 ✗ | 39 | | ✓ 39 ✗ |
| 20 | | ✓ 20 ✗ | 40 | | ✓ 40 ✗ |

| Marker 2 Signature | Marker 1 Signature | Reading Total |
|---|---|---|
| | | |